THE SHAKESPEARE FOLIOS

General Editor: Nick de Somogyi
Typographical Consultant: Simon Trussler

Measure for Measure

Measvre, For Measure

NICK DE SOMOGYI

Nick de Somogyi was educated at Dulwich College, and at Pembroke College, Cambridge (where he gained his doctorate), and now works in London as a freelance writer and researcher, and as a genealogist at the College of Arms. His publications include *Shakespeare's Theatre of War* (1998), *Jokermen and Thieves: Bob Dylan and the Ballad Tradition* (1986), and, as editor, *The Little Book of War Poems* (1999). He is the founding editor of the Globe Quartos series, and has also lectured on Shakespearean drama for the Museum of London, the Rose Theatre Trust, and Shakespeare's Globe. His media work includes contributions to the Open University, BBC Radio 4, and Carlton Television.

SIMON TRUSSLER

Simon Trussler is co-editor of *New Theatre Quarterly* and author or editor of numerous books on drama and theatre, including *Shakespearean Concepts* (1989) and the award-winning *Cambridge Illustrated History of British Theatre* (1993). Formerly Reader in Drama in the University of London, he is now Senior Research Fellow at Rose Bruford College.

This edition of the plays of William Shakespeare has a simple aim: to present to modern readers the full text of the 1623 First Folio in as accessible a form as possible, and without altering or editing it, either in substance or in detail.

Each play has therefore been carefully reproduced with all the idiosyncrasies (in spelling, punctuation, and layout) of the First Folio – but in modern type. Instead of the cramped, double-column typography of the early seventeenth century, our reproductions provide freshly legible and accessible texts that preserve their original quirks. We offer readers the opportunity to draw their own conclusions about the form, validity, and significance of the First Folio's every line.

The 'rules' underpinning our transcription from ancient to modern are spelled out in the Series Introduction, but our watchword has been to maintain the absolute integrity of the First Folio – even when it seems to make no sense at all. For there is no doubt that it does contain mistakes, occasioned by the slips and inattentions that inevitably accompanied the process of publication.

For this reason, we have also prepared a modernized version of the Folio text, which appears on every facing page of our editions. This provides a line-by-line parallel script in which spelling and punctuation are standardized, and which adopts the familiar conventions of printed plays – italicized stage-directions, capitalized character names, and so on.

In addition, whenever the Folio text seems indefensible, this modern edition offers an alternative reading taken from another edition of the play (often a Quarto published during Shakespeare's lifetime). These occasions – and others, where the Folio presents a significant problem – are explained in the Textual Notes at the end of each of our volumes. These Textual Notes (it should be remarked) do not provide a glossary for difficult words and phrases: they are solely concerned with clarifying the particular difficulties posed by the First Folio text. Their function is simply to ask, 'Does the Folio mean what it says? And, if not, what might it have meant to say?'

As our individual Introductions explain, each of Shakespeare's plays found its own distinctive way into the 1623 First Folio. We have therefore occasionally supplemented our parallel editions with an Appendix, detailing (for example) additional material included in earlier Quarto editions of a play but omitted from its Folio version.

Finally, and simply, our aim is to afford our readers access to the earliest definitive edition of Shakespeare's plays, and so reveal the First Folio in all its problematic glory.

Nick Hern
Nick de Somogyi
Simon Trussler

THE SHAKESPEARE FOLIOS

Measure for Measure

Measvre, For Measure

The First Folio of 1623
and a parallel modern edition

edited by
NICK DE SOMOGYI

London
NICK HERN BOOKS
www.nickhernbooks.co.uk

The Shakespeare Folios

This edition of *Measure for Measure / Measvre, For Measure*
first published in Great Britain in 2002 as a paperback original
by Nick Hern Books Limited, 14 Larden Road, London W3 7ST

Cover Design: Ned Hoste
Cover Photography: Graham Price

A CIP catalogue record for this book
is available from the British Library

ISBN 1 85459 647 0

Typeset by Country Setting, Kingsdown, Kent CT14 8ES

Printed and bound in Great Britain by Biddles of Guildford

Contents

Acknowledgements

It is a cause for regret that John Heminge and William Condell did not include a full Acknowledgements page in the prefatory material to their First Folio of Shakespeare's works. True, they included fulsome praise for their aristocratic patrons, the brothers William and Philip Herbert, and appended a list of 26 'Names of the Principal Actors in all these Plays'; but there is no namecheck for those who procured the 'True Original Copies' from which their collection was printed; nor for all the many publishers, scribes, typesetters, editors, and proof-readers who lent a hand in its production.

As editor of the Shakespeare Folios series, my principal debts are to Nick Hern, whose vision and patience have steered the project to fruition; and to Simon Trussler, whose inspiring expertise in both 17th- and 21st-century technologies has lent 'to airy nothing | A local habitation and a name'. The detail and colour of our series have depended upon the kindness and dedication of its many assistant contributors. I should therefore like to record my thanks to Ned Hoste and Graham Price for their cover design; and to the Governors of Dulwich College for their kind permission to reproduce images from Philip Henslowe's manuscript diary, and from the copy of the First Folio, held in its library. Dr Jan Piggott, the Archivist at Dulwich College, has been characteristically generous with both his time and mind; as has Thomas Woodcock, Norroy and Ulster King of Arms, whose assistance in securing access to the manuscript archive of the College of Arms is greatly appreciated. Ann Cooke's contribution to the series has been invaluable, both for her scrupulous attention to detail, and for her expert advice in establishing a systematic editorial policy. The perspicacity of Caroline Downing's quick and fresh eye has also illuminated much that was dark.

Heminge and Condell, Shakespeare's first editors, concluded the dedication of their volume with the hope that whatever 'delight' their edition contained would reflect upon their patrons, while acknowledging full responsibility for all its 'faults'. Both the sentiment and substance of this courtesy is true of the Shakespeare Folios, a series dedicated to all anonymous contributors.

NICK DE SOMOGYI

Series Introduction

The First Folio of 1623: 'True Original Copies'

When the time came for Shakespeare to emulate his own Richard II, and 'choose executors, and talk of wills' (3.2), he chose to remember just three of his theatrical colleagues from London. He drafted his own will in the Winter of 1615–16, after retiring to Stratford, where he died the following April. In it he bequeathed 26 shillings and eightpence to each of 'my fellows John Heminge, Richard Burbage and Henry Condell . . . to buy them rings.' All three were actors, senior members of the King's Men, as Shakespeare himself had lately been. It was Burbage who had first given voice to Richard II's 'talk of graves, of worms, and epitaphs,' twenty-odd years before, and who had premièred the roles of Richard III, Brutus (in *Julius Caesar*), King Lear, 'young Hamlet . . . the grievèd Moor [Othello, that is], and more beside.' Those parts 'That lived in him,' as an Elegy on Burbage lamented in 1619, 'have now for ever died.'[1]

Well, not quite 'for ever'. For soon after Heminge and Condell inherited the mantle of Burbage's leadership of the King's Men, they performed for Shakespeare what they called a further 'office to the dead . . . only to keep the memory of so worthy a friend and fellow alive' – and one far more substantial than wearing a mourning ring, or even composing an elegy. Taking upon themselves the role of literary executors, they struck a complicated deal with a consortium of London publishers; squared the tangled demands of primitive copyright; and, after years of work, at last 'collected and published' *Mr. William Shakespeares Comedies, Histories, & Tragedies* in a lavish 900-page volume, now known as the First Folio. ('Folio' refers to the large format of its page, as we might describe a 'coffee-table book'; second, third, and fourth editions of the Folio collection were published in 1632, 1663–4, and 1685.) Heminge and Condell's book was published ('in the best Crown paper, far better than most Bibles', as one Puritan critic sniffed)[2] towards the end of 1623, in a run of around a thousand copies, 'by Isaac Jaggard, and Ed. Blount', Isaac's father William having supervised the printing process.[3] Readers could buy an unbound copy – in paperback, as it were – for about fifteen shillings; but a hardbacked copy bound in calfskin sold for a pound: the monthly salary of a Jacobean schoolteacher.[4]

It is clear that Heminge and Condell thought of their book in terms of a Last Will and Testament. Their dedicatory epistle to their aristocratic patrons – William Herbert, Earl of Pembroke and his brother Philip – wittily appoints them 'guardians' to plays that are now Shakespeare's 'orphans', 'outliving him, and he not having the fate, common with some, to be executor to his own writings.' Perhaps they were thinking of Ben Jonson, who had set a precedent in 1616 by compiling his own collected *Workes* into a Folio edition, and who now contributed two prefatory poems to Shakespeare's: one, 'To the Reader' (printed opposite Shakespeare's famous portrait), which diverts our attention from the actor's appearance to the playwright's legacy ('look | Not on his picture, but his book'); and the other his honest and affectionate lines 'To the memory of my beloved, The Author Mr William Shakespeare: And what he hath left us'.

Something of the same sense of bequest playfully haunts Heminge and Condell's preface, 'To the Great Variety of Readers', in the legalese with which they set out their stall:

> It had been a thing, we confess, worthy to have been wished that the author himself had lived to have set forth and overseen his own writings. But since it hath been ordained otherwise, and he by death departed from that right, we pray you do not envy his friends the office of their care and pain, to have collected and published them; and so to have published them, as where (before) you were abused with diverse stolen and surreptitious copies, maimed and deformed by the frauds and stealths of injurious impostors that exposed them: even those are now offered to your view, cured and perfect of their limbs; and all the rest, absolute in their numbers, as he conceived them.

Of the 36 plays included in the First Folio, around half had never been printed before. These range across Shakespeare's working life, including early and late Histories (*1 Henry VI*, *Henry VIII*), early and mature Comedies (*Two Gentlemen of Verona*, *Twelfth Night*, *Measure for Measure*), and middle and late Tragedies (*Julius Caesar*, *Antony and Cleopatra*), as well as most of his so-called 'Romances' (*The Tempest*, *The Winter's Tale*, *Cymbeline*) – though the Folio editors' threeway division fails to distinguish this last category. It is these previously unpublished plays, some of them over thirty years old, which Heminge and Condell claimed to be presenting 'as he conceived them'.

The remaining plays represent some of the most popular successes of Shakespeare's dramatic career. These had already been published, between 1594 (*Titus Andronicus*, *2 Henry VI*) and 1622 (*Othello*), in the slim paperback editions known, from the four-way folding of their printed sheets, as Quartos, which sold for about sixpence. Often, more than one such edition was produced: there had been six Quartos, for example, of *Richard III* by the time the Folio was published in 1623. These successive editions were usually little more than reissues, typeset from their immediate Quarto predecessor. Sometimes these plays had been pirated (we might say 'bootlegged') in opportunistic Quarto versions whose mangled texts at best approximate the scripts Shakespeare's company had successfully performed. 'To be, or not to be,' says Hamlet in the First Quarto of his play (1603), 'ay, there's the point. | To die, to sleep: is that all? Ay, all.'[5] The first Quartos of *Romeo and Juliet* (1597), *Henry V* (1600), and *The Merry Wives of Windsor* (1602) contain similar abridgements and abbreviations. It is these flawed editions (long known as 'bad Quartos') which Heminge and Condell describe as 'diverse stolen and surreptitious copies, maimed and deformed by the frauds and stealths of injurious impostors,' and which their Folio has restored, so they claim, to their proper health, 'cured and perfect of their limbs'. The status of these 'bad Quartos' is currently the subject of much reappraisal by a new generation of critics objecting to the moral overtones of the term: plays were inherently collaborative enterprises, it is argued, so any discrepancies from the Folio's 'authorized' texts recorded in the 'bad Quartos' do not necessarily render them 'inferior', 'corrupt', or 'debased'; they are merely differently abled. Heminge and Condell's preface is the starting-point for this debate.[6]

Not all of the Quartos, however, were quite as 'maimed and deformed' as they claimed. For the pirated texts of *Romeo and Juliet* and *Hamlet*, for example, were swiftly superseded into print by apparently authoritative versions – the so-called 'good Quartos'. Other plays, including *Much Ado About Nothing* and *The Merchant of Venice*, were simply reprinted from their ('good') Quartos in the Folio text.[7] But even when such authoritative editions were used in preparing the Folio, they were often supplemented by 'new' (previously unpublished) material, procured, evidently with some care, by Heminge and Condell.

These authentically Shakespearean 'additions' range from a previously unknown prologue (*Troilus and Cressida*) or extra speech (*2 Henry IV*), via passages of supplementary dialogue (*Hamlet*), to entire scenes (*Titus Andronicus*). The Folio texts of *Othello* and *King Lear*, furthermore, effectively present, by a series of sometimes minute but often substantial differences from their Quarto editions, entirely distinct – but equally authorial – versions of the same play. It is now generally accepted, in other words, that the Folio versions of these, and certain other plays, are the product of a systematic set of second thoughts by Shakespeare himself; that they represent the equivalent of Pope's re-aimed and revised *New Dunciad* (1742); Coleridge's reworded and poignantly glossed 'Rime of the Ancient Mariner' (1817); or the subtly reworked ending Dickens provided for *Great Expectations* (1868).[8]

Ben Jonson, after all, likened poets to blacksmiths in his lines 'To the memory of my beloved': each 'must sweat . . . and strike the second heat | Upon the Muse's anvil . . . For a good poet's made, as well as born. | And such wert thou.' This is not to say, of course, that the First Folio can exactly be likened, for example, to the Macmillan 'Wessex Edition' of Thomas Hardy's novels (1912), the 1850 edition of Wordsworth's *Prelude*, or even the Folio *Workes of Benjamin Jonson* (1616), all of which the authors themselves prepared, revising and annotating as they went. Shakespeare inconveniently 'departed from that right' by dying, as Heminge and Condell remind us. But their 1623 Folio, assiduously and laboriously compiled,[9] and 'Published,' as its title-page promises, 'according to the True Original Copies', presents seventeen previously unpublished plays; the full text of five plays previously available only in abbreviated 'bad' Quartos; and the handsome reprints of fourteen others, variously supplemented with new material.

The exact nature of these 'True Original Copies' – the material procured by Heminge and Condell from which their Folio was typeset – remains an enormously complicated matter, and one subject to a baffling variety of contending theories. It is important to stress, however, that by no means all the Folio plays were printed from Shakespeare's 'quill-inscribed' manuscripts (the so-called 'foul papers' of his working drafts); nor yet from the polished 'fair copy' he may have prepared.[10] Some, for example, were apparently set from transcripts *of* those manuscripts, prepared by a professional scribe; others from the so-called 'prompt-book' or 'theatre copy' – the transcript prepared from Shakespeare's draft as a guide to its original performance; still others from professional transcripts *of* those transcripts. Finally, while some Folio plays were straightforward reprints of good Quartos, others apparently made use of annotated, pasted, and interleaved copies of those Quartos.

The problem is rendered thornier still by the fact that to speak of 'the' Folio text is potentially misleading. As the outstanding research of Charlton Hinman demonstrates, the volume was (rudimentarily) proof-read in two-page sections while they were being printed; these corrections were then incorporated on the galleys; but the uncorrected pages that had meanwhile come off the press were nevertheless subsequently included in finished copies of the book.[11] Because of this arbitrary mixture of corrected and uncorrected pages, it is thought that no copy of *Mr. William Shakespeares Comedies, Histories, & Tragedies* is minutely identical to another; and therefore that no single copy represents 'the' ideal Folio text. Hinman's facsimile edition of *The First Folio of Shakespeare* (1968, 2nd edition 1996) magnificently supplied this want, providing a composite sequence of its most legible pages, in their most fully corrected state, compiled and reproduced from about thirty surviving copies. (Around 250 copies of the 1623 volume are thought to be extant worldwide.) Our Shakespeare Folios series, however, is based upon a single surviving edition rather than what Hinman himself called the 'theoretical entity' of his reconstructed volume (xxii).

Our copy-text is that of the facsimile edition prepared by Helge Kökeritz (1954) from a single copy, formerly owned by the nineteenth-century collector Henry Huth (1815–78), and subsequently presented by Alexander Smith Cochran to the Elizabethan Club at Yale University. Kökeritz's facsimile, however, has occasionally – and then very obviously – been 'touched up', presumably where the 1623 original is illegible.[12] Such impositions have been checked and, where necessary, corrected, against Hinman's facsimile, the critical apparatus of modern editions, and the (imperfect) copy of the 1623 Folio held at the library of Dulwich College.[13]

Fuller accounts of the paperchase of 'textual transmission' particular to each Folio play (from page to stage, manuscript to transcript, Quarto to Folio) can be found in the individual introductions to each of our editions, and in the diagrams that preface them. It will be clear from this brief summary, however, that we must take care to recognize that none of these texts exactly reproduces the 'original', authorial scripts that Shakespeare wrote – even supposing that any of them ever achieved this definitive form: do an author's revised second thoughts still count as 'original'? Is the mere script of a play (of all things) ever 'definitive'? 'Look how the father's face | Lives in his issue,' reads Jonson's memorial poem; the fact is, though, that the plays' family trees are far more complicated than that, and include whole collateral branches of orphaned cousins twice-removed. 'All men make faults,' as Shakespeare's own Sonnet 35 reminds us, and the line resounds through the multiple chains of copyists, annotators, actors, editors, typesetters ('compositors'), and proof-readers that stretch out behind the Folio texts of his plays – not to mention the equally complex pedigrees of the Quarto texts used in creating them.

Heminge and Condell's advertisement of the credentials for their book ('according to the True Original Copies'), then, must be treated with a pinch of salt. (How, after all, can *anything* be at once a copy and an original?) Yet their First Folio substantially contains what they call the literary 'remains of your servant Shakespeare': a canon of plays collected by the men who had acted in most of them; in a form which they took pains to establish as the most authoritative versions available; and by which they chose to remember them, and him, to posterity. These are the texts which our series of Shakespeare Folios reproduces, that they may, as Othello says there, 'a round unvarnish'd tale deliver' (1.3). His words provide the opportunity to explain both what our parallel play-texts are, and, equally importantly, what they are not.

Facsimile or Restoration? Reproducing the Folio

Each volume of our Shakespeare Folios comprises a parallel edition. The right-hand page of each spread reproduces the text of the 1623 First Folio; the facing page presents that text in a modernized form. The editorial policy governing this running 'translation' is detailed in the next section. It remains here to explain the procedures we have adopted in restoring the Folio text to modern readers.

As with the cleaning of an old painting, the chief aim in reproducing the Folio has been delicately to strip away the accumulated varnish, candle-soot, and overpainting of the centuries, in order to restore to the piece the vigour and clarity of its original colours, while remaining true to the precise nuances of its graphic form. Our texts therefore scrupulously reproduce in modern type the exact spelling, punctuation, and layout of a single edition of the 1623 First Folio, dissolving the patina of age that any mere facsimile would necessarily present. It is the distinctive typographic appearance of those seventeenth-century pages, invisible to their first readers, which lends them an inescapably 'antique' look to modern eyes, like the atmospheric (but entirely accidental) gloom of an Old Master.

Nothing looks older, or more misleadingly 'quaint' than old technology. It is therefore the aim of our reprocessed Folio texts to maintain the fertile impact of their original verbal form, while removing all purely incidental or superficial distractions. We have therefore replaced with its modern form the Folio's potentially misleading use of the 'long *s*' ('Where the bee ſucks, there ſuck I', *The Tempest*, 5.1), a typographic remnant current only in the German use of 'ß' to represent a double-*s*. For the same reason, while meticulously retaining the spelling, punctuation, lineation, use of capital letters and italic font of its model, our Folio texts have systematically applied this fidelity according to modern typographic procedures, as follows.

Readers wishing to avoid the minutiae of this process may care to turn to p. xv.

As the facsimile page reproduced below (p. 210) demonstrates, the 1623 Folio (known for convenience as 'F') is printed in double columns, with the first word of the following page, the so-called 'catch-word', appearing at the bottom right of each page's right-hand column. (This was a printer's safeguard to ensure that the pages followed on correctly.) A series of so-called 'signatures' ('C2' or 'bb3', for example), which refer to the alphabetical sequencing of the printed sheets into their assembled form, also intermittently appears beneath the right-hand column of F's right-hand ('recto') pages. The text is also paginated at the top left and right of each double-spread, with the relevant title running across the uppermost border of each page.[14] Since each of our Folio pages occupies slightly less than half of each of the 1623 columns, we have silently removed these technical marks, while imposing a border around each page in simulation of those surrounding the original columns. The width of those 1623 columns is sometimes too narrow to accommodate the final word, or part-word, of a verse line, and the original compositors set the overspill wherever it would fit:

> *Ham.* Very like, very like : ſtaid it long ? (dred.
> *Hor*. While one with moderate haſt might tell a hun-

For the same reason, they sometimes crammed a particularly lengthy line flush to its speech-prefix:

> *B.Cant.*God and his Angels guard your ſacred Throne,

Our Folio texts seek to avoid these unsightly and accidental interruptions and conflations. We have therefore throughout applied a standard space between speech-prefixes and their corresponding text; and have wherever possible set overspilled lines in full, while registering the procedure, in the case of divided words, with a vertical stroke. We therefore set these lines from *Hamlet* (1.2) and *Henry V* (1.2) as follows:

> *Ham.* Very like, very like: staid it long?
> *Hor.* While one with moderate hast might tell a hun|dred.

> *B. Cant.* God and his Angels guard your sacred Throne,

When our own Folio pages cannot accommodate a full verse-line, we reproduce the position and form of the original overspill. The lineation and word-breaks of all prose passages are exactly retained from F.

Shakespeare, in common with most of his fellow dramatists, seems to have used punctuation sparingly; and it is more likely the original compositors who are responsible for F's (to modern eyes sometimes eccentric, sometimes misleading) scattering of commas, colons, and brackets.[15] Nevertheless, as G. Blakemore Evans reminds us, these were 'men who had a contemporary feeling for the spoken relation of words and the rhythm and emphasis of Elizabethan English.'[16] We therefore reproduce exactly the Folio's original 'pointing', though our fidelity to F has once again been enhanced and clarified by modern procedures: all punctuation marks have been set flush to their preceding words, and automatically followed by a single space (as in this sentence).

By the same token, while F sometimes uses italic punctuation marks within normal 'upright' passages, and *vice versa*, our texts automatically deploy italic punctuation within italic passages, and upright punctuation elsewhere. F uses italics not only to designate speech-prefixes and stage-directions, to distinguish the on-stage recital of songs, letters, sonnets, bills, and so on, but also in setting most proper names, foreign languages, and exotic terms: 'When he himselfe might his *Quietus* make | With a bare Bodkin? . . . Soft you now, | The faire *Ophelia*?'). We reproduce all these decisions, even on those rare occasions when the original compositors mixed italic and upright type within a single word or speech-prefix. We have, however, ignored all instances of what might appear to our eyes as 'bold' type: this is a nineteenth-century typographic form, and merely an accidental irregularity of ink or type in the 1623 volume.

Having 'cleaned' the 1623 Folio's typography in this way, it seemed immediately apparent that the scale of other potential obstacles to its direct understanding was dramatically reduced. The Jacobean custom of printing 'i' for 'j', and 'u' for 'v', and *vice versa* (so that Othello promises to 'deliuer' an 'vn-varnish'd Tale'), seemed of a piece with the fresh, fluid, and often illuminating spellings used throughout the collection. (The idiosyncracies of its spelling, however, may equally reflect the habits of the Folio's compositors as Shakespeare's own.) We have likewise retained its use of superior letters and contracted abbreviations – 'Which in th'eleuēth yere of yͤ last Kings reign' (*Henry V*, 1.1) – as part of the same high fidelity towards it, while acknowledging that F's deployment of these abbreviations, and its sometimes irregular lineation, are often the result of the particular process by which its pages were printed.[17] The slight oddity of such occasions, especially when shorn of their Jacobean type, soon evaporates from the forefront of a reader's mind. And, in any case, each of our Folio pages is accompanied by its facing text: a parallel edition which provides a fully modernized and theatrically coherent 'running commentary' on the original.

'So all my best is dressing old words new.' The aspiration of Shakespeare's Sonnet 76 is one shared by our Folio reproductions, in the crisp typography of their renewed form. The process of clarification they embody may perhaps be likened to a digitally remastered CD of a 78 r.p.m. analogue recording: we have sought to remove the distracting hiss and clicks of its early mediation, while enhancing the volume, tone, and range of the original recording. The parallel scripts that appear on their facing pages re-record that material in a more immediately accessible form, as the following section details.

Edition or Imposition? Modernizing the Folio

The modern edition that accompanies the text of our Folio reproductions seeks to install a finer filter still between the 1623 text and its modern readers, by refining out the grosser elements of the First Folio's impurities. It therefore modernizes all spelling; introduces the principles of a systematic punctuation; and inserts, where strictly necessary, a number of stage-directions ('SDs'). The SDs we impose are dictated either by the needs of stage-practice – where characters enter but do not exit from a scene, for example – or by reference to the descriptions offered in the text itself.[18] It indicates, by a system of aligned indentations ('staircases') those occasions where a verse-line is divided between two or more speakers.[19] It prints as regular verse those lines which the F compositors either set as successive half-lines, to fill out their page, or as prose, to save them space (see below, note 17). It introduces into verse-lines an indication of the stress required in pronouncing the final *–ed* of verbs (though elided *–ued* and *–ied* endings are not so shown):

> Why thy **canoniz'd** bones, **hearsèd** in death,
>
> (*Hamlet*, 1.5, pp. 38–9)

> But **died** thy sister of her love, my boy?
>
> (*Twelfth Night*, 2.4, pp. 62–3)

And it highlights, by a system of end-notes, a series of occasions of particular textual interest and complexity. These Textual Notes range from the simple attribution of those generally accepted emendations which significantly re-interpret F's readings – or those of the Quarto ('Q') where such texts exist; via the signalling of arguably more valid readings, where F nonetheless makes good sense; and the noting of substantial passages that are unique either to F or Q; to lengthier appraisals of more stubbornly intractable textual problems.

Each of Shakespeare's plays brings with it a discrete set of textual problems, and our procedures in dealing with them are explained at length in our individual introductions, together with a full account of that play's textual pedigree. Broadly speaking, however, the editorial policy of our facing editions has been as far as possible to maintain the integrity of the Folio texts they modernize – the most authoritative versions Heminge and Condell were able to provide.

All additional material – the editorial apparatus we have imposed – is set within square brackets, unless otherwise stated in the particular introduction. So, where the Folio text reads:

Enter the King, Humfrey, Bedford, Clarence,
Warwick, Westmerland, and Exeter.

our modern edition reads:

[1.2]

Enter the KING, GLOUCESTER, BEDFORD, *Clarence,* WARWICK, WESTMORLAND, *and* EXETER [*and attendants*]

(*Henry V*, 1.2, pp. 10–11)

As in this example from *Henry V*, we introduce act- and scene-numbers when F omits them; modernize and retain, where possible, the exact wording of F's SDs; and capitalize the form of the character's name used in its speech-prefixes ('SPs'). Where necessary, we supplement those SDs, in this example with the attendants later instructed to fetch in the French ambassador. The names of mute characters – those, like Clarence here, who nowhere speak in the play, but whose presence is nevertheless signalled – are not capitalized. The choice of SP is sometimes complicated by F's occasionally expressive variations, as the Duke of Gloucester's appearance here as '*Humfrey*'. Later in the same play, Fluellen is suddenly designated '*Welch*' when he converses with Captains MacMorris ('*Irish*') and Jamy ('*Scot*') (3.2, pp. 72–3); and in *Romeo and Juliet*, Lady Capulet is variously referred to as '*Wife*', '*Lady of the house*', and '*Mother*', according to the function she performs. Our modern texts render all such SPs and SDs consistent (he is '*Fluellen*' throughout, she '*Lady Capulet*', and Prince Humphrey '*Gloucester*'), in order to provide an immediate gloss for the benefit of a momentarily confused reader of the Folio. Sometimes, however, our process of clarification has had to deal more substantially than with matters of spelling, punctuation, or stage-business.

Some of these necessary intercessions are more straightforward than others; as when, for example, in F *Hamlet*, Laertes bafflingly vows to behave towards his dead father's friends 'like the kinde Life-rend'ring Polititian,' providing them 'Repast . . . with my blood' (4.5, pp. 172–3). Cross-reference to that play's 1604 Second Quarto ('Q2') reveals the mistake – and a mistake it certainly is, apparently by a careless compositor of the Folio page. For in that text it is the 'kind life-rendring Pelican' – the bird popularly thought to feed its young with blood pecked from its own breast – to which Laertes compares himself. On occasions like these, our Folio page retains 'Polititian', as part of its scrupulous fidelity to the 1623 text; but our parallel edition imports and modernizes the Q2 reading: 'And, like the kind life-rend'ring pelican, | Repast them with my blood.'

On the other side of the critical field are those occasions, in plays which have survived in both Quarto and Folio forms, which present a straight choice between two equally legible alternatives. Thus, while Old Hamlet's corpse has been 'quietly interr'd' in Q2, in F it has been 'quietly enurn'd' (1.4, pp. 38–9). It is the constant policy of our parallel editions to allow the 1623 First Folio to speak for itself whenever it speaks sense. In this case, therefore, our Folio text crisply resets the original line, and our edition merely modernizes its spelling (according to the version given in the *Oxford*

English Dictionary), signalling the required stress as described above, to read 'Wherein we saw thee quietly inurn'd.'

Sometimes, however, such a choice turns out to be less straightforward than it seems. Perhaps the most famous of these textual problems – or 'cruxes', as they are known – occurs in *Othello*. In his final speech, its hero presents himself as 'one, whose hand . . . threw a Pearle away | Richer then all his Tribe' (5.2) – but in doing so, is he 'like the base *Indian*' (Q, 1622) or 'the base Iudean' (F, 1623)? The problem is intricate with the various textual entanglements we have discussed, not least since both readings make more than good sense.

In Q, the Moor abjectly compares himself to a native of the newly colonized Indies, proverbially indifferent to the priceless natural resources around him, carelessly discarding Desdemona's love and life; 'her bed is *India*,' exclaims Shakespeare's Troilus of his Cressida, 'there she lies, a Pearle' (1.1). In F, on the other hand, Othello likens himself to Judas Iscariot, the disciple from Judaea ('Iudean'), who betrayed Jesus with a kiss (as Othello did Desdemona: 'I kist thee, ere I kill'd thee'); killed himself (as Othello is shortly to do); and squandered his chances of salvation – the 'one pearl of great price' of St Matthew's Gospel (14, 46). The word 'Tribe' allows both biblical and ethnic contexts.

The problem is that whichever reading is correct, the other is most probably an error for it, since the letters 'i' and 'j' were used interchangeably, and the letters 'n' and 'u' were easily confused, whether when read from manuscript, or handled as a piece of letter-type. In such keenly contested cases as these, we reproduce Othello's words exactly from the Folio ('Like the base Iudean'), and amplify that voice in our modernized version ('Like the base Judaean'), while signalling the difficulty in a Textual Note.

In many of the plays contained in the Folio, of course, there is no other text with which to compare a doubtful reading; or if there is, like the abbreviated 'bad' Quarto of *Henry V* (1600), it is of limited use. Mistress Quickly's account of Falstaff's death in that play is justly famous: 'I knew there was but one way: for his nose was as sharp as a pen, and 'a babbled of green fields' (2.3, pp. 50–51). The trouble is that the lines did not appear in this form until Lewis Theobald devised them for his edition of the *Works* in 1733. In the Folio, they read as follows: 'I knew there was but one way: for his Nose was as sharpe as a Pen, and a Table of greene fields.' As the relevant note in our edition of the play details, critical interpretation of these last six words (which have no exact equivalent in the Quarto) has ranged from the probable – 'he talked ['Table' misread from 'talkd'] of green fields [the 'green pastures' of Psalm 23]' – to the bizarre – '[his face was] a table [the spitting image] of [Sir Richard] Grenville's [the captain of the ship *Revenge*, killed in 1591]'. Theobald's 'babbled', with its subtle play between the trill of a stream narrowing through pasture, and the fluent gibberish of a dying man, has itself snaked its way into the standard reading. For all its enduring brilliance, however, Shakespeare himself may never have written it. 'To alter,' as Dr Johnson, one of his greatest editors, commented, 'is more easy than to explain.'[20]

Puzzles like these are generally tucked away in the small print, copious notes, and appendices of Shakespearean editions. Our own facing texts provide the standard reading for passages that make doubtful sense, like this one; but our hope remains that by affording plain access to the Folio originals, their occasional difficulties may be aired as simply as possible. It is not the aim of our series, however, to provide a full 'critical apparatus' for the plays. Glossaries, commentaries, lists of variant readings, accounts of stage histories and of the vast critical and editorial tradition – all these remain the invaluable function of the great modern editions (the Oxford, the Cambridge, the Arden, the Riverside) to which our series is indebted. Each of our volumes merely supplements its parallel text with the notes mentioned above, and with an introduction which explains the nature of the Folio text we reproduce, and details some of the effects uniquely achieved by the contours of its original appearance.

The chimera of a true Shakespearean 'original' seems to have gone up in the smoke of a great fire that swept through Warwick in 1694 – according to a report by a 'Stroling Player' in 1729. '*Two* large *Chests* full of this GREAT MAN's *loose Papers* and *Manuscripts*,' he bemoaned, 'were carelessly scatter'd and thrown about, as Garret Lumber and Litter . . . till they were all consum'd in the general Fire and Destruction of that Town'.[21] Shakespeare's King John (5.7) seems to have been prophetic:

> I am a scribled forme drawne with a pen
> Vpon a Parchment, and against this fire
> Do I shrinke vp.

The sole exception to this gloomy likelihood are three or four manuscript pages, now in the British Library, that form part of *Sir Thomas More*, a play by Anthony Munday, Thomas Dekker, and others, which was conceived around 1593, later much revised, but probably never performed, and certainly never published in their lifetime. It is now generally accepted that the so-called 'Hand D' of these pages is William Shakespeare's.[22] They remain the sum-total of his theatrical manuscripts – two hundred lines or so, from a body of work totalling around a hundred and twenty thousand.

It is true that Heminge and Condell's Shakespeare Folio, unlike Jonson's, omits all his narrative verse and sonnets, but these have survived from their original editions; so, thankfully, have *Edward III* and *The Two Noble Kinsmen*, the collaborative plays with which Shakespeare topped and tailed his career; the absence of a First Folio text of *Pericles* is more grievous, for the Quarto of that play – one of the author's greatest popular successes – is a poor shadow indeed; two further plays have fared still worse: *Love's Labour's Won* (1597) and *Cardenio* (1613) remain mere ghosts. But the labour of love, and monumental act of remembrance, that is *Mr. William Shakespeares Comedies, Histories, & Tragedies* (1623) remains the nearest thing we have to the contents of those '*Two* large *Chests*' last heard of in 1729.

The parallel texts which our series of Shakespeare Folios presents have a simple aim: to provide readers, actors, students, teachers, and directors with an uncomplicated and accessible purchase on the canonical form by which Shakespeare's colleagues first commended his 'printed worth' to posterity. In the absence of a 'definitive' version of any of Shakespeare's plays, the modern scripts we have edited from the Folio can only ever be provisional. But our readers are actively invited to test their findings against our own meticulously recreated 'true original copies'. So, with Heminge and Condell, we ask you to 'Reade him, therefore; and againe, and againe'; and with Shakespeare's own Armado we exclaim, 'Deuise Wit, write Pen, for I am for whole volumes in folio.'[23]

Notes

1. 'An Elegie on the death of the famous actor Rich: Burbage' (1619), E.K. Chambers, *The Elizabethan Stage*, 4 vols (Oxford, 1923), 2, 309.
2. William Prynne, *Histrio-Mastix* (1633), Preface 'To the Christian Reader'.
3. See W.W. Greg, *The Shakespeare First Folio: Its Bibliographical and Textual History* (Oxford, 1955); Charlton Hinman's Introduction to *The Norton Facsimile: The First Folio of Shakespeare* (Hamlyn, 1968); and Peter Blayney's Introduction to its second edition (1996).
4. Edward Alleyn, the actor who later founded Dulwich College, noted the payment of £3 to 'Mr Younge, my chapline and schoole-master, for his quarters wages' on 24 March 1618, in his Diary and Account-Book (Dulwich College MSS, IX). The same document notes that Alleyn dined with John Heminge ('M[r] Hemings') on 4 June 1622, possibly in connection with the compilation of the First Folio.
5. *The First Quarto of Hamlet*, ed. Kathleen O. Irace (Cambridge, 1998), Scene 7.
6. The debate has recently issued into two useful series of Quarto-based editions: Graham Holderness and Bryan Loughrey's old-spelling 'Shakespearean Originals: First Editions' (Harvester, 1992–3); and the modern-spelling 'Early Quartos' volumes of The New Cambridge Shakespeare (1994–2000).
7. It is probably for copyright reasons that the names of two other publishers, John Smethwick and William Aspley, were acknowledged on its final page: 'Smethwick and Aspley both owned the copyrights of plays already published in quarto, and were presumably named because they (unlike half a dozen more cautious copyright owners) chose to join the venture as proportional shareholders rather than to sell or lease their rights to the principals' (Peter Blayney, Introduction to the Second Edition of *The Norton Facsimile*, 1996, p. xxviii).
8. See Maynard Mack, *Alexander Pope: A Life* (Yale, 1985), pp. 774–96; Richard Holmes, *Coleridge: Darker Reflections* (Flamingo, 1999), pp. 418–20; and *Great Expectations*, ed. Angus Calder (Penguin, 1965), pp. 494–6. Among other notable revisers may be counted Tennyson ('The Charge of the Light Brigade', 1854 and 1855); Brecht (*Leben des Galilei*, 1938, 1943, and 1944–7); and Evelyn Waugh (*Brideshead Revisited*, 1945 and 1959: 'here re-issued with many small additions and some substantial cuts'). For an enthralling summary, see John Kerrigan, 'Shakespeare as Reviser', in *English Drama to 1710*, ed. Christopher Ricks (Oxford, 1987).
9. 'Shakespeare, *at length* thy pious fellows give | The world thy works,' reads Leonard Digges's dedicatory poem in the Folio (my italics). 'Half of the plays were still in manuscript, many of them old and annotated prompt-copies, and if each editor prepared for the press an average of two a year, it was as much

as could be expected' (F.E. Halliday, *Shakespeare in his Age*, 1956, reprinted 1971, p. 347). Halliday counts Burbage as a third editor.

10. 'A Shakespeare play first assumed material form as the author's bundle of manuscript sheets. The company of players required a manuscript fair copy of the play . . . Into the fair copy were entered playhouse changes' (Brian Gibbons, Preface to The New Cambridge Shakespeare: The Early Quartos, 1994–2000).
11. *The Norton Facsimile* (1968), pp. xv–xxii.
12. Kökeritz's 'facsimile' of *Hamlet* (5.2), for example, reads 'They are not neere my Conference' (p. 769), which falsely emends the true reading, 'neere my Conscience'.
13. The editor and publisher gratefully acknowledge the Master and Governors of Dulwich College for their permission to reproduce details from Henslowe's Diary and the 1623 First Folio on the cover of this volume; and Dr Jan Piggott, Keeper of Archives, for his generously invaluable assistance with this series.
14. The lengthy titles of *The Tragedie of Othello | the Moore of Venice* and *The Tragedie of | Anthony and Cleopatra* are set across the upper borders of the full double-spread, divided as shown here.
15. That the Folio's punctuation can be misleading is illustrated by Horatio's description of the ghost in *Hamlet*, who

    with solemn march
    Goes slow and stately by them. Thrice he walk'd
    By their oppress'd and fear-surprisèd eyes.
    (1.2, pp. 24–5)

    In the Folio, the second line reads, 'Goes slow and stately: By them thrice he walkt,' which sits rather awkwardly with the subsequent repetition of 'by'. The compositor who set the line in the play's Second Quarto (1604) seems to have understood the syntax rather better: 'Goes slowe and stately by them; thrice he walkt . . .'
16. G. Blakemore Evans, 'Shakespeare's Text: Approaches and Problems', in *A New Companion to Shakespeare Studies*, ed. Kenneth Muir and S. Schoenbaum (Cambridge, 1971), pp. 222–38 (p. 234).
17. In order to distribute the work more efficiently, the Folio printers would estimate the amount of space required for each play, then mark up the manuscript or Quarto copy-text they were using. The process is known as 'casting off copy'. If the calculations went awry, the compositors would have to artificially fill out or compress their material in setting it. 'Much of the verse that appears as prose in the Folio probably reflects a need to save space, and prose was sometimes printed as verse in order to waste space' (*The Norton Facsimile* (1968), p. xvii).

18. In *Hamlet*, for example, the Folio notes that the Prince '*Killes Polonius*', but the Queen later elaborates the sequence of events: 'Behind the arras hearing something stir, | He whips his rapier out, and . . . kills | The unseen good old man' (4.1, pp. 154–5). Our modern script therefore introduces the direction '[POLONIUS *withdraws behind the arras*]', and later supplements F as follows: '[*He runs his sword through the arras and*] *kills* POLONIUS' (pp. 140–43). We have also sometimes incorporated the evidence of contemporary stage-practice provided by a play's Quarto edition(s).
19. Sometimes F presents three successive half-lines, as in the first scene of *Henry V* (pp. 5–7), when its clergymen debate the King's recent Budget:

    Bish. Ely. This would drinke deepe.
    Bish. Cant. 'Twould drinke the Cup and all,
    Bish. Ely. But what preuention?

    In common with most editions, our modern text treats Canterbury's words as a swift riposte, and therefore part of the same verse-line as Ely's first comment. Such an arrangement lays a weighted pause (or 'caesura') after Ely's question, before the full pentameter of Canterbury's reply:

    Ely This would drink deep.
    Canterbury 'Twould drink the cup and all.
    Ely But what prevention?
    Canterbury The King is full of grace and fair regard.

    But the lines might equally be arranged as follows, lending the subtle sense of urgency to Ely:

    Ely This would drink deep.
    Canterbury 'Twould drink the cup and all.
    Ely But what prevention?
    Canterbury The King is full of grace and fair regard.

    Since our parallel edition sets the generally adopted nuance opposite its Folio original, our readers can test, or challenge, that consensus.
20. Quoted in Leslie Hotson, 'Falstaff's Death and Greenfield's', *Times Literary Supplement* (6 April, 1956), p. 212.
21. *An Answer to Mr. Pope's Preface to Shakespear* (1729), quoted in S. Schoenbaum, *William Shakespeare: A Compact Documentary Life* (Oxford, 1977), pp. 305–6.
22. British Library, Harleian MS. 7368. Opinion is divided as to the extent of Shakespeare's contribution. For a full account, see *Sir Thomas More: A Play by Anthony Munday and others, revised by Henry Chettle, Thomas Dekker, Thomas Heywood and William Shakespeare*, ed. Vittorio Gabrieli and Giorgio Melchiori (Manchester, 1990), 1–53.
23. *Love's Labour's Lost*, 1.2. This is the only occurrence of the word 'folio' in the whole of Shakespeare's works.

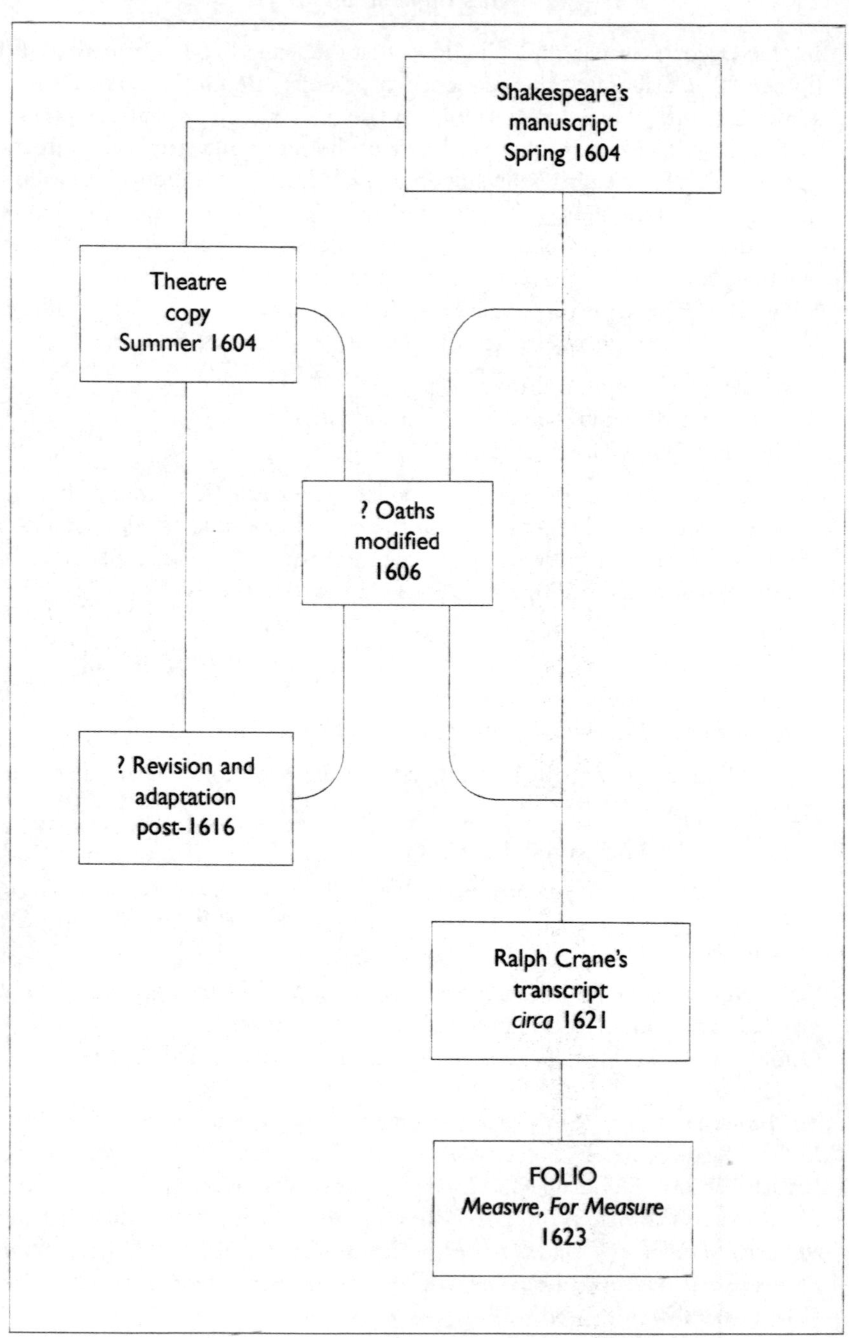

Measure for Measure: a Genealogy of the Text

Introduction

'To stage me to their eyes': *Measure for Measure* in context

'A play Caled Mesur for Mesur' was acted before King James I in the Banqueting Hall of Whitehall Palace on the evening of 26 December 1604.[1] The entry in the court accounts further notes that the play was performed 'By his Ma^{tis} Plaiers', and written by one 'Shaxberd'; this is the earliest record we have of Shakespeare's *Measure for Measure*.[2] That play formed part of a Winter season of royal command performances which, despite also featuring work by Ben Jonson and George Chapman, resembled something of a 'Shakespeare retrospective'. The clerkly audit of these productions – including the by now rather elderly *Comedy of Errors* and *Love's Labour's Lost*, *Henry V* (his most recent history play), and the brand-new *Othello* – implies as unbroken a sequence to Shakespeare's career as his new King had sought to impose upon the succession. In fact, these revels marked the end of nearly two years of turbulent anxiety for the kingdom, the King's Men, and the capital.

The last occasion that Shakespeare's company had performed at Whitehall Palace, on Twelfth Night (6 January) 1603, must have been a notably gloomy affair: for all that the Lord Chamberlain's Men (as they still were) 'flourished more than ordinary', Queen Elizabeth's age and frailty were obvious to all.[3] 'Youth's a stuff will not endure,' sang Feste the Clown, in the play named for the same festival a year before (2.3);[4] and so, protractedly, it proved. Two weeks later, 'in very foul and wet weather', Elizabeth removed her court up-river to Richmond, where, on 2 February 1603, Shakespeare's company again performed for her.[5] But as her condition worsened, a general 'restraint of stage-plays' in London was issued by the Privy Council on 19 March;[6] four days later she died. And so began the so-called 'Wonderful Year' of 1603: the death of Queen Elizabeth, the accession of King James, and the massive outbreak of plague that by the end of August was claiming over 2,000 Londoners a week.[7] Shakespeare's fortunes – and those of his fellow actors and dramatists – were intimately bound up in this 'three-fold Metamorphosis'.[8]

The new King arrived in London from Scotland on 7 May 1603 (more or less at the same time as the plague bacillus), and theatrical companies were soon performing again 'by the king's licence'.[9] The Lord Chamberlain's Men were swiftly elevated to the status of royal servants ('the King's Men') later that month; but then, as plague deaths steadily rose in the capital, the theatres were once again closed, this time for the best part of a year, and James's triumphal progress through the city was also indefinitely postponed. Contemporary logic associated physical with moral hygiene, and the crisis played into the hands of those Puritan dogmatists whose anti-theatrical polemic had threatened Shakespeare's livelihood for most of his career. In September a proclamation was issued demanding the demolition of suburban houses frequented by 'dissolute and dangerous persons' in an attempt to staunch the ravaging infection,[10] while 'necessary and requisite laws' were enforced elsewhere in London 'for the supplanting and depopulating of vice'.[11]

Shakespeare's social elevation coincided with the closure of the Globe, his chief source of income; such was the virulence of the plague that provincial tours were likewise prohibited.[12] So, as he had done ten years before during a previous outbreak, he seems to have turned his pen to non-dramatic work (for why write plays for an empty theatre?): revising, sequencing, and supplementing his *Sonnets*, and composing a pendant, or coda, to them, *A Lover's Complaint*.[13] But this universal anxiety (what he called in his topical Sonnet 107 'the prophetic soul | Of the wide world') proved overly pessimistic. The plague receded, and the King's smooth succession seemed at last to herald an era of stability and peace.

James's formal progress through the City of London finally went ahead on 15 March 1604, when (attended by Shakespeare's company, the King's Men, clad in sumptuous 'red cloth') he was treated to a 'Magnificent Entertainment': an elaborate pageant devised by Thomas Dekker and Ben Jonson, that included a speech of welcome by Edward Alleyn, the Olivier of the age, personifying the 'Genius of the City'.[14] In April the theatres were at last re-opened ('except there shall happen weekly to die of the plague above the number of thirty').[15] And in May peace-talks began between the new government and delegates from Spain and the Austrian Netherlands, negotiations that culminated in the Somerset House Conference where, on 19 August 1604, James ratified the peace treaty that brought nearly twenty years of European war to an end. The Spanish ambassador-extraordinary, the Duke of Frias, was attended at these talks by the King's Men – William Shakespeare among them – in the ceremonial rôle of 'grooms of the chamber'.[16] By the time of *Measure for Measure*'s royal première at Whitehall that December, the 'Wonderful Year' was just a memory: 'Uncertainties now crown themselves assur'd, | And peace proclaims olives of endless age' (Sonnet 107 again).

The aim of this lengthy preamble is to demonstrate the extraordinary timeliness and comprehensive topicality of *Measure for Measure*, a play devoted to exploring what its Duke calls 'The nature of our people, | Our city's institutions, and the terms | For common justice' (1.1, pp. 2–3). The play begins, after all, with the transference of political power, from Duke to Deputy, after a period of international conflict (the subject of Lucio's chatter about 'composition with the King of Hungary', 1.2, 8–9).[17] 'Thus,' complains the seamy procuress, Mistress Overdone the Bawd, 'what with the war, what with the sweat, what with the gallows, and what with poverty, I am custom-shrunk.' As the Globe stood empty, month after month, hers was not the only business to have been starved of customers; nor she the only victim of the new regime's policy of zero tolerance ('for the supplanting and depopulating of vice'). 'You have not heard of the proclamation, have you?' asks Pompey, the play's even seamier Clown. 'But shall all our houses of resort in the suburbs be pulled down?' exclaims the Bawd. 'To the ground, mistress,' comes the reply (1.2, pp. 12–13).

Some critics have gone so far as to view the Duke as a flattering portrait of King James himself.[18] 'I love the people,' says the Duke, shortly before adopting his disguise as Friar Lodowick, 'But do not like to stage me to their eyes . . . I do not relish well | Their loud applause and "*Aves*" vehement' (1.1, pp. 6–7); the King had paid an incognito visit to the Royal Exchange in March 1604, but word got out, and the royal party found themselves besieged by a jostling throng of well-wishers, much to the King's displeasure.[19] (The episode, to which Shakespeare may well have been an eye-witness, perhaps also informs the elaborate simile by which Angelo likens his choked heart to a 'well-wish'd king' overwhelmed by members of the public who 'Crowd to his presence', 2.4, pp. 62–3). It is surely no coincidence that the Duke's resumption of power in Act Five takes place 'at the gates' of the city (4.4, pp. 136–7) – the scene of another pageant in London that March, 'upon the entrance of her long-expected comfort'.[20]

It is possible to overstate such parallels; *Measure for Measure* is much more, after all, than a sycophantic manifesto (of which there were plenty at the time). But the themes it explores – the principles of government and the law, the relationship between justice and mercy, or liberty and licence –

were at least opportune. The focus of the new administration had indeed shifted from Elizabethan foreign policy to (as it were) the Jacobean Home Office. It is often remarked, for example, that King James commanded a repeat performance of *The Merchant of Venice* – another play about the quality of mercy – during the same Winter season at Whitehall that saw *Measure for Measure*'s first documented performance; and James's own disquisition on governance, *Bazilikon Doron* (Edinburgh, 1599), which dealt with comparable themes ('A King's Duty in his Office'), was republished in London in 1603.[21] It is generally assumed, on the grounds that the King's Men would scarcely have premièred 'an untried play at court',[22] that *Measure for Measure* had been tried and tested the previous Summer in the newly re-opened Globe. Certainly the play seems to have marked a fresh beginning, both for Shakespeare's temporarily suspended dramatic career, and for the world in which he variously worked – a world that extended from the city's palaces to its pubs.

Eighteenth-century editors of the play, influenced by the scenic design of the contemporary stage's 'flats', spelled out the various settings in which Shakespeare's action is played. 1.1: 'A Palace' (Alexander Pope, 1723–5); 1.2: 'The Street'; 1.4: 'A Monastery'; 1.5: 'A Nunnery'; 2.3: 'A Prison' (Nicholas Rowe, 1709); 5.1: 'The City Gate' (Edward Capell, 1767–8).[23] Twentieth-century directors have included 'The Brothel' among the 'city's institutions' the play inhabits.[24] The play's topography bears an uncanny similarity to the auspices of its first performances at the Globe on Bankside, an area documented in detail by John Stow, in his masterpiece of place, *A Survey of London* (the second edition of which was published in 1603). To read Stow's account of the 'Houses most notable' in Southwark is to find one's bearings among the 'houses of resort in the suburbs' of Shakespeare's 'Vienna':[25]

> The antiquities most notable in this borough be these: First, for ecclesiastical, there was . . . St Mary Overy, a priory of canons . . . St Margaret on the Hill being put down is now a court for justice . . . There be also these five prisons or jails: The Clink on the Bank. The Counter . . . The Marshalsea. The King's Bench. And the White Lion, all in Long Southwark. Houses most notable be these: The Bishop of Winchester's house . . . The Tabard, an hostelry or inn . . . The Abbot of Hyde his house . . . The Stews on the bank of Thames . . . a place so called of certain stew-houses privileged there, for the repair of incontinent men to the like women.[26]

In strict contrast to the rural settings of his recent comedies,[27] Shakespeare plots the moral coordinates of his play within an identifiably urban landscape, from high 'cloister' (where the novice nun Isabel is 'enskied and sainted') to low slum (where the Duke has 'seen corruption boil and bubble | Till it o'errun the stew').[28] Such is Angelo's puritanical zeal, we are told, that 'Sparrows must not build in his house-eaves, because they are lecherous' (3.1, pp. 100–1); but one result of his stringent regime is that prisons become almost indistinguishable from brothels: 'I am as well acquainted here,' says Pompey the clownish pimp from within prison-walls, 'as I was in our house of profession: one would think it were Mistress Overdone's own house, for here be many of her own customers' (4.3, pp. 124–5).[29] (No wonder that the long arm of the law, in the guileless shape of Constable Elbow, struggles to grasp the distinction between 'benefactors' and 'malefactors'.)[30] When Isabel first lodges her appeal for Claudio's life, she bids Angelo visit his own conscience as one might a neighbour's house:

> Go to your bosom,
> Knock there, and ask your heart what it doth know
> That's like my brother's fault.
>
> (2.2, pp. 54–5)

And when she is then cornered by Angelo's devilish blackmail – her brother's life in exchange for sexual favours – her outrage is once again couched in a sort of moral architecture: 'Ignomy in ransom and free pardon | Are of two houses: lawful mercy | Is nothing kin to foul redemption' (2.4, pp. 68–9). Something of the same perspective attaches to the Duke's ironic praise in Act Five for Angelo's lieutenancy: his conduct, he says, deserves a 'forted residence 'gainst the tooth of time' (5.1, pp. 142–3). How appropriate, then, that Lucio should describe him – the mediating agent of this providential comedy – as the 'Duke of dark corners' (4.3, pp. 134–5). According to Stow, the Borough of Southwark 'consisteth of divers streets, ways, and winding lanes, all full of buildings, inhabited'; the same might be said of *Measure for Measure*.[31]

Perhaps uniquely among Shakespeare's plays, *Measure for Measure* belongs to the time and place of its first performances; belongs, that is, to the London Summer of 1604, at the outset of the Jacobean age. It was not published, however, until nearly twenty years later, in the closing years of James's reign, when it emerged as the fourth comedy (and play) of the First

Folio, occupying pp. 61–84 (sig. F1r– G6v).[32] Its name appears in the entry for 'Mr. William Shakspeers Comedyes Histories, & Tragedyes' in the Stationers' Register on 8 November 1623, with fifteen other titles 'not formerly entred to other men' – those plays, in other words, being printed there for the first time, 'absolute in their numbers,' so Heminge and Condell claimed, 'as he conceived them'.[33] Scholarly opinion is divided over the degree to which *Measure for Measure* fulfils this claim. It is the object of the following section, then, to consider the extent to which the twenty-odd years between playhouse and printing house have left their mark upon the text of Shakespeare's script.

'There is a kind of character in thy life': the text of *Measure for Measure*

One of the most interesting figures to have emerged from the shadowy history of the First Folio is the scrivener Ralph Crane. Scriveners were professional copyists of formal documents, generally employed (until the advent of the typewriter and the photocopier) in the corridors of the Law. They were also familiar figures in the milieu of the contemporary stage. The dramatist Thomas Kyd was the son of a senior member of the Company of Scriveners, and may well have started out in the same trade; Shakespeare included a fascinating cameo in his *Richard III* of a soliloquizing Scrivener '*with a paper in his hand*' (3.6); and in 1589 the literary factotum Thomas Lodge dedicated one of his poems to Ralph Crane himself, 'and the rest of his most entire well-willers, the gentlemen of the Inns of Court and Chancery'.[34]

The details of the freelance career Crane fashioned from his 'ready writer's pen' are well documented. Probably born around 1560, he was variously a private secretary in an aristocratic household; a 'painful [= *painstaking*] clerk' at the fringes of the Privy Council; but chiefly (like Dickens's Nemo in *Bleak House*) he was a 'law-writer', a scribe in the employ of 'renown'd and learned lawyers'. He was also a minor poet, the author of a collection of religious verse, *The Works of Mercy*, which was published in 1621.[35] This work includes a lengthy autobiographical preface, in rhyming couplets, which is why so much is known about Crane's life. It is a passage from towards the end of this preface that first set in train, nearly eighty years ago, an inspiring sequence of detective scholarship that has demonstrated, with increasing certainty, the pivotal rôle that Crane played in the preparation of Shakespeare's First Folio. The relevant passage reads as follows:

And some employment hath my useful pen
Had 'mongst those civil, well-deserving men
That grace the stage with honour and delight,
Of whose true honesties I much could write,
But will comprise't (as in a cask of gold)
Under the Kingly service they do hold.[36]

The reference to those 'well-deserving men | That grace the stage . . . Under the Kingly service' is unambiguous: Crane has been employed by the company of players known (since 1603) as the King's Men, whose senior partners were even then (1621) engaged in assembling the material for Shakespeare's collected works.

The sequence of scholarship is worth summarizing. In 1925 W.W. Greg published an article suggesting that, from the style of their handwriting, two extant theatrical transcripts can be identified as having been prepared by the same man.[37] That man, according to F.P. Wilson's pioneering study in 1927, was Ralph Crane, who signed and dated his transcript of Fletcher's *The Humorous Lieutenant* on 27 November 1625.[38] Wilson identified four extant manuscript play-texts as Crane's work, whose authors (John Fletcher, Philip Massinger, and Thomas Middleton) had variously inherited Shakespeare's mantle as principal dramatist to the King's Men. The same article advanced the brilliant theory, based on the tics and mannerisms of this limited manuscript corpus, that Crane's 'useful pen' had played its part in the preparation of the Shakespeare Folio. The theory has since been confirmed in a series of specialist studies that have demonstrated Crane's connection with the company as early as 1618 (when he wrote out a fair copy of Jonson's masque, *Pleasure Reconciled to Virtue*); and that the 1623 Quarto of John Webster's *The Duchess of Malfi* (another Globe play) was printed from another of Crane's transcripts.[39]

By a further stroke of good fortune, not only did Crane compose an autobiography of sorts, but the style and manner of his calligraphy are also enormously distinctive. His punctuation, for example, was 'plentiful and even fussy',[40] with lavish sprinklings of hyphens, brackets, colons, and apostrophes; and his spelling was systematically eccentric, even by the erratic standards of the day. It is the survival of these idiosyncratic elements into printed texts – into the 1623 First Folio in particular – that proves those texts were typeset from a Crane transcript. Five of the Folio's 36 plays (*The Tempest*, *The Two Gentlemen of Verona*, *The Merry Wives of Windsor*, *Measure for Measure*, and *The Winter's Tale*) have long been accounted Crane's work;

E.A.J. Honigmann has recently and persuasively added *Othello* to the list.[41] The first four of those plays are also the first four plays of the Folio itself, and may therefore also have been the first four to have been prepared for publication. Scholars agree that *The Tempest* was probably the first, and Crane's handiwork may have consciously emulated Ben Jonson's literary presentation of his own 1616 Folio *Workes* – dividing the play into acts and scenes, for example, supplying a list of characters, and specifying the location of the play's action ('The Scene, an vn-inhabited Island').[42]

Measure for Measure is a classic example of Ralph Crane's work, replete with his characteristically liberal punctuations,[43] peculiar spellings, and supplementary information for a reader ('*The Scene Vienna*', 'The names of all the Actors').

That list of dramatis personae (see below, p. 177) in fact rather well illustrates the potential consequences of Crane's workmanship for subsequent readers of Shakespeare's play, for whom 'the kindly, philosophical Vincentio' is Duke of Vienna, and 'Isabella' the novitiate nun for whose chastity Vincentio's deputy corruptly bargains.[44] For although '*Vincentio: the Duke*' heads Crane's list in the Folio, the character is nowhere named in the play itself, and it remains something of a mystery as to where Crane found it. Perhaps (as in the case of Hamlet's uncle 'Claudius') Shakespeare came up with an appropriate name in the early stages of his composition, but then realized that some characters best remain anonymous (the usurping 'King', the shadowy 'Duke'), and swiftly abandoned its resonances.[45] As for the play's heroine, while it is true that its dialogue sometimes refers to her as 'Isabella', the far more 'usual form' of her name in the Folio is 'Isabell', and this is the form that Shakespeare himself 'seems to have preferred';[46] but this is not the form by which she is generally known to scholars, editors, and actors, the vast majority of whom favour the name that Ralph Crane preferred in his list of characters ('*Isabella, sister to Claudio*'). Our modern edition reverses this quirk of editorial history.

Crane's transcript of *Measure for Measure* has not survived; nor has any of his work on the First Folio, which remains – let it not be forgotten – an entirely theoretical entity. It is evident, however, from those of his manuscripts that are extant, that Crane's draftsmanship was both elegant and legible. Comparison with what is probably Shakespeare's own handwriting (see Series Introduction, pp. xix–xx) explains at a glance why Heminge and Condell should have paid for his labour. With Crane's transcript before them, the Folio compositors were that much less likely to misread their copy as they worked at typesetting their Folio pages. The arrangement seems to have been calculated to avoid the sort of errors that had appeared, for example, in the 1604 edition of *Hamlet*. In that text, evidently printed 'according to the true and perfect copy' of Shakespeare's own manuscript, the King meaninglessly refers to 'arrowes | Too slightly tymberd for so loued Arm'd' (4.7); the Folio text both corrects the error ('. . . for so loud a Winde') and demonstrates its origins in a compositor's misreading.[47] Mistakes such as these would have been minimized by the clarity of Crane's calligraphy, and so the unique Folio text of *Measure for Measure* probably reproduces with more than usual accuracy the transcript of the play he had prepared. But how accurately did Crane himself reproduce the script of that twenty-year-old play?

The answer to that question is not encouraging. Although none of Crane's Folio manuscripts survive, much of his other theatrical work does – and, crucially, so do a number of independently printed texts of the same plays. But the most detailed evidence for Crane's accuracy derives from Thomas Middleton's scandalous political allegory *A Game at Chess*, which broke box-office records at the Globe in August 1624, before being suppressed by the Privy Council.[48] Because of its incendiary nature, Middleton's play exists in a series of contemporary manuscripts, including versions by Thomas Middleton himself *and* by Ralph Crane, Scrivener to the King's Men. Comparison between the two reveals a rather worrying latitude in Crane's professional habits.

'Fidelity to his original copy,' writes T.H. Howard-Hill in his authoritative study, 'was not one of his foremost concerns'; nor was he 'reluctant to interfere with his text, consciously or unconsciously, when its meaning was obscure to him'.[49] He 'took many liberties,' comments Honigmann, 'eliminating colloquialisms and profanity, changing words and omitting words, lines and longer passages.'[50] The case can be overstated, of course: there may be other reasons for Crane's truncation of Middleton's play; and non-specialist readers may question the severity with which scholars have noted his tendency to introduce apostrophes and elisions to his texts, or to replace 'has' with 'hath', or the colloquial 'a purpose' with 'on purpose'.[51] Readers of our Folio text of *Measure for Measure*, exactly reproduced from the 1623 text, should nevertheless bear in mind that the slightly eccentric shadow of Ralph Crane – more copy editor than photocopier – falls upon it. And in one important aspect, that shadow may be impenetrable.

It is a notable fact that, for all the moral seriousness of its concerns, the overtly Christian profile of many of its characters, and the biblical quotation of its title,[52] the word 'God' is nowhere spoken in *Measure for*

Measure. One famous passage, indeed, positively cries out for an editorial emendation of 'heaven' to 'God': Angelo mouths the 'empty words' of his prayers, he bemoans, but his sexual imagination

> Anchors on Isabel – heaven in my mouth,
> As if I did but only chew his name . . .
>
> (2.4, pp. 62–3)

Both the metre and sense ('chew *his* name') of this line encourage the view that Shakespeare's original has been tampered with, a theory all but clinched by J.W. Lever's analogous quotation from James I's *Bazilikon Doron*: 'Keep God more sparingly in your mouth, but abundantly in your heart'.[53] Scholars have detected similar possible substitutions among the play's other references to 'heaven' (or 'heavens'), and deduce that the Folio text has been systematically expurgated. But by whom?

Two principal theories have been advanced, and these have a bearing on the larger question as to precisely what document it was that Ralph Crane copied out in his elegant hand. For on 27 May 1606 James I's government passed an Act 'for the preventing and avoiding of the great abuse of the Holy Name of God in stage-plays', which threatened with a heavy fine anyone who 'jestingly or profanely speak or use the Name of God or of Christ Jesus'.[54] Little is known of the stringency with which the law was enforced, but it seems possible that if *Measure for Measure* had been revived, two or more years after its première, the script would have been pruned of any reference to 'the Name of God'. If so, these changes would have been made in the so-called 'theatre-copy' (or 'prompt-book') – the annotated version of the play that would have been prepared from Shakespeare's manuscript to include all the props, cues, stage-directions, and effects necessary to ensure a smooth performance. If Crane worked from the prompt-book, then, faithfully reproducing its sometimes clumsy avoidance of the word 'God', one would expect the Folio text that was typeset from his transcript to be 'playable' as a theatrical script.

The alternative view is that Crane prepared his transcript from Shakespeare's own manuscript – the so-called 'foul papers' the dramatist would have presented to the company in advance of rehearsals in the early Summer of 1604. If so, since this manuscript must have predated the 1606 Act, it follows that the Folio's expurgation probably dates from the period of Crane's workmanship in the early 1620s. Crane seems to have taken it upon himself to tone down the oaths in a number of his surviving transcripts, and it seems increasingly likely that he performed the same function in preparing *Measure for Measure* for the press.[55] In the Folio, both the Provost and Isabel greet Angelo with the words ''Saue your Honour' (2.2, pp. 49, 57); it is the view of at least one modern editor that Shakespeare's original script, subsequently obscured by Crane's pious predilection for apostrophes, read 'God save your honour'.[56] Early on in the play, Claudio explains the circumstances of his imprisonment: he and his girlfriend have enjoyed premarital sex, he says, but she is now pregnant: the secretive 'stealth of our most mutual entertainment | With character too gross is writ on Juliet' (1.3, pp. 16–17). *Too* gross, so the theory goes, for Ralph Crane, the elderly scrivener who was shortly to publish a collection of his own devotional verse.

That theory gains support from those elements in the Folio text that point towards its origin in Shakespeare's finished draft of the play rather than in the annotated 'theatre-copy' that would have been marked up for performance. The more 'playable' the Folio text (the tidier its entrances and exits), the more likely is its basis in such a theatre-copy; the less evidence there is for this organizing process, the likelier its derivation from Shakespearean manuscript. While the matter is complicated by the fact that Crane's workmanship 'obscures evidence of the kind of manuscript which he transcribed',[57] the 1623 text of *Measure for Measure* retains at least the impression of some of its author's creative processes some twenty years before.

Why, for example, should Isabel's guardian in her cloister be named '*Francisca a Nun*' in a stage-direction (1.5, pp. 22–3), when the name of this minor character is nowhere spoken, and therefore surely surplus to the play's requirements? And why should it be Friar Peter, first abruptly mentioned by the Duke in Act Four (4.3, pp. 134–5), who plays his part in the final revelatory scene, when it is Friar Thomas who was in on the Duke's imposture from the start (1.4, pp. 22–3)? And what about the Justice in Act Two, who silently presides over the ludicrous 'trial' of Pompey the Clown, and then speaks just ten rather flat words when Escalus invites him to lunch (2.1, pp. 44–5)? The role scarcely counts among Shakespeare's more vivid cameos, after all, and even the wording of his entrance at the beginning of the scene looks like an afterthought: '*Enter Angelo, Escalus, and seruants, Iustice*' (pp. 28–9) – probably because that is exactly what it was. Shakespeare (so the theory goes) originally gave the lines to the Provost (who enters on pp. 30–31), 'and then changed his mind . . . Possibly [the Justice] was invented when Shakespeare noticed that the

Provost begins the next scene'.[58] Perhaps, and by the same token, Shakespeare simply forgot the Friar's name by the time he was needed again; and called his Nun 'Francisca', but then scaled down the character's part as he worked. Such sketched details remain, like so many pencil marks, barely visible beneath the creative wash of Shakespeare's working method and the approximate reproduction of Crane's copy.

On even the most optimistic analysis, then, the Folio text of *Measure for Measure* that we reproduce stands at some remove from the play Shakespeare composed in 1604. A chain of potential human error extends from every page, and readers must exercise their own measure of critical vigilance. Not only was Shakespeare's handwriting potentially misleading, but his manuscript-bundle was getting on for twenty years old by the time Crane transcribed it; 'it is not known whether anyone connected with the King's Men read the transcripts he . . . made for the Folio',[59] Crane certainly respelled and probably reworded as he worked; and while the Folio compositors had a relatively easy task in typesetting Crane's transcript, nobody's perfect, and their text has its share of typographical slips ('Rather reioycing to see another merry, then merrrie [*sic*] at anie thing . . .', 3.1, pp. 102–3).[60]

There is, however, an even more pessimistic view, perhaps most extremely set out by John Dover Wilson,[61] which claims that the Folio text preserves a revised adaptation of the play, and incorporates additional material stitched into Shakespeare's original design for a subsequent revival. It is certainly true that contemporary theatrical companies treated their repertoire merely as the raw material for performance. In December 1602, for example, the rival impresario Philip Henslowe commissioned the young Thomas Middleton to provide a new prologue and epilogue 'for the play of bacon' – Robert Greene's *Friar Bacon and Friar Bungay* – 'for the court';[62] and when Shakespeare's own company, the King's Men, somehow gained the performance rights to John Marston's *The Malcontent* in around 1604, the young John Webster was employed to provide 'additions'.[63] 'Faith, sir, the book was lost,' says 'Harry Condell' (played by Henry Condell), in Webster's new Induction to the play; 'we found it and play it'. 'What are your additions?' asks 'Will Sly' (played by William Sly); 'Sooth, not greatly needful,' replies 'Dick Burbage' (played by Richard Burbage), 'only as your salad to your great feast, to entertain a little more time, and to abridge the not-received custom of music in our theatre'.

There is simply no way of knowing whether the version of *Measure for Measure* performed for King James at court in December 1604 was identical to the version that had (probably) premièred at the Globe the previous Summer; nor whether either of these scripts is preserved in the 1623 Folio; nor whether that text indeed betrays the sorts of casual tampering that Dick Burbage describes – here the padding of a scene 'to entertain a little more time', there the cutting of a sequence to accommodate the auspices of a revival. The details of these scholarly suspicions are given in our Textual Notes (see below, pp. 179–206), but it is worth rehearsing here the principles upon which they have been advanced.

The nightmare of the play's hypothetical chronology centres on the song the Boy performs for Mariana 'at the moated grange' at the beginning of Act Four (pp. 106–7). The same song appears in a collaborative play, the unpromisingly titled *Rollo, Duke of Normandy*, which was first performed around 1616, but not printed until a 1639 Quarto, in which the song included a second stanza. Scholars are agreed that John Fletcher composed the scene in which the song appears, but there the consensus ends. Did Fletcher appropriate and supplement Shakespeare's original song? Or was Fletcher's (or somebody else's) original song in part transplanted onto Shakespeare's script as part of a wholesale revision and revival?

If the song *is* a posthumous interpolation, then so must be Mariana's command to 'Break off thy song'; and so, too, must be the Duke's account of the musical 'measure' of his play ('though music oft hath such a charm | To make bad good, and good provoke to harm') – and so the Folio text begins to unravel before our eyes. For without the song, and its consequent discussion, the scene must begin with the Duke greeting Isabel ('Very well met, and welcome', pp. 108–9); in which case why provide the Duke with an exit after his strange, ritual soliloquy ('He who the sword of heaven will bear', 3.1, pp. 104–7)? And if the Duke indeed remains on-stage, does it not make better sense for him to deliver that long soliloquy while Isabel explains to Mariana the complicated details of the 'bed-trick'? And if so, surely, might not that speech simply be transposed with the Duke's later and shorter speech ('O place and greatness!', pp. 110–11)? And isn't it slightly odd that the Duke's mysterious octosyllabic couplets divide into four distinct sections of six, six, *four*, and six lines? And (come to think of it, and while we're about it) wouldn't the Duke's two short speeches on the subject of vulgar rumour – 'O place and greatness!' (pp. 110–11) and 'No might nor greatness in mortality' (pp. 100–1) – be altogether more impressive if they were run together into a single speech?[64]

Well, maybe so. But for almost every gloomily expert prognosis of Shakespeare's limited responsibility for the form in which *Measure for*

Measure has endured, there is a second opinion that seeks to justify the posthumous authority with which Harry Condell and his fellows prepared it, 'and all the rest, absolute in their numbers, as he conceived them'.

'A good thing being often read': modernizing *Measure for Measure*

'There is perhaps not one of Shakespeare's plays,' wrote Samuel Johnson at the outset of his edition of *Measure for Measure* (1765), 'more darkened than this by the peculiarities of its author, and the unskilfulness of its editors, by distortions of phrase or negligence of transcription'.[65] Johnson's appraisal (delivered long before 'foul papers', 'prompt-books', and Ralph Crane became the common currency of its critical discussion) continues to define the basis of that debate. The principle of our series is to allow the Folio to speak for itself wherever it makes sense. Our modern edition of *Measure for Measure* therefore seeks, wherever possible, to illuminate 'the peculiarities of its author' (via a coherent system of punctuation and spelling) rather than to reverse any theoretically substantial 'distortions of phrase or negligence of transcription'. If, as seems on balance credible, the Folio was typeset from Crane's transcript of Shakespeare's working papers, the modern edition we provide in parallel to our Folio reproduction provides much the same service as the prompt-book that would originally have been prepared from them. The editorial procedures we have adopted are detailed above in our Series Introduction (pp. xv–xix), and the extent of their imposition may be illustrated by reference to the facsimile reproduction (on p. 210 below) of p. 74 of the Folio play (sig. G1v), which corresponds to pp. 98–107 of our parallel edition.

Since it is Crane's specifically idiosyncratic habits of punctuation and spelling that have helped construct the play's textual pedigree, it might be thought that the reproduction of these mannerisms in the 1623 Folio presents an anachronistic obstacle to Shakespeare's play rather than affording it any special access. It is true, for example, that the Clown's mention of 'stewd prewyns' deposits an unwanted layer of obfuscation to his cock-and-bull testimony (2.1, pp. 34–5);[66] and true, too, that scholars have long laboured in vain to interpret Claudio's reference to 'The prenzie, *Angelo*' (3.1, pp. 80–81).[67] Elsewhere, however, it could be argued that the spelling of the play's Folio form repeatedly demonstrates a magnetic attachment to the original poetry of its themes.

As when Claudio, for example, in his desperate Death Row interview with his sister, imagines the alternative destinies for his liberated soul:

And the delighted spirit
To bath in fierie floods, or to recide
In thrilling Region of thicke-ribbed Ice . . .

(3.1, pp. 82–3)

(For does it not lend a fleeting, sibilant chill to Claudio's elemental fears to spell that word 'reside' with a 'c' instead of its modern 's', lending still further claustrophobic force to the lines' accumulated echoes by having 'Ice' indeed reside within 'r**eci**de'?)

Or when the word 'Friar' is spelled with an 'e' ('Frier'), as it is repeatedly in the Folio text. Incorrect to modern eyes, such a spelling in fact enhances the word's etymological meaning – 'brother', as in the French *frère* – in a manner arguably pertinent to the play's treatment of spiritual and human relationships. Isabel is Claudio's sister, but she is also 'to be shortlie of a Sister-hood' (2.2, pp. 46–7); 'He is my brother too:' says the Duke, when his disguise as '*Frier Lodowick*' is revealed, 'But fitter time for that' (5.1, pp. 150–51).

Or when, to go from the sublime to the ridiculous (a return-journey which the structure of the play perfects), the Second Gentleman trumps Lucio's brag: 'I haue purchas'd as many diseases under her Roofe,' says the play's libertine go-between of Mistress Overdone, its madam, 'As come to' – 'To three thousand Dollours a yeare' (1.2, pp. 10–11). Not quite 'dolours' (the miserable pains of venereal disease), nor yet, quite, 'dollars' (then the German currency – the '*Thaler*' – of a high-denomination silver coin), but 'Dollours': the portmanteau spelling clinches the gamy joke in a manner simply beyond the resources of a modernized script to convey.

Such effects may be incidental (or indeed accidental) to Shakespeare's play; but if they are Crane's, they comprise a graphic, near-contemporary commentary on Shakespeare's art by an (admittedly minor) fellow-poet. And while many of the typographic conventions observed in its Folio text seem alien to modern eyes, they may, on closer inspection, seem apt. Among Crane's documented habits, for example, is his tendency to signal the occurrence of so-called 'sententiae' – a sort of pithy, detachable maxim:

Well: heauen forgiue him; and forgiue vs all:
Some rise by sinne, and some by vertue fall:

(2.1, pp. 30–31)

Then *Isabell* liue chaste, and brother die;
"More then our Brother, is our Chastitie.

(2.4, pp. 72–3)

Modern editors of the play dispense with these typographic 'frames' (the italic phrase, the open-ended quotation-mark) presumably on the grounds that the practice makes the text look old-fashioned. But there was 'concern for such detail in the printing-shop' when Crane's transcript of *The Duchess of Malfi* was being typeset;[68] and besides, much of *Measure for Measure* seems specifically designed to have appeared slightly old-fashioned: 'As with some Elizabethan mansion built from the stones of a ruined abbey, [it] abounds in instances of morality and interlude devices made to serve new ends.'[69]

One such instance is its taste for allegorical personifications: 'the dribling dart of Loue' (1.4, pp. 18–19); 'And libertie plucks Iustice by the nose' (1.4, pp. 20–21); 'Lord *Angelo* . . . Stands at a guard with Enuie' (1.4, pp. 22–3); 'blossoming Time' (1.5, pp. 24–5); 'Which is wiser here; *Iustice* or *Iniquitie*?' (2.1, pp. 38–9); 'hee is indeede Iustice' (3.1, pp. 104–5). The problem for an editor, of course, is that, while modern practice is to capitalize personifications, capitals are elsewhere freely used in the Folio (much as modern German capitalizes its nouns). Modern editors therefore prefer, for example, to have the Duke speak of the 'dart of love' (not 'Love'), and elsewhere to submit the play to the levelling process of modern conventions:

> Let's write good Angell on the Deuills horne
> 'Tis not the Deuills Crest:
>
> (1623)

> Let's write 'good angel' on the devil's horn,
> 'Tis not the devil's crest.
>
> (Bawcutt, 1991)

N.W. Bawcutt's latter version of the lines (2.4, pp. 62–3) certainly gains a purchase both on their difficult sense (*whatever the motto on the Devil's coat-of-arms, his picture is plain to see*), and its application: 'Angelo has discovered with horror that his angelic appearance . . . masks a devilish nature' (p. 233). But doesn't the Folio text spell out Angelo's 'angelic appearance' by capitalizing both his name and the word 'Angell'?[70]

Our own modern edition capitalizes a wider range of words than others in the Shakespeare Folios series, in order to reflect some of the originally conscious 'antiquity' to the play; and restores a discreet set of quotation marks, like raised eyebrows,[71] to the sententiae described above. Some of the Folio's unique effects, however, are beyond the means of a modern text to imply. That text, for example, may be promiscuous in its use of capital letters; but only such a context can accommodate the quietly profound way in which its nameless, shadowy, and providential Duke is referred to as 'Father' (not 'father') when clad in his friar's disguise, and as 'my Lord' (not 'my lord') in his proper person.[72] It is the Duke who moves through *Measure for Measure*, his – more properly, perhaps, 'His' – wonders to perform.

And 'perform' is the operative word. In a period when Puritan opposition to London's 'houses of resort in the suburbs' was gaining ground, Shakespeare's first play since the plague defends the personal services of drama itself, and makes a case for its moral health. As the Duke (not 'Vincentio') himself says to Isabel (not 'Isabella'), 'the doublenes of the benefit defends the deceit from reproofe' (3.1, pp. 88–9). The parallel text of *Measure for Measure* that follows pleads the same defence.

Notes

1. *Jacobean and Caroline Revels Accounts, 1603–42*, ed. W.R. Streitberger, Malone Society (Oxford, 1986), p. 8.
2. It has been suggested that the clerk who spelled Shakespeare's name in this way 'was a newly arrived Scot who indulged his burr orthographically' (Samuel Schoenbaum, *William Shakespeare: A Compact Documentary Life* (Oxford, 1977), p. 253, f.n.).
3. Paul Johnson, *Elizabeth I: A Study in Power and Intellect* (Weidenfeld and Nicolson, 1974, repr. 1988), p. 433; F.E. Halliday, *Shakespeare in his Age* (1956, reprinted 1971), p. 250.
4. On the naming of *Twelfth Night*, see our Shakespeare Folios edition (Nick Hern, 2000), p. xxvi.
5. Johnson, *Elizabeth I*, p. 434; Halliday, *Shakespeare in his Age*, p. 250.
6. *Documents of the Rose Playhouse*, ed. Carol Chillington Rutter (rev. ed., Manchester, 1999), p. 211.
7. Thomas Dekker titled his harrowing account of the plague's visitation *The Wonderfull Yeare. 1603* (London, 1604) ('wonderful' in the sense of 'prodigious', 'ominous'); on London's weekly plague-figures, see Leeds Barroll, *Politics, Plague, and Shakespeare's Theater: The Stuart Years* (Cornell, 1991), pp. 223–6.
8. John Hanson titled his verbose contribution to the flood of congratulatory material addressed to the new king *Time is a Turne-Coate. or England's three-fold Metamorphosis* (London, 1604).
9. *Henslowe's Diary*, ed. R.A. Foakes and R.T. Rickerts (Cambridge, 1961), p. 225 (9 May 1603) (modernized text).

10. *Stuart Royal Proclamations*, ed. J.F. Larkin and P.L. Hughes (Oxford, 1973), 1, 47. The relevance of this legislation was influentially proposed by J.W. Lever in his edition of *Measure for Measure* (Arden, 1965), pp. xxxii–xxxiii. This introduction, and the parallel texts themselves, are particularly indebted to three modern editions of the play: Lever's Arden edition (1965); N.W. Bawcutt's Oxford edition (1991); and Brian Gibbons's New Cambridge edition (1991).
11. John Hanson, *Time is a Turne-Coate* (1604), ¶3v–4r.
12. Malvolio's puritanical vow to 'be reveng'd on the whole pack of you' (*Twelfth Night*, 5.1) must have come to seem prophetic.
13. These poems were not published until 1609, the year of a renewed epidemic. On Shakespeare's personal 'wonderful year', see *Shakespeare's Sonnets*, ed. Katherine Duncan-Jones (Arden, 1997), pp. 8–10; on *A Lover's Complaint*, see *The Sonnets and A Lover's Complaint*, ed. John Kerrigan (Penguin, 1986), pp. 389–94: 'Notice, too, the [poem's] overlap with *Measure for Measure* through its interest in sexual irregularity, confessional utterance, problematic judgement, the cloistered life, worldly grace, and a fiend as an angel' (p. 394).
14. Schoenbaum, *William Shakespeare*, pp. 251–2; Dekker and Jonson's collaboration ended in acrimony, and each writer published his contribution separately (Dekker's as *The Magnificent Entertainment*, Jonson's as *Part of the King's Entertainment in passing to his Coronation*).
15. *Documents of the Rose*, ed. Rutter, p. 217.
16. Barroll, *Politics, Plague, and Shakespeare's Theater*, pp. 50–52. The Duke of Frias features in the anonymous group-portrait commissioned to celebrate the talks' success, *The Somerset House Peace Conference, 1604*, in the National Portrait Gallery in London: he is the delegate sitting furthest away, on the left-hand side.
17. Lucio's reference to 'the sanctimonious pirate that went to sea' has likewise been linked to James's hatred of piracy (*Measure for Measure*, ed. Bawcutt (1991), p. 2; ed. Gibbons (1991), p. 23).
18. See David L. Stevenson, 'The Role of James I in Shakespeare's *Measure for Measure*', *English Literary History* 26 (1959), 188–208; and Josephine Waters Bennett, *'Measure for Measure' as Royal Entertainment* (Columbia, 1966), pp. 79–104.
19. See J.W. Lever, 'The Date of *Measure for Measure*', *Shakespeare Quarterly* 10 (1959), 381–4.
20. Hanson, *Time is a Turne-Coate* (1604), title-page.
21. *Jacobean and Caroline Revels Accounts*, ed. Streitberger, p. 9 (12 February 1605: 'The Martchaunt of Venis Againe Cōmanded By the Kings Ma[tie]'); James I, *Bazilikon Doron, or His Majesties Instructions to his Dearest Sonne* (London, 1603), p. 23.
22. *Measure for Measure*, ed. Bawcutt (1991), p. 2.
23. On the numbering of Act One's scenes, see below, Textual Note 4 (p. 181); for full publication details of quoted editions, see Authorities Cited below, pp. 206–9).

24. *Measure for Measure*, ed. Bawcutt (1991), p. 35, n.1.
25. For an absorbing account of the play that takes '*The Scene Vienna*' (p. 177) at its face-value, see Leah Marcus, *Puzzling Shakespeare: Local Reading and Its Discontents* (Los Angeles, 1988), pp. 184–202.
26. John Stow, *A Survey of London*, ed. Henry Morley (1912; reprinted Sutton Publishing, 1994), pp. 369–70. (Stow uses the past tense to speak of 'the Bordello, or Stews', but the Red Light district he detailed endured at least until the Civil War.)
27. Compare, for example, the country-houses of Navarre (*Love's Labour's Lost*, 1595) and Illyria (*Twelfth Night*, 1602); and the forests of Athens (*A Midsummer Night's Dream*, 1595) and Arden (*As You Like It*, 1598–9). On the other hand, as always, must be acknowledged the London topicalities of Falstaff's scenes in the two parts of *Henry IV* (1596–8).
28. 1.3, pp. 18–19; 1.5, pp. 24–5; 5.1, pp. 160–61.
29. Pompey's jocular comment may in fact reflect a contemporary scandal since, in 1602, the running of Bridewell Prison was contracted out to four entrepreneurs; within the year, the prison had indeed become a brothel. (See Philip Shaw, 'The Position of Thomas Dekker in Jacobean Prison Literature', *PMLA* 42 (1927), 366–91.)
30. 2.1, pp. 32–3. Elbow's comic malapropisms here serve a serious moral purpose, slurring those black-and-white absolutes (*detesting* his wife when he means to *protest* her innocence) which the play so systematically questions.
31. Stow, *Survey of London*, p. 369.
32. Technically speaking, the First Folio is a 'folio in sixes', by which three sheets of paper, folded once (<<<), were bound into a single three-sheet, six-page, twelve-sided 'quire' (or 'signature'). This 'quire' was identified by a letter of the alphabet (e.g. 'M'), whose pages were numbered from 1–6 (e.g. 'M4'), the two sides of which are known as the 'recto' (on the right-hand side of the page-spread: 'M2r') and the 'verso' (on the reverse of that page: 'M2v'). When the letters of the alphabet were exhausted, these successive quires used double ('bb 6') or treble ('aaa 3') letters.
33. W.W. Greg, *The Shakespeare First Folio: Its Bibliographical and Textual History* (Oxford, 1955), p. 59; see Series Introduction above, p. viii.
34. For Thomas Kyd as scrivener, see Arthur Freeman, *Thomas Kyd: Facts and Problems* (Oxford, 1967), p. 12; on the Scrivener in Shakespeare's *Richard III*, see the Introduction to our Shakespeare Folios edition (2002), pp. xxxix–xl; Thomas Lodge, *Scillaes Metamorphosis* (London, 1590), 'To his Especiall good friend Master Raph Crane'.
35. The work was republished as *The Pilgrimes New-yeares-Gift* in 1625.
36. *The Pilgrimes New-yeares-Gift*, A3v (modernized text).
37. W.W. Greg, 'Prompt Copies, Private Transcripts, and "The Playhouse Scrivener"', *The Library* 6 (1926), 148–56.

38. F.P. Wilson, 'Ralph Crane, Scrivener to the King's Players', *The Library* 7 (1927), 194–215. (Wilson reproduces a facsimile of Crane's signed dedication to Fletcher's play, then known as *Demetrius and Enanthe*.)
39. See W.W. Greg, 'Some Notes on Crane's Manuscript of *The Witch*', *The Library* 22 (1942), 208–19; T.H. Howard-Hill, *Ralph Crane and Some Shakespeare First Folio Comedies* (Virginia, 1972); John Russell Brown, 'The Printing of John Webster's Plays', *Studies in Bibliography* 6 (1954), 117–40; 8 (1956), 113–27; 15 (1962), 57–69.
40. John Fletcher, *Demetrius and Enanthe* [*The Humorous Lieutenant*], ed. Margaret McLaren Cook, Malone Society Reprints (Oxford, 1951), p. ix.
41. Howard-Hill, *Ralph Crane*; E.A.J. Honigmann, *The Texts of 'Othello' and Shakespearian Revision* (Routledge, 1998), pp. 66–70.
42. Howard-Hill, *Ralph Crane*, pp. 9–10.
43. Hyphens: 'Of the all-building-Law' (2.4, p. 69); 'palsied-Eld' (3.1, p. 77); 'A creature vnpre-par'd' (4.3, p. 129). Apostrophes: 'Good'euen, good Father' (3.1, p. 103); 'Ha'st thou or word, or wit' (5.1, p. 165). Brackets: 'Now (pious sir)' (1.4, p. 21); 'But (oh) how much is the good Duke deceiu'd' (3.1, p. 87). See *Measure for Measure*, ed. Lever (1965), pp. xi–xii, and Howard-Hill, *Ralph Crane*, pp. 122–8.
44. Shakespeare, *Complete Works*, ed. William Aldis Wright, illustrated by Rockwell Kent (New York, 1936), p. 899.
45. On King Claudius's name, see our Shakespeare Folios edition of *Hamlet* (2001), pp. xxxiv–xxxv; the name 'Vincentio' apparently elides his Viennese authority with his ultimate triumph (Latin *vincere*). If a connection was intended between the play's Duke of Vienna and the Hapsburg dynasty, the name of Vincentio Gonzaga, Duke of Mantua (and cousin to the Holy Roman Emperor Rudolf II) brings with it a wealth of scholarly potential. For the names Vincentio, Isabel, Claudio, Claudius, Albertus, and Gonzago form a relatively unexplored relationship within the textual histories of *Hamlet* and *Measure for Measure*. (See Marcus, *Local Reading and its Discontents*, pp. 189, 255 nn. 44–8; Nick de Somogyi, *Shakespeare's Theatre of War* (Ashgate, 1998), pp. 242–3.)
46. *A New Variorum Edition of Shakespeare: Measure for Measure*, ed. Mark Eccles (New York, 1980), p. 5. She appears as 'Isabella' just five times in the play's dialogue, 24 times as 'Isabel(l)'.
47. See *The Tragicall Historie of Hamlet* (Q2, 1604–5), t.p, L3r. The Folio text of *Henry V*, likewise printed from authorial manuscript, probably includes a comparable compositorial misreading: F's 'ay, or goe to death' might properly read 'I owe God a death' (see *King Henry V*, ed. T.W. Craik (1995), p. 102).
48. See *A Game at Chess*, ed. J.W. Harper (New Mermaid, 1966), pp. xii–xv.
49. Howard-Hill, *Ralph Crane*, pp. 13, 133.
50. Honigmann, *The Texts of 'Othello'*, p. 75.

51. For examples, see Honigmann, *The Texts of 'Othello'*, pp. 66–70.
52. The title derives from Jesus's sermon on the mount: 'Judge not, that ye be not judged. For with what judgment ye judge, ye shall be judged: and with what measure ye mete, it shall be measured to you again' (Matthew, 7, 1–2).
53. James I, *Bazilikon Doron*, p. 20.
54. See *Measure for Measure*, ed. Bawcutt, pp. 68–9.
55. See Honigmann, *The Texts of 'Othello'*, pp. 78–80.
56. *Measure for Measure*, ed. J.M. Nosworthy (Penguin, 1969).
57. Howard-Hill, *Ralph Crane*, p. 138.
58. *Measure for Measure*, ed. Gibbons (1991), p. 201.
59. Howard-Hill, *Ralph Crane*, p. 15.
60. A vast complexity attaches to scholarly attempts to identify the compositors responsible for typesetting *Measure for Measure*. As many as eight (perhaps nine) separate compositors are thought to have worked on the First Folio. They are known to scholarship by the initial letters A to H (or I), and distinguished by the distinct characteristics of their work. Almost all of them have been suspected of involvement in this play. (For a maddening table, see *Measure for Measure*, ed. Gibbons (1991), p. 195.)
61. *Measure for Measure*, ed. John Dover Wilson and Arthur Quiller Couch (Cambridge, 1922), pp. 97–113.
62. *Henslowe's Diary*, ed. R.A. Foakes and R.T. Rickert (Cambridge, 1961), p. 207.
63. John Marston, *The Malcontent*, ed. M.L. Wine (Regents Renaissance Drama, 1965), p. xiii. The plot of Marston's play concerns a Duke who disguises himself in order to scrutinize corruption in high places.
64. See below, Textual Notes 50, 49, and 47. The Oxford editors (1986) further suspect that Thomas Middleton (fresh from his presumably successful top-and-tailing of Greene's *Friar Bacon*) devised most of the gamier conversation at the outset of 1.2 (see Textual Note 4 below).
65. *Johnson on Shakespeare*, ed. Arthur Sherbo, 2 vols (Yale, 1968), 1, 174.
66. 'Stewed prunes' were repeatedly associated with brothels ('the Bordello, or Stews') in the period, as Thomas Dekker's *Seven Deadly Sins of London* (1606) makes clear: 'Nay, the sober Perpetuana-suited Puritan . . . dares not (so much as by moonlight) come near the suburb-shadow of a house where they set stewed prunes before you'.
67. See Textual Note 36 below, p. 193.
68. John Webster, *The Duchess of Malfi*, ed. John Russell Brown (Revels, 1964), p. lxx.
69. *Measure for Measure*, ed. Lever, p. xciii.
70. Shakespeare's taste for medieval allegory in **Angel**o's name probably extends to the almost exactly contemporary Des**demon**a in *Othello*.
71. Geoffrey Hill, *The Lords of Limit* (Andre Deutsch, 1984), p. 1.
72. See for example 2.3, pp. 60–61, 3.1, pp. 88–9; 1.1, pp. 2–3, 5.1, 150–51.

The Actors' Names

In Order of Appearance

The DUKE *of Vienna*
Old ESCALUS } *his deputies*
ANGELO }
LUCIO, *a fantastic gentleman*
Two GENTLEMEN *of Vienna*
Mistress Overdone, a BAWD
Pompey Bum, a CLOWN
The PROVOST
CLAUDIO, *a young gentleman*
JULIET, *Claudio's betrothed*
Friar THOMAS
ISABEL, *Claudio's sister*
Francisca, a NUN
A JUSTICE *of the Peace*
ELBOW, *a simple constable*
FROTH, *a foolish gentleman*
A SERVANT *to Angelo*
MARIANA, *Angelo's betrothed*
A BOY, *servant to Mariana*
ABHORSON, *an executioner*
A MESSENGER
BARNARDINE, *a dissolute prisoner*
Friar PETER
Varrius

lords, officers, servants, citizens

Measure for Measure

a parallel text

Measvre, For Measure

Measure for Measure

1.1

Enter DUKE, ESCALUS, *and lords*

Duke Escalus.
Escalus My lord.
Duke Of government the properties to unfold
Would seem in me t'affect speech and discourse,
Since I am put to know that your own science
Exceeds, in that, the lists of all advice
My strength can give you. Then no more remains
But that, to your sufficiency, as your worth is able,
And let them work.[1] The nature of our people,
Our city's institutions, and the terms
For common justice you're as pregnant in
As art and practice hath enrichèd any
That we remember. There is our commission,
From which we would not have you warp. Call hither,
I say, bid come before us Angelo. [*Exit a lord*]
What figure of us, think you, he will bear?
For you must know, we have with special soul
Elected him our absence to supply,
Lent him our terror, dress'd him with our love,
And given his deputation all the organs
Of our own power. What think you of it?
Escalus If any in Vienna be of worth
To undergo such ample grace and honour,

MEASVRE, For Measure.

Actus primus, Scena prima.

Enter Duke, Escalus, Lords.

Duke.
E*Scalus.*
Esc. My Lord.
Duk. Of Gouernment, the properties to vn|fold,
Would seeme in me t'affect speech & discourse,
Since I am put to know, that your owne Science
Exceedes (in that) the lists of all aduice
My strength can giue you: Then no more remaines
But that, to your sufficiency, as your worth is able,
And let them worke: The nature of our People,
Our *Cities Institutions*, and the Termes
For Common Iustice, y'are as pregnant in
As Art, and practise, hath inriched any
That we remember: There is our Commission,
From which, we would not haue you warpe; call hither,
I say, bid come before vs *Angelo*:
What figure of vs thinke you, he will beare.
For you must know, we haue with speciall soule
Elected him our absence to supply;
Lent him our terror, drest him with our loue,
And giuen his Deputation all the Organs
Of our owne powre: What thinke you of it?
Esc. If any in *Vienna* be of worth
To vndergoe such ample grace, and honour,

It is Lord Angelo.

Enter ANGELO

Duke Look where he comes.

Angelo Always obedient to your grace's will,
I come to know your pleasure.

Duke Angelo,
There is a kind of character in thy life
That to th'observer doth thy history
Fully unfold. Thyself and thy belongings
Are not thine own so proper as to waste
Thyself upon thy virtues, they on thee.
Heaven doth with us as we with torches do,
Not light them for themselves: for if our virtues
Did not go forth of us, 'twere all alike
As if we had them not. Spirits are not finely touch'd
But to fine issues; nor nature never lends
The smallest scruple of her excellence
But, like a thrifty goddess, she determines
Herself the glory of a creditor,
Both thanks and use. But I do bend my speech
To one that can my part in him advèrtise.
Hold therefore, Angelo.
In our remove be thou at full ourself.
Mortality and mercy in Vienna
Live in thy tongue and heart. Old Escalus,
Though first in question, is thy secondary.
Take thy commission.

Angelo Now, good my lord,
Let there be some more test made of my metal
Before so noble and so great a figure
Be stamp'd upon it.

Duke No more evasion.
We have with a leaven'd and preparèd choice

It is Lord *Angelo*.

Enter Angelo.

Duk. Looke where he comes.
Ang. Alwayes obedient to your Graces will,
I come to know your pleasure.
Duke. Angelo:
There is a kinde of Character in thy life,
That to th'obseruer, doth thy history
Fully vnfold: Thy selfe, and thy belongings
Are not thine owne so proper, as to waste
Thy selfe vpon thy vertues; they on thee:
Heauen doth with vs, as we, with Torches doe,
Not light them for themselues: For if our vertues
Did not goe forth of vs, 'twere all alike
As if we had them not: Spirits are not finely tonch'd,
But to fine issues: nor nature neuer lends
The smallest scruple of her excellence,
But like a thrifty goddesse, she determines
Her selfe the glory of a creditour,
Both thanks, and vse; but I do bend my speech
To one that can my part in him aduertise;
Hold therefore *Angelo*:
In our remoue, be thou at full, our selfe:
Mortallitie and Mercie in *Vienna*
Liue in thy tongue, and heart: Old *Escalus*
Though first in question, is thy secondary.
Take thy Commission.
Ang. Now good my Lord
Let there be some more test, made of my mettle,
Before so noble, and so great a figure
Be stamp't vpon it.
Duk. No more euasion:
We haue with a leauen'd, and prepared choice

Proceeded to you; therefore take your honours.
Our haste from hence is of so quick condition
That it prefers itself, and leaves unquestion'd
Matters of needful value. We shall write to you,
As time and our concernings shall importune,
How it goes with us, and do look to know
What doth befall you here. So fare you well.
To th' hopeful execution do I leave you
Of your commissions.

Angelo Yet give leave, my lord,
That we may bring you something on the way.

Duke My haste may not admit it,
Nor need you, on mine honour, have to do
With any scruple. Your scope is as mine own,
So to enforce or qualify the laws
As to your soul seems good. Give me your hand;
I'll privily away. I love the people,
But do not like to stage me to their eyes:
Though it do well, I do not relish well
Their loud applause and '*Ave*s' vehement,
Nor do I think the man of safe discretion
That does affect it. Once more, fare you well.

Angelo The heavens give safety to your purposes!

Escalus Lead forth and bring you back in happiness!

Duke I thank you. Fare you well. *Exit* 2

Escalus I shall desire you, sir, to give me leave
To have free speech with you; and it concerns me
To look into the bottom of my place.
A power I have, but of what strength and nature
I am not yet instructed.

Angelo 'Tis so with me. Let us withdraw together,
And we may soon our satisfaction have
Touching that point.

Escalus I'll wait upon your honour.

Exeunt

Proceeded to you; therefore take your honors:
Our haste from hence is of so quicke condition,
That it prefers it selfe, and leaues vnquestion'd
Matters of needful value: We shall write to you
As time, and our concernings shall importune,
How it goes with vs, and doe looke to know
What doth befall you here. So fare you well:
To th' hopefull execution doe I leaue you,
Of your Commissions.

Ang. Yet giue leaue (my Lord,)
That we may bring you something on the way.

Duk. My haste may not admit it,
Nor neede you (on mine honor) haue to doe
With any scruple: your scope is as mine owne,
So to inforce, or qualifie the Lawes
As to your soule seemes good: Giue me your hand,
Ile priuily away: I loue the people,
But doe not like to stage me to their eyes:
Though it doe well, I doe not rellish well
Their lowd applause, and Aues vehement:
Nor doe I thinke the man of safe discretion
That do's affect it. Once more fare you well.

Ang. The heauens giue safety to your purposes.

Esc. Lead forth, and bring you backe in happinesse. *Exit.*

Duk. I thanke you, fare you well.

Esc. I shall desire you, Sir, to giue me leaue
To haue free speech with you; and it concernes me
To looke into the bottome of my place:
A powre I haue, but of what strength and nature,
I am not yet instructed.

Ang. 'Tis so with me: Let vs with-draw together,
And we may soone our satisfaction haue
Touching that point.

Esc. Ile wait vpon your honor. *Exeunt.*

1.2

Enter LUCIO *and two other* GENTLEMEN

Lucio If the Duke, with the other dukes, come not to composition with the King of Hungary, why then all the dukes fall upon the King.

1 Gentleman Heaven grant us its peace – but not the King of Hungary's.

2 Gentleman Amen.

Lucio Thou conclud'st like the sanctimonious pirate that went to sea with the Ten Commandments, but scraped one out of the table.

2 Gentleman 'Thou shalt not steal'?

Lucio Ay, that he razed.

1 Gentleman Why, 'twas a commandment to command the captain and all the rest from their functions: they put forth to steal. There's not a soldier of us all that in the thanksgiving before meat do relish the petition well that prays for peace.

2 Gentleman I never heard any soldier dislike it.

Lucio I believe thee, for I think thou never wast where grace was said.

2 Gentleman No? A dozen times at least!

1 Gentleman What, in metre?

Lucio In any proportion, or in any language.

2 Gentleman I think – or in any religion.

Lucio Ay, why not? Grace is grace, despite of all controversy; as, for example, thou thyself art a wicked villain, despite of all grace.

1 Gentleman Well, there went but a pair of shears between us.

Lucio I grant – as there may between the lists and the velvet. Thou art the list.

1 Gentleman And thou the velvet. Thou art good velvet: thou'rt

Scena Secunda.

Enter Lucio, and two other Gentlemen.

Luc. If the *Duke*, with the other Dukes, come not to composition with the King of *Hungary*, why then all the Dukes fall vpon the King.

I. *Gent.* Heauen grant vs its peace, but not the King of *Hungaries*.

2. *Gent.* Amen.

Luc. Thou conclud'st like the Sanctimonious Pirat, that went to sea with the ten Commandements, but scrap'd one out of the Table.

2. *Gent.* Thou shalt not Steale?

Luc. I, that he raz'd.

I. *Gent.* Why? 'twas a commandement, to command the Captaine and all the rest from their functions: they put forth to steale: There's not a Souldier of vs all, that in the thanks-giuing before meate, do rallish the petition well, that praies for peace.

2. *Gent.* I neuer heard any Souldier dislike it.

Luc. I beleeue thee: for I thinke thou neuer was't where Grace was said.

2. *Gent.* No? a dozen times at least.

I. *Gent.* What? In meeter?

Luc. In any proportion. or in any language.

I. *Gent.* I thinke, or in any Religion.

Luc. I, why not? Grace, is Grace, despight of all controuersie: as for example; Thou thy selfe art a wicked villaine, despight of all Grace.

I. *Gent.* Well: there went but a paire of sheeres betweene vs.

Luc. I grant: as there may betweene the Lists, and the Veluet. Thou art the List.

I. *Gent.* And thou the Velvet; thou art good veluet;

three-piled piece, I warrant thee. I had as lief be a list of an English kersey as be piled – as thou art pilled – for a French velvet.[3] Do I speak feelingly now?

Lucio I think thou dost, and indeed with most painful feeling of thy speech. I will, out of thine own confession, learn to begin thy health; but, whilst I live, forget to drink after thee.

1 Gentleman I think I have done myself wrong, have I not?

2 Gentleman Yes, that thou hast – whether thou art tainted or free.

Enter BAWD

Lucio Behold, behold, where 'Madam Mitigation' comes. I have purchased as many diseases under her roof as come to –

2 Gentleman To what, I pray?

Lucio Judge.

2 Gentleman To three thousand dolours a year.

1 Gentleman Ay, and more.

Lucio A French crown more!

1 Gentleman Thou art always figuring diseases in me, but thou art full of error. I am sound.

Lucio Nay, not (as one would say) healthy, but so sound as things that are hollow. Thy bones are hollow: impiety has made a feast of thee.

1 Gentleman How now? Which of your hips has the most profound sciatica?

Bawd Well, well. There's one yonder arrested and carried to prison was worth five thousand of you all.

2 Gentleman Who's that, I pray thee?

Bawd Marry, sir, that's Claudio, Signor Claudio.

1 Gentleman Claudio to prison? 'Tis not so!

Bawd Nay, but I know 'tis so. I saw him arrested; saw him carried away; and – which is more – within these three days his head to be chopped off.

Lucio But, after all this fooling, I would not have it so. Art thou sure of this?

thou'rt a three pild-peece I warrant thee: I had as liefe be a Lyst of an English Kersey, as be pil'd, as thou art pil'd, for a French Velvet. Do I speake feelingly now?

Luc. I thinke thou do'st: and indeed with most painfull feeling of thy speech: I will, out of thine owne confession, learne to begin thy health; but, whilst I liue forget to drinke after thee.

1. *Gen.* I think I haue done my selfe wrong, haue I not?

2. *Gent.* Yes, that thou hast; whether thou art tainted, or free. *Enter Bawde.*

Luc. Behold, behold, where Madam *Mitigation* comes. I haue purchas'd as many diseases vnder her Roofe,
As come to

2. *Gent.* To what, I pray?

Luc. Iudge.

2. *Gent.* To three thousand Dollours a yeare.

1. *Gent.* I, and more.

Luc. A French crowne more.

1. *Gent.* Thou art alwayes figuring diseases in me; but thou art full of error, I am sound.

Luc. Nay, not (as one would say) healthy: but so sound, as things that are hollow; thy bones are hollow; Impiety has made a feast of thee.

1. *Gent.* How now, which of your hips has the most profound Ciatica?

Bawd. Well, well: there's one yonder arrested, and carried to prison, was worth fiue thousand of you all.

2. *Gent.* Who's that I pray'thee?

Bawd. Marry Sir, that's *Claudio*, Signior *Claudio*.

1. *Gent.* *Claudio* to prison? 'tis not so.

Bawd. Nay, but I know 'tis so: I saw him arrested: saw him carried away: and which is more, within these three daies his head to be chop'd off.

Luc. But, after all this fooling, I would not haue it so: Art thou sure of this?

Bawd I am too sure of it; and it is for getting Madam Julietta with child.

Lucio Believe me, this may be. He promised to meet me two hours since, and he was ever precise in promise-keeping.

2 Gentleman Besides, you know, it draws something near to the speech we had to such a purpose.

1 Gentleman But most of all agreeing with the proclamation.

Lucio Away. Let's go learn the truth of it.

Exeunt LUCIO [*and* GENTLEMEN]

Bawd Thus, what with the war, what with the sweat, what with the gallows, and what with poverty, I am custom-shrunk.

Enter CLOWN

How now? What's the news with you?

Clown Yonder man is carried to prison.

Bawd Well! What has he done?

Clown A woman.

Bawd But what's his offence?

Clown Groping for trouts in a peculiar river.

Bawd What? Is there a maid with child by him?

Clown No, but there's a woman with maid by him. You have not heard of the proclamation, have you?

Bawd What proclamation, man?

Clown All houses in the suburbs of Vienna must be plucked down.

Bawd And what shall become of those in the city?

Clown They shall stand for seed. They had gone down too, but that a wise burgher put in for them.

Bawd But shall all our houses of resort in the suburbs be pulled down?

Clown To the ground, mistress.

Bawd Why, here's a change indeed in the commonwealth! What shall become of me?

Clown Come, fear not you. Good counsellors lack no clients. Though you change your place, you need not change

Bawd. I am too sure of it: and it is for getting Madam *Iulietta* with childe.

Luc. Beleeue me this may be: he promis'd to meete me two howres since, and he was euer precise in promise keeping.

2. *Gent.* Besides you know, it drawes somthing neere to the speech we had to such a purpose.

1. *Gent.* But most of all agreeing with the proclamatiō.

Luc. Away: let's goe learne the truth of it. *Exit.*

Bawd. Thus, what with the war; what with the sweat, what with the gallowes, and what with pouerty, I am Custom-shrunke. How now? what's the newes with you. *Enter Clowne.*

Clo. Yonder man is carried to prison.

Baw. Well: what has he done?

Clo. A Woman.

Baw. But what's his offence?

Clo. Groping for Trowts, in a peculiar Riuer.

Baw. What? is there a maid with child by him?

Clo. No: but there's a woman with maid by him: you haue not heard of the proclamation, haue you?

Baw. What proclamation, man?

Clow. All howses in the Suburbs of *Vienna* must bee pluck'd downe.

Bawd. And what shall become of those in the Citie?

Clow. They shall stand for seed: they had gon down to, but that a wise Burger put in for them.

Bawd. But shall all our houses of resort in the Suburbs be puld downe?

Clow. To the ground, Mistris.

Bawd. Why heere's a change indeed in the Commonwealth: what shall become of me?

Clow. Come: feare not you: good Counsellors lacke no Clients: though you change your place, you neede your trade. I'll be your tapster still. Courage! There will be pity taken on you; you that have worn your eyes almost out in the service, you will be considered.

Bawd What's to do here, Thomas Tapster? Let's withdraw.

Clown Here comes Signor Claudio, led by the Provost to prison; and there's Madam Juliet. *Exeunt*[4]

1.3

Enter PROVOST, CLAUDIO, JULIET, *and officers,*
LUCIO, *and two* GENTLEMEN [*after them*]

Claudio Fellow, why dost thou show me thus to th' world?
Bear me to prison, where I am committed.

Provost I do it not in evil disposition,
But from Lord Angelo by special charge.

Claudio Thus can the demi-god, Authority,
Make us pay down for our offence by weight
The words of heaven. On whom it will, it will;
On whom it will not, so; yet still 'tis just.

Lucio Why, how now, Claudio? Whence comes this restraint?

Claudio From too much liberty, my Lucio, liberty.
As surfeit is the father of much fast,
So every scope by the immoderate use
Turns to restraint. Our natures do pursue,
Like rats that ravin down their proper bane,
A thirsty evil, and when we drink, we die.

Lucio If I could speak so wisely under an arrest, I would send for certain of my creditors. And yet, to say the truth, I had as lief have the foppery of freedom as the mortality of imprisonment.[5] What's thy offence, Claudio?

Claudio What but to speak of would offend again.

not change your Trade: Ile bee your Tapster still; courage, there will bee pitty taken on you; you that haue worne your eyes almost out in the seruice, you will bee considered.

Bawd. What's to doe heere, *Thomas* Tapster? let's withdraw?

Clo. Here comes Signior *Claudio*, led by the Prouost to prison: and there's Madam *Iuliet*. *Exeunt.*

Scena Tertia.

Enter Prouost, Claudio, Iuliet, Officers, Lucio, & 2. Gent.

Cla. Fellow, why do'st thou show me thus to th'world?
Beare me to prison, where I am committed.

Pro. I do it not in euill disposition,
But from Lord *Angelo* by speciall charge.

Clau. Thus can the demy-god (Authority)
Make vs pay downe, for our offence, by waight
The words of heauen; on whom it will, it will,
On whom it will not (soe) yet still 'tis iust. (straint.

Luc. Why how now *Claudio*? whence comes this re-

Cla. From too much liberty, (my *Lucio*) Liberty
As surfet is the father of much fast,
So euery Scope by the immoderate vse
Turnes to restraint: Our Natures doe pursue
Like Rats that rauyn downe their proper Bane,
A thirsty euill, and when we drinke, we die.

Luc. If I could speake so wisely vnder an arrest, I would send for certaine of my Creditors: and yet, to say the truth, I had as lief haue the foppery of freedome, as the mortality of imprisonment: what's thy offence, *Claudio*?

Cla. What (but to speake of) would offend againe.

Lucio What, is't murder?
Claudio No.
Lucio Lechery?
Claudio Call it so.
Provost Away, sir, you must go.
Claudio One word, good friend. – Lucio, a word with you.
Lucio A hundred, if they'll do you any good. Is lechery so looked after?
Claudio Thus stands it with me: upon a true contract
I got possession of Julietta's bed.
You know the lady; she is fast my wife,
Save that we do the denunciation lack
Of outward order. This we came not to
Only for propagation of a dower [6]
Remaining in the coffer of her friends,
From whom we thought it meet to hide our love
Till time had made them for us. But it chances
The stealth of our most mutual entertainment
With character too gross is writ on Juliet.
Lucio With child, perhaps?
Claudio Unhappily, even so.
And the new Deputy now for the Duke –
Whether it be the fault and glimpse of newness,
Or whether that the body public be
A horse whereon the governor doth ride,
Who, newly in the seat, that it may know
He can command, lets it straight feel the spur;
Whether the tyranny be in his place,
Or in his eminence that fills it up,
I stagger in – but this new governor
Awakes me all the enrollèd penalties
Which have, like unscour'd armour, hung by th' wall
So long that nineteen zodiacs have gone round,[7]
And none of them been worn; and for a name

Luc. What, is't murder?
Cla. No.
Luc. Lecherie?
Cla. Call it so.
Pro. Away, Sir, you must goe.
Cla. One word, good friend:
Lucio, a word with you.
Luc. A hundred:
If they'll doe you any good: Is *Lechery* so look'd after?
Cla. Thus stands it with me: vpon a true contract
I got possession of *Iulietas* bed,
You know the Lady, she is fast my wife,
Saue that we doe the denunciation lacke
Of outward Order. This we came not to,
Onely for propogation of a Dowre
Remaining in the Coffer of her friends,
From whom we thought it meet to hide our Loue
Till Time had made them for vs. But it chances
The stealth of our most mutuall entertainment
With Character too grosse, is writ on *Iuliet*.
Luc. With childe, perhaps?
Cla. Vnhappely, euen so.
And the new Deputie, now for the Duke,
Whether it be the fault and glimpse of newnes,
Or whether that the body publique, be
A horse whereon the Gouernor doth ride,
Who newly in the Seate, that it may know
He can command; lets it strait feele the spur:
Whether the Tirranny be in his place,
Or in his Eminence that fills it vp
I stagger in: But this new Gouernor
Awakes me all the inrolled penalties
Which haue (like vn-scowr'd Armor) hung by th'wall
So long, that ninteene Zodiacks haue gone round,
And none of them beene worne; and for a name

Now puts the drowsy and neglected Act
Freshly on me. 'Tis surely for a name.

Lucio I warrant it is. And thy head stands so tickle on thy shoulders that a milkmaid, if she be in love, may sigh it off. Send after the Duke, and appeal to him.

Claudio I have done so, but he's not to be found.
I prithee, Lucio, do me this kind service:
This day my sister should the cloister enter,
And there receive her approbation.
Acquaint her with the danger of my state;
Implore her, in my voice, that she make friends
To the strict Deputy; bid herself assay him.
I have great hope in that, for in her youth
There is a prone and speechless dialect [8]
Such as move men; beside, she hath prosperous art
When she will play with reason and discourse,
And well she can persuade.

Lucio I pray she may – as well for the encouragement of the like, which else would stand under grievous imposition, as for the enjoying of thy life, who I would be sorry should be thus foolishly lost at a game of tick-tack. I'll to her.

Claudio I thank you, good friend Lucio.

Lucio Within two hours.

Claudio Come, officer, away. *Exeunt*

1.4

Enter DUKE *and Friar* THOMAS

Duke No, holy father, throw away that thought;
Believe not that the dribbling dart of Love
Can pierce a còmplete bosom. Why I desire thee
To give me secret harbour hath a purpose

Now puts the drowsie and neglected Act
Freshly on me: 'tis surely for a name.

Luc. I warrant it is: And thy head stands so tickle on thy shoulders, that a milke-maid, if she be in loue, may sigh it off: Send after the Duke, and appeale to him.

Cla. I haue done so, but hee's not to be found.
I pre'thee (*Lucio*) doe me this kinde seruice:
This day, my sister should the Cloyster enter,
And there receiue her approbation.
Acquaint her with the danger of my state,
Implore her, in my voice, that she make friends
To the strict deputie: bid her selfe assay him,
I haue great hope in that: for in her youth
There is a prone and speechlesse dialect,
Such as moue men: beside, she hath prosperous Art
When she will play with reason, and discourse,
And well she can perswade.

Luc. I pray shee may; aswell for the encouragement of the like, which else would stand vnder greeuous imposition: as for the enioying of thy life, who I would be sorry should bee thus foolishly lost, at a game of ticke-tacke: Ile to her.

Cla. I thanke you good friend *Lucio*.

Luc. Within two houres.

Cla. Come Officer, away. *Exeunt.*

Scena Quarta.

Enter Duke and Frier Thomas.

Duk. No: holy Father, throw away that thought,
Beleeue not that the dribling dart of Loue
Can pierce a compleat bosome: why, I desire thee
To giue me secret harbour, hath a purpose

More grave and wrinkled than the aims and ends
Of burning youth.

Thomas May your grace speak of it?

Duke My holy sir, none better knows than you
How I have ever lov'd the life remov'd,
And held in idle price to haunt assemblies
Where youth and cost witless bravery keeps.
I have deliver'd to Lord Angelo –
A man of stricture and firm abstinence –
My absolute power and place here in Vienna;
And he supposes me travell'd to Poland,
For so I have strew'd it in the common ear,
And so it is receiv'd. Now, pious sir,
You will demand of me why I do this.

Thomas Gladly, my lord.

Duke We have strict statutes and most biting laws,
The needful bits and curbs to headstrong weeds,[9]
Which for this fourteen years we have let slip,
Even like an o'ergrown lion in a cave
That goes not out to prey. Now, as fond fathers,
Having bound up the threatening twigs of birch
Only to stick it in their children's sight
For terror, not to use – in time the rod
More mock'd than fear'd – so our decrees,[10]
Dead to infliction, to themselves are dead,
And Liberty plucks Justice by the nose,
The baby beats the nurse, and quite athwart
Goes all decorum.

Thomas It rested in your grace
To unloose this tied-up justice when you pleas'd,
And it in you more dreadful would have seem'd
Than in Lord Angelo.

Duke I do fear, *too* dreadful.
Sith 'twas my fault to give the people scope,
'Twould be my tyranny to strike and gall them

More graue, and wrinkled, then the aimes, and ends
Of burning youth.
Fri. May your Grace speake of it?
Duk. My holy Sir, none better knowes then you
How I haue euer lou'd the life remoued
And held in idle price, to haunt assemblies
Where youth, and cost, witlesse brauery keepes.
I haue deliuerd to Lord *Angelo*
(A man of stricture and firme abstinence)
My absolute power, and place here in *Vienna*,
And he supposes me trauaild to *Poland*,
(For so I haue strewd it in the common eare)
And so it is receiu'd: Now (pious Sir)
You will demand of me, why I do this.
Fri. Gladly, my Lord.
Duk. We haue strict Statutes, and most biting Laws,
(The needfull bits and curbes to headstrong weedes,)
Which for this foureteene yeares, we haue let slip,
Euen like an ore-growne Lyon in a Caue
That goes not out to prey: Now, as fond Fathers,
Hauing bound vp the threatning twigs of birch,
Onely to sticke it in their childrens sight,
For terror, not to vse: in time the rod
More mock'd, then fear'd: so our Decrees,
Dead to infliction, to themselues are dead,
And libertie, plucks Iustice by the nose;
The Baby beates the Nurse, and quite athw art
Goes all decorum.
Fri. It rested in your Grace
To vnloose this tyde-vp Iustice, when you pleas'd:
And it in you more dreadfull would haue seem'd
Then in Lord *Angelo*.
Duk. I doe feare: too dreadfull:
Sith 'twas my fault, to giue the people scope,
'T would be my tirrany to strike and gall them,

For what I bid them do: for we bid this be done
When evil deeds have their permissive pass
And not the punishment. Therefore indeed, my father,
I have on Angelo impos'd the office,
Who may in th'ambush of my name strike home,
And yet my nature never in the fight
To do in slander. And, to behold his sway,
I will, as 'twere a brother of your order,
Visit both prince and people. Therefore I prithee
Supply me with the habit, and instruct me
How I may formally in person bear
Like a true friar. More reasons for this action
At our more leisure shall I render you –
Only this one: Lord Angelo is precise;
Stands at a guard with Envy; scarce confesses
That his blood flows, or that his appetite
Is more to bread than stone. Hence shall we see,
If power change purpose, what our seemers be.

Exeunt

1.5

Enter ISABEL *and Francisca, a* NUN

Isabel And have you nuns no farther privileges?
Nun Are not these large enough?
Isabel Yes, truly. I speak not as desiring more,
But rather wishing a more strict restraint
Upon the sisterhood, the votarists of Saint Clare.[11]
Lucio (*Within*) Ho! Peace be in this place!
Isabel Who's that which calls?
Nun It is a man's voice. Gentle Isabella,
Turn you the key, and know his business of him.

For what I bid them doe: For, we bid this be done
When euill deedes haue their permissiue passe,
And not the punishment: therefore indeede (my father)
I haue on *Angelo* impos'd the office,
Who may in th'ambush of my name, strike home,
And yet, my nature neuer in the fight
To do in slander: And to behold his sway
I will, as 'twere a brother of your Order,
Visit both Prince, and People: Therefore I pre'thee
Supply me with the habit, and instruct me
How I may formally in person beare
Like a true *Frier*: Moe reasons for this action
At our more leysure, shall I render you;
Onely, this one: Lord *Angelo* is precise,
Stands at a guard with Enuie: scarce confesses
That his blood flowes: or that his appetite
Is more to bread then stone: hence shall we see
If power change purpose: what our Seemers be. *Exit.*

Scena Quinta.

Enter Isabell and Francisca a Nun.

Isa. And haue you *Nuns* no farther priuiledges?
Nun. Are not these large enough?
Isa. Yes truely; I speake not as desiring more,
But rather wishing a more strict restraint
Vpon the Sisterstood, the Votarists of Saint *Clare.*
Lucio within.
Luc. Hoa? peace be in this place.
Isa. Who's that which cals?
Nun. It is a mans voice: gentle *Isabella*
Turne you the key, and know his businesse of him;

You may, I may not; you are yet unsworn.
When you have vow'd, you must not speak with men
But in the presence of the Prioress.
Then, if you speak, you must not show your face;
Or, if you show your face, you must not speak.
He calls again. I pray you answer him.

Isabel Peace and prosperity! Who is't that calls?

[*Enter* LUCIO][12]

Lucio Hail, virgin, if you be – as those cheek-roses
Proclaim you are no less. Can you so stead me
As bring me to the sight of Isabella,
A novice of this place, and the fair sister
To her unhappy brother Claudio?

Isabel Why 'her unhappy brother'? Let me ask,
The rather for I now must make you know
I am that Isabella, and his sister.

Lucio Gentle and fair, your brother kindly greets you.
Not to be weary with you, he's in prison.

Isabel Woe me! For what?

Lucio For that which, if myself might be his judge,
He should receive his punishment in thanks:
He hath got his friend with child.

Isabel Sir, make me not your story.

Lucio 'Tis true!
I would not – though 'tis my familiar sin
With maids to seem the lapwing, and to jest,
Tongue far from heart – play with all virgins so.
I hold you as a thing enskied and sainted
By your renouncement, an immortal spirit,
And to be talk'd with in sincerity
As with a saint.

Isabel You do blaspheme the good in mocking me.

Lucio Do not believe it. Fewness and truth, 'tis thus:
Your brother and his lover have embrac'd.
As those that feed grow full; as blossoming Time
That from the seedness the bare fallow brings

You may; I may not: you are yet vnsworne:
When you haue vowd, you must not speake with men,
But in the presence of the *Prioresse*;
Then if you speake, you must not show your face;
Or if you show your face, you must not speake.
He cals againe: I pray you answere him.
Isa. Peace and prosperitie: who is't that cals?
Luc. Haile Virgin, (if you be) as those cheeke-Roses
Proclaime you are no lesse: can you so steed me,
As bring me to the sight of *Isabella*,
A Nouice of this place, and the faire Sister
To her vnhappie brother *Claudio*?
Isa. Why her vnhappy Brother? Let me aske,
The rather for I now must make you know
I am that *Isabella*, and his Sister.
Luc. Gentle & faire: your Brother kindly greets you;
Not to be weary with you; he's in prison.
Isa. Woe me; for what?
Luc. For that, which if my selfe might be his Iudge,
He should receiue his punishment, in thankes:
He hath got his friend with childe.
Isa. Sir, make me not your storie.
Luc. 'Tis true; I would not, though 'tis my familiar sin,
With Maids to seeme the Lapwing, and to iest
Tongue, far from heart: play with all Virgins so:
I hold you as a thing en-skied, and sainted,
By your renouncement, an imortall spirit
And to be talk'd with in sincerity,
As with a Saint.
Isa. You doe blaspheme the good, in mocking me.
Luc. Doe not beleeue it: fewnes, and truth; tis thus,
Your brother, and his louer haue embrac'd;
As those that feed, grow full: as blossoming Time
That from the seednes, the bare fallow brings

To teeming foison; even so her plenteous womb
Expresseth his full tilth and husbandry.

Isabel Someone with child by him? My cousin Juliet?

Lucio Is she your cousin?

Isabel Adoptedly, as schoolmaids change their names
By vain though apt affection.

Lucio She it is.

Isabel Oh, let him marry her!

Lucio This is the point.
The Duke is very strangely gone from hence;
Bore many gentlemen – myself being one –
In hand, and hope of action; but we do learn,
By those that know the very nerves of state,
His giving-out were of an infinite distance
From his true-meant design. Upon his place,
And with full line of his authority,
Governs Lord Angelo: a man whose blood
Is very snow-broth, one who never feels
The wanton stings and motions of the sense,
But doth rebate and blunt his natural edge
With profits of the mind, study and fast.
He, to give fear to use and liberty –
Which have for long run by the hideous law,
As mice by lions – hath pick'd out an Act
Under whose heavy sense your brother's life
Falls into forfeit; he arrests him on it,
And follows close the rigour of the statute
To make him an example. All hope is gone,
Unless you have the grace by your fair prayer
To soften Angelo. And that's my pith of business
'Twixt you and your poor brother.

Isabel Doth he so
Seek his life?

Lucio Has censur'd him already,
And, as I hear, the Provost hath a warrant

To teeming foyson: euen so her plenteous wombe
Expresseth his full Tilth, and husbandry.
Isa. Some one with childe by him? my cosen *Iuliet*?
Luc. Is she your cosen?
Isa. Adoptedly, as schoole-maids change their names
By vaine, though apt affection.
Luc. She it is.
Isa. Oh, let him marry her.
Luc. This is the point.
The Duke is very strangely gone from hence;
Bore many gentlemen (my selfe being one)
In hand, and hope of action: but we doe learne,
By those that know the very Nerues of State,
His giuing-out, were of an infinite distance
From his true meant designe: vpon his place,
(And with full line of his authority)
Gouernes Lord *Angelo*; A man, whose blood
Is very snow-broth: one, who neuer feeles
The wanton stings, and motions of the sence;
But doth rebate, and blunt his naturall edge
With profits of the minde: Studie, and fast
He (to giue feare to vse, and libertie,
Which haue, for long, run-by the hideous law,
As Myce, by Lyons) hath pickt out an act,
Vnder whose heauy sence, your brothers life
Fals into forfeit: he arrests him on it,
And followes close the rigor of the Statute
To make him an example: all hope is gone,
Vnlesse you haue the grace, by your faire praier
To soften *Angelo*: And that's my pith of businesse
'Twixt you, and your poore brother.
Isa. Doth he so,
Seeke his life?
Luc. Has censur'd him already,
And as I heare, the Prouost hath a warrant

For's execution.

Isabel Alas, what poor ability's in me
To do him good?

Lucio Assay the power you have.

Isabel My power? Alas, I doubt.

Lucio Our doubts are traitors,
And makes us lose the good we oft might win
By fearing to attempt. Go to Lord Angelo
And let him learn to know, when maidens sue,
Men give like gods, but when they weep and kneel,
All their petitions are as freely theirs
As they themselves would owe them.

Isabel I'll see what I can do.

Lucio But speedily.

Isabel I will about it straight,
No longer staying but to give the Mother
Notice of my affair. I humbly thank you.
Commend me to my brother; soon at night
I'll send him certain word of my success.

Lucio I take my leave of you.

Isabel Good sir, adieu. *Exeunt*

2.1

Enter ANGELO, ESCALUS, *servants, and a* JUSTICE

Angelo We must not make a scarecrow of the law,
Setting it up to fear the birds of prey,
And let it keep one shape till custom make it
Their perch, and not their terror.

Escalus Ay, but yet
Let us be keen, and rather cut a little
Than fall, and bruise to death. Alas, this gentleman
Whom I would save had a most noble father.

For's execution.
Isa. Alas: what poore
Abilitie's in me, to doe him good.
Luc. Assay the powre you haue.
Isa. My power? alas, I doubt.
Luc. Our doubts are traitors
And makes vs loose the good we oft might win,
By fearing to attempt: Goe to Lord *Angelo*
And let him learne to know, when Maidens sue
Men giue like gods: but when they weepe and kneele,
All their petitions, are as freely theirs
As they themselues would owe them.
Isa. Ile see what I can doe.
Luc. But speedily.
Isa. I will about it strait;
No longer staying, but to giue the Mother
Notice of my affaire: I humbly thanke you:
Commend me to my brother: soone at night
Ile send him certaine word of my successe.
Luc. I take my leaue of you.
Isa. Good sir, adieu. *Exeunt.*

Actus Secundus. Scœna Prima.

Enter Angelo, Escalus, and seruants, Iustice.

Ang. We must not make a scar-crow of the Law,
Setting it vp to feare the Birds of prey,
And let it keepe one shape, till custome make it
Their pearch, and not their terror.
Esc. I, but yet
Let vs be keene, and rather cut a little
Then fall, and bruise to death: alas, this gentleman
Whom I would saue, had a most noble father,

Let but your honour know –
Whom I believe to be most strait in virtue –
That in the working of your own affections,
Had time coher'd with place, or place with wishing,
Or that the resolute acting of our blood [13]
Could have attain'd th'effect of your own purpose,
Whether you had not sometime in your life
Err'd in this point which now you censure him,
And pull'd the law upon you.

Angelo 'Tis one thing to be tempted, Escalus,
Another thing to fall. I not deny
The jury passing on the prisoner's life
May in the sworn twelve have a thief or two
Guiltier than him they try. What's open made to justice,
That justice seizes. What knows the laws
That thieves do pass on thieves? 'Tis very pregnant,
The jewel that we find, we stoop and take't,
Because we see it; but what we do not see
We tread upon and never think of it.
You may not so extenuate his offence
For I have had such faults; but rather tell me,
When I that censure him do so offend,
Let mine own judgement pattern out my death
And nothing come in partial. Sir, he must die.

Enter PROVOST

Escalus Be it as your wisdom will.

Angelo Where is the Provost?

Provost Here, if it like your honour.

Angelo See that Claudio
Be executed by nine tomorrow morning.
Bring him his confessor, let him be prepar'd,
For that's the utmost of his pilgrimage.

[*Exit* PROVOST]

Escalus Well, heaven forgive him, and forgive us all:
'Some rise by sin, and some by virtue fall.'

Let but your honour know
(Whom I beleeue to be most strait in vertue)
That in the working of your owne affections,
Had time coheard with Place, or place with wishing,
Or that the resolute acting of our blood
Could haue attaind th'effect of your owne purpose,
Whether you had not sometime in your life
Er'd in this point, which now you censure him,
And puld the Law vpon you.
Ang. 'Tis one thing to be tempted (*Escalus*)
Another thing to fall: I not deny
The Iury passing on the Prisoners life
May in the sworne-twelue haue a thiefe, or two
Guiltier then him they try; what's open made to Iustice,
That Iustice ceizes; What knowes the Lawes
That theeues do passe on theeues? 'Tis very pregnant,
The Iewell that we finde, we stoope, and take't,
Because we see it; but what we doe not see,
We tread vpon, and neuer thinke of it.
You may not so extenuate his offence,
For I haue had such faults; but rather tell me
When I, that censure him, do so offend,
Let mine owne Iudgement patterne out my death,
And nothing come in partiall. Sir, he must dye.
Enter Prouost.
Esc. Be it as your wisedome will.
Ang. Where is the *Prouost*?
Pro. Here if it like your honour.
Ang. See that *Claudio*
Be executed by nine to morrow morning,
Bring him his Confessor, let him be prepar'd,
For that's the vtmost of his pilgrimage.
Esc. Well: heauen forgiue him; and forgiue vs all:
Some rise by sinne, and some by vertue fall:

Some run from brakes of ice, and answer none,
And some condemnèd for a fault alone.[14]

Enter ELBOW, *with* FROTH
and CLOWN *in the custody of officers*

Elbow Come, bring them away. If these be good people in a commonweal that do nothing but use their abuses in common houses, I know no law. Bring them away.

Angelo How now, sir, what's your name, and what's the matter?

Elbow If it please your honour, I am the poor Duke's constable, and my name is Elbow. I do lean upon justice, sir, and do bring in here before your good honour two notorious benefactors.

Angelo 'Benefactors'? Well, what benefactors are they? Are they not malefactors?

Elbow If it please your honour, I know not well what they are. But precise villains they are, that I am sure of, and void of all profanation in the world that good Christians ought to have.

Escalus This comes off well; here's a wise officer.

Angelo Go to. What quality are they of? Elbow is your name? Why dost thou not speak, Elbow?

Clown He cannot, sir: he's out at elbow.

Angelo What are you, sir?

Elbow He, sir? A tapster, sir; parcel bawd; one that serves a bad woman, whose house, sir, was, as they say, plucked down in the suburbs; and now she professes a hot-house which I think is a very ill house too.

Escalus How know you that?

Elbow My wife, sir, whom I detest before heaven and your honour –

Escalus How? Thy wife?

Elbow Ay, sir: whom I thank heaven is an honest woman –

Some run from brakes of Ice, and answere none,
And some condemned for a fault alone.

Enter Elbow, Froth, Clowne, Officers.

Elb. Come, bring them away: if these be good people in a Common-weale, that doe nothing but vse their abuses in common houses, I know no law: bring them away.

Ang. How now Sir, what's your name? And what's the matter?

Elb. If it please your honour, I am the poore Dukes Constable, and my name is *Elbow*; I doe leane vpon Iustice Sir, and doe bring in here before your good honor, two notorious Benefactors.

Ang. Benefactors? Well: What Benefactors are they? Are they not Malefactors?

Elb. If it please your honour, I know not well what they are: But precise villaines they are, that I am sure of, and void of all prophanation in the world, that good Christians ought to haue.

Esc. This comes off well: here's a wise Officer.

Ang. Goe to: What quality are they of? *Elbow* is your name?
Why do'st thou not speake *Elbow*?

Clo. He cannot Sir: he's out at Elbow.

Ang. What are you Sir?

Elb. He Sir: a Tapster Sir: parcell Baud: one that serues a bad woman: whose house Sir was (as they say) pluckt downe in the Suborbs: and now shee professes a hot-house; which, I thinke is a very ill house too.

Esc. How know you that?

Elb. My wife Sir? whom I detest before heauen, and your honour.

Esc. How? thy wife?

Elb. I Sir: whom I thanke heauen is an honest woman.

Escalus Dost thou 'detest' her therefore?

Elbow I say, sir, I will detest myself also, as well as she, that this house, if it be not a bawd's house, it is pity of her life, for it is a naughty house.

Escalus How dost thou know that, Constable?

Elbow Marry, sir, by my wife, who, if she had been a woman cardinally given, might have been accused in fornication, adultery, and all uncleanliness there.

Escalus By the woman's means?

Elbow Ay, sir, by Mistress Overdone's means. But as she spit in his face, so she defied him.

Clown Sir, if it please your honour, this is not so.

Elbow Prove it before these varlets here, thou honourable man, prove it!

Escalus Do you hear how he misplaces?

Clown Sir, she came in great with child, and longing (saving your honour's reverence) for stewed prunes. Sir, we had but two in the house, which at that very distant time stood,[15] as it were, in a fruit dish – a dish of some threepence: your honours have seen such dishes. They are not china dishes, but very good dishes –

Escalus Go to, go to. No matter for the dish, sir.

Clown No indeed, sir, not of a pin, you are therein in the right. But to the point. As I say, this Mistress Elbow, being (as I say) with child, and being great-bellied, and longing (as I said) for prunes, and having but two in the dish (as I said), Master Froth here, this very man, having eaten the rest (as I said) and (as I say) paying for them very honestly – for, as you know, Master Froth, I could not give you threepence again –

Froth No indeed.

Clown Very well. You being then (if you be remembered) cracking the stones of the foresaid prunes –

Froth Ay, so I did indeed.

Clown Why, very well. I telling you then (if you be

Esc. Do'st thou detest her therefore?

Elb. I say sir, I will detest my selfe also, as well as she, that this house, if it be not a Bauds house, it is pitty of her life, for it is a naughty house.

Esc. How do'st thou know that, Constable?

Elb. Marry sir, by my wife, who, if she had bin a woman Cardinally giuen, might haue bin accus'd in fornication, adultery, and all vncleanlinesse there.

Esc. By the womans meanes?

Elb. I sir, by Mistris *Ouer-dons* meanes: but as she spit in his face, so she defide him.

Clo. Sir, if it please your honor, this is not so.

Elb. Proue it before these varlets here, thou honorable man, proue it.

Esc. Doe you heare how he misplaces?

Clo. Sir, she came in great with childe: and longing (sauing your honors reuerence) for stewd prewyns; sir, we had but two in the house, which at that very distant time stood, as it were in a fruit dish (a dish of some three pence; your honours haue seene such dishes) they are not China-dishes, but very good dishes.

Esc. Go too: go too: no matter for the dish sir.

Clo. No indeede sir not of a pin; you are therein in the right: but, to the point: As I say, this Mistris *Elbow*, being (as I say) with childe, and being great bellied, and longing (as I said) for prewyns: and hauing but two in the dish (as I said) Master *Froth* here, this very man, hauin g eaten the rest (as I said) & (as I say) paying for them very honestly: for, as you know Master *Froth*, I could not giue you three pence againe.

Fro. No indeede.

Clo. Very well: you being then (if you be remembred) cracking the stones of the foresaid prewyns.

Fro. I, so I did indeede.

Clo. Why, very well: I telling you then (if you be

remembered) that such-a-one and such-a-one were past cure of the thing you wot of, unless they kept very good diet, as I told you –

Froth All this is true.

Clown Why, very well then –

Escalus Come, you are a tedious fool. To the purpose. What was done to Elbow's wife that he hath cause to complain of? Come me to what was done to her.

Clown Sir, your honour cannot come to that yet!

Escalus No, sir, nor I mean it not.

Clown Sir, but you shall come to it, by your honour's leave. And I beseech you, look into Master Froth here, sir, a man of four-score pound a year, whose father died at Hallowmas – was't not at Hallowmas, Master Froth?

Froth All Hallow Eve.

Clown Why, very well. I hope here be truths. He, sir, sitting (as I say) in a lower chair, sir – 'twas in the Bunch of Grapes, where indeed you have a delight to sit, have you not?

Froth I have so, because it is an open room, and good for winter.

Clown Why, very well then. I hope here be truths.

Angelo This will last out a night in Russia
When nights are longest there. I'll take my leave,
And leave you to the hearing of the cause,
Hoping you'll find good cause to whip them all.

Escalus I think no less. Good morrow to your lordship.

Exit ANGELO

Now, sir, come on. What was done to Elbow's wife, once more?

Clown Once, sir? There was nothing done to her once.

Elbow I beseech you, sir, ask him what this man did to my wife.

Clown I beseech your honour, ask me.

Escalus Well, sir, what did this gentleman to her?

remembred) that such a one, and such a one, were past cure of the thing you wot of, vnlesse they kept very good diet, as I told you.

Fro. All this is true.

Clo. Why very well then.

Esc. Come: you are a tedious foole: to the purpose: what was done to *Elbowes* wife, that hee hath cause to complaine of? Come me to what was done to her.

Clo. Sir, your honor cannot come to that yet.

Esc. No sir, nor I meane it not.

Clo. Sir, but you shall come to it, by your honours leaue: And I beseech you, looke into Master *Froth* here sir, a man of foure-score pound a yeare; whose father died at *Hallowmas*: Was't not at *Hallowmas* Master *Froth*?

Fro. Allhallond-Eue.

Clo. Why very well: I hope here be truthes: he Sir, sitting (as I say) in a lower chaire, Sir, 'twas in the bunch of Grapes, where indeede you haue a delight to sit, haue you not?

Fro. I haue so, because it is an open roome, and good for winter.

Clo. Why very well then: I hope here be truthes.

Ang. This will last out a night in *Russia*
When nights are longest there: Ile take my leaue,
And leaue you to the hearing of the cause;
Hoping youle finde good cause to whip them all. *Exit.*

Esc. I thinke no lesse: good morrow to your Lordship. Now Sir, come on: What was done to *Elbowes* wife, once more?

Clo. Once Sir? there was nothing done to her once.

Elb. I beseech you Sir, aske him what this man did to my wife.

Clo. I beseech your honor, aske me.

Esc. Well sir, what did this Gentleman to her?

Clown I beseech you, sir, look in this gentleman's face. Good Master Froth, look upon his honour; 'tis for a good purpose. Doth your honour mark his face?

Escalus Ay, sir, very well.

Clown Nay, I beseech you, mark it well.

Escalus Well, I do so.

Clown Doth your honour see any harm in his face?

Escalus Why, no.

Clown I'll be supposed upon a book, his face is the worst thing about him. Good, then. If his face be the worst thing about him, how could Master Froth do the constable's wife any harm? I would know that of your honour.

Escalus He's in the right, Constable. What say you to it?

Elbow First, an it like you, the house is a respected house; next, this is a respected fellow; and his mistress is a respected woman.

Clown By this hand, sir, his wife is a more respected person than any of us all.

Elbow Varlet, thou liest! Thou liest, wicked varlet! The time is yet to come that she was ever respected with man, woman, or child!

Clown Sir, she was respected with him before he married with her.

Escalus Which is the wiser here, Justice or Iniquity? – Is this true?

Elbow Oh, thou caitiff! Oh, thou varlet! Oh, thou wicked Hannibal! I, respected with her before I was married to her? – If ever I was respected with her, or she with me, let not your worship think me the poor Duke's officer. – Prove this, thou wicked Hannibal, or I'll have mine action of battery on thee.

Escalus If he took you a box o'th'ear, you might have your action of slander too.

Elbow Marry, I thank your good worship for it. What is't

Clo. I beseech you sir, looke in this Gentlemans face: good Master *Froth* looke vpon his honor; 'tis for a good purpose: doth your honor marke his face?

Esc. I sir, very well.

Clo. Nay, I beseech you marke it well.

Esc. Well, I doe so.

Clo. Doth your honor see any harme in his face?

Esc. Why no.

Clo. Ile be supposd vpon a booke, his face is the worst thing about him: good then: if his face be the worst thing about him, how could Master *Froth* doe the Constables wife any harme? I would know that of your honour.

Esc. He's in the right (Constable) what say you to it?

Elb. First, and it like you, the house is a respected house; next, this is a respected fellow; and his Mistris is a respected woman.

Clo. By this hand Sir, his wife is a more respected person then any of vs all.

Elb. Varlet, thou lyest; thou lyest wicked varlet: the time is yet to come that shee was euer respected with man, woman, or childe.

Clo. Sir, she was respected with him, before he married with her.

Esc. Which is the wiser here; *Iustice* or *Iniquitie*? Is this true?

Elb. O thou caytiffe: O thou varlet: O thou wicked *Hanniball*; I respected with her, before I was married to her? If euer I was respected with her, or she with me, let not your worship thinke mee the poore *Dukes* Officer: proue this, thou wicked *Hanniball*, or ile haue mine action of battry on thee.

Esc. If he tooke you a box 'oth'eare, you might haue your action of slander too.

Elb. Marry I thanke your good worship for it: what

your worship's pleasure I shall do with this wicked caitiff?

Escalus Truly, officer, because he hath some offences in him that thou wouldst discover if thou couldst, let him continue in his courses till thou know'st what they are.

Elbow Marry, I thank your worship for it. – Thou seest, thou wicked varlet now, what's come upon thee. Thou art to continue now, thou varlet, thou art to continue.

Escalus Where were you born, friend?

Froth Here in Vienna, sir.

Escalus Are you of four-score pounds a year?

Froth Yes, an't please you, sir.

Escalus So. – What trade are you of, sir?

Clown A tapster, a poor widow's tapster.

Escalus Your mistress' name?

Clown Mistress Overdone.

Escalus Hath she had any more than one husband?

Clown Nine, sir; Overdone by the last.

Escalus Nine? – Come hither to me, Master Froth. Master Froth, I would not have you acquainted with tapsters: they will draw you, Master Froth, and you will hang them. Get you gone, and let me hear no more of you.

Froth I thank your worship. For mine own part, I never come into any room in a tap-house, but I am drawn in.

Escalus Well, no more of it, Master Froth. Farewell.

[*Exit* FROTH]

Come you hither to me, Master Tapster. What's your name, Master Tapster?

Clown Pompey.

Escalus What else?

Clown Bum, sir.

Escalus Troth, and your bum is the greatest thing about you, so that, in the beastliest sense, you are 'Pompey the Great'. Pompey, you are partly a bawd, Pompey, howsoever you colour it in being a tapster, are you

is't your Worships pleasure I shall doe with this wicked Caitiffe?

Esc. Truly Officer, because he hath some offences in him, that thou wouldst discouer, if thou couldst, let him continue in his courses, till thou knowst what they are.

Elb. Marry I thanke your worship for it: Thou seest thou wicked varlet now, what's come vpon thee. Thou art to continue now thou Varlet, thou art to continue.

Esc. Where were you borne, friend?

Froth. Here in *Vienna*, Sir.

Esc. Are you of fourescore pounds a yeere?

Froth. Yes, and 't please you sir.

Esc. So: what trade are you of, sir?

Clo. A Tapster, a poore widdowes Tapster.

Esc. Your Mistris name?

Clo. Mistris *Ouer-don*.

Esc. Hath she had any more then one husband?

Clo. Nine, sir: *Ouer-don* by the last.

Esc. Nine? come hether to me, Master *Froth*; Master *Froth*, I would not haue you acquainted with Tapsters; they will draw you Master *Froth*, and you will hang them: get you gon, and let me heare no more of you.

Fro. I thanke your worship: for mine owne part, I neuer come into any roome in a Tap-house, but I am drawne in.

Esc. Well: no more of it Master *Froth*: farewell: Come you hether to me, M^{r}. Tapster: what's your name M^{r}. Tapster?

Clo. Pompey.

Esc. What else?

Clo. Bum, Sir.

Esc. Troth, and your bum is the greatest thing about you, so that in the beastliest sence, you are *Pompey* the great; *Pompey*, you are partly a bawd, *Pompey*; howsoeuer you colour it in being a Tapster, are you not? come, not? Come, tell me true, it shall be the better for you.

Clown Truly, sir, I am a poor fellow that would live.

Escalus *How* would you live, Pompey? By being a bawd? What do you think of the trade, Pompey? Is it a lawful trade?

Clown If the law would allow it, sir.

Escalus But the law will not allow it, Pompey, nor it shall not be allowed in Vienna.

Clown Does your worship mean to geld and spay all the youth of the city?

Escalus No, Pompey.

Clown Truly, sir, in my poor opinion, they will to't then. If your worship will take order for the drabs and the knaves, you need not to fear the bawds.

Escalus There is pretty orders beginning, I can tell you. It is but heading and hanging.

Clown If you head and hang all that offend that way but for ten year together, you'll be glad to give out a commission for more heads. If this law hold in Vienna ten year, I'll rent the fairest house in it after threepence a bay. If you live to see this come to pass, say Pompey told you so.

Escalus Thank you, good Pompey. And in requital of your prophecy, hark you: I advise you, let me not find you before me again upon any complaint whatsoever; no, not for dwelling where you do. If I do, Pompey, I shall beat you to your tent, and prove a shrewd Caesar to you. In plain dealing, Pompey, I shall have you whipped. So for this time, Pompey, fare you well.

Clown I thank your worship for your good counsel – [*Aside*] but I shall follow it as the flesh and fortune shall better determine.

Whip me? No, no, let car-man whip his jade:
The valiant heart's not whipp'd out of his trade. *Exit*

Escalus Come hither to me, Master Elbow, come hither,

tell me true, it shall be the better for you.

Clo. Truly sir, I am a poore fellow that would liue.

Esc. How would you liue *Pompey*? by being a bawd? what doe you thinke of the trade *Pompey*? is it a lawfull trade?

Clo. If the Law would allow it, sir.

Esc. But the Law will not allow it *Pompey*; nor it shall not be allowed in *Uienna*.

Clo. Do's your Worship meane to geld and splay all the youth of the City?

Esc. No, *Pompey*.

Clo. Truely Sir, in my poore opinion they will too't then: if your worship will take order for the drabs and the knaues, you need not to feare the bawds.

Esc. There is pretty orders beginning I can tell you: It is but heading, and hanging.

Clo. If you head, and hang all that offend that way but for ten yeare together; you'll be glad to giue out a Commission for more heads: if this law hold in *Vienna* ten yeare, ile rent the fairest house in it after three pence a Bay: if you liue to see this come to passe, say *Pompey* told you so.

Esc. Thanke you good *Pompey*; and in requitall of your prophesie, harke you: I aduise you let me not finde you before me againe vpon any complaint whatsoeuer; no, not for dwelling where you doe: if I doe *Pompey*, I shall beat you to your Tent, and proue a shrewd *Cæsar* to you: in plaine dealing *Pompey*, I shall haue you whipt; so for this time, *Pompey*, fare you well.

Clo. I thanke your Worship for your good counsell; but I shall follow it as the flesh and fortune shall better determine. Whip me? no, no, let Carman whip his Iade,
The valiant heart's not whipt out of his trade. *Exit.*

Esc. Come hether to me, Master *Elbow*: come hither

Master Constable. How long have you been in this place of constable?

Elbow Seven year and a half, sir.

Escalus I thought, by the readiness in the office, you had continued in it some time. You say seven years together?

Elbow And a half, sir.

Escalus Alas, it hath been great pains to you; they do you wrong to put you so oft upon't. Are there not men in your ward sufficient to serve it?

Elbow Faith, sir, few of any wit in such matters. As they are chosen, they are glad to choose me for them. I do it for some piece of money, and go through with all.

Escalus Look you bring me in the names of some six or seven, the most sufficient of your parish.

Elbow To your worship's house, sir?

Escalus To my house. Fare you well. [*Exit* ELBOW]
What's o'clock, think you?

Justice Eleven, sir.

Escalus I pray you home to dinner with me.

Justice I humbly thank you.

Escalus It grieves me for the death of Claudio,
But there's no remedy.

Justice Lord Angelo is severe.

Escalus It is but needful.
Mercy is not itself that oft looks so;
Pardon is still the nurse of second woe.
But yet, poor Claudio! There is no remedy.
Come, sir. *Exeunt*

Master Constable: how long haue you bin in this place of Constable?

Elb. Seuen yeere, and a halfe sir.

Esc. I thought by the readinesse in the office, you had continued in it some time: you say seauen yeares together.

Elb. And a halfe sir.

Esc. Alas, it hath beene great paines to you: they do you wrong to put you so oft vpon't. Are there not men in your Ward sufficient to serue it?

Elb. 'Faith sir, few of any wit in such matters: as they are chosen, they are glad to choose me for them; I do it for some peece of money, and goe through with all.

Esc. Looke you bring mee in the names of some sixe or seuen, the most sufficient of your parish.

Elb. To your Worships house sir?

Esc. To my house: fare you well: what's a clocke, thinke you?

Iust. Eleuen, Sir.

Esc. I pray you home to dinner with me.

Iust. I humbly thanke you.

Esc. It grieues me for the death of *Claudio*
But there's no remedie:

Iust. Lord *Angelo* is seuere.

Esc. It is but needfull.
Mercy is not it selfe, that oft lookes so,
Pardon is still the nurse of second woe:
But yet, poore *Claudio*; there is no remedie.
Come Sir. *Exeunt.*

2.2

Enter PROVOST *and a* SERVANT

Servant He's hearing of a cause; he will come straight.
I'll tell him of you.

Provost Pray you do. [*Exit* SERVANT]
I'll know
His pleasure; maybe he will relent. Alas,
He hath but as offended in a dream.
All sects, all ages smack of this vice – and he
To die for't?

Enter ANGELO

Angelo Now, what's the matter, Provost?

Provost Is it your will Claudio shall die tomorrow?

Angelo Did not I tell thee yea? Hadst thou not order?
Why dost thou ask again?

Provost Lest I might be too rash.
Under your good correction, I have seen
When, after execution, Judgement hath
Repented o'er his doom.

Angelo Go to; let that be mine.
Do you your office, or give up your place,
And you shall well be spar'd.

Provost I crave your honour's pardon.
What shall be done, sir, with the groaning Juliet?
She's very near her hour.

Angelo Dispose of her
To some more fitter place, and that with speed.

[*Enter* SERVANT]

Servant Here is the sister of the man condemn'd
Desires access to you.

Angelo Hath he a sister?

Provost Ay, my good lord, a very virtuous maid,
And to be shortly of a sisterhood,
If not already.

Angelo Well; let her be admitted. [*Exit* SERVANT]

Scena Secunda.

Enter Prouost, Seruant.

Ser. Hee's hearing of a Cause; he will come straight, I'le tell him of you.

Pro. 'Pray you doe; Ile know
His pleasure, may be he will relent; alas
He hath but as offended in a dreame,
All Sects, all Ages smack of this vice, and he
To die for't?

Enter Angelo.

Ang. Now, what's the matter *Prouost*?

Pro. Is it your will *Claudio* shall die to morrow?

Ang. Did not I tell thee yea? hadst thou not order?
Why do'st thou aske againe?

Pro. Lest I might be too rash:
Vnder your good correction, I haue seene
When after execution, Iudgement hath
Repented ore his doome.

Ang. Goe to; let that be mine,
Doe you your office, or giue vp your Place,
And you shall well be spar'd.

Pro. I craue your Honours pardon:
What shall be done Sir, with the groaning *Iuliet*?
Shee's very neere her howre.

Ang. Dispose of her
To some more fitter place; and that with speed.

Ser. Here is the sister of the man condemn'd,
Desires accesse to you.

Ang. Hath he a Sister?

Pro. I my good Lord, a very vertuous maid,
And to be shortlie of a Sister-hood,
If not alreadie.

Ang. Well: let her be admitted,

See you the fornicatress be remov'd.
Let her have needful but not lavish means.
There shall be order for't.

Enter LUCIO *and* ISABEL

Provost Save your honour.
Angelo Stay a little while. – You're welcome. What's your will?
Isabel I am a woeful suitor to your honour,
Please but your honour hear me.
Angelo Well; what's your suit?
Isabel There is a vice that most I do abhor,
And most desire should meet the blow of justice;
For which I would not plead, but that I must,
For which I must not plead, but that I am
At war 'twixt will and will not.
Angelo Well; the matter?
Isabel I have a brother is condemn'd to die:
I do beseech you, let it be his fault,
And not my brother.
Provost [*Aside*] Heaven give thee moving graces![16]
Angelo Condemn the fault, and not the actor of it?
Why, every fault's condemn'd ere it be done.
Mine were the very cipher of a function
To fine the faults, whose fine stands in record,
And let go by the actor.
Isabel O just but severe law!
I *had* a brother, then. Heaven keep your honour.
Lucio [*Aside*] Give't not o'er so. To him again, entreat him,
Kneel down before him, hang upon his gown.
You are too cold. If you should need a pin,
You could not with more tame a tongue desire it.
To him, I say.
Isabel Must he needs die?
Angelo Maiden, no remedy.
Isabel Yes: I do think that you might pardon him,
And neither heaven nor man grieve at the mercy.

See you the Fornicatresse be remou'd,
Let her haue needfull, but not lauish meanes,
There shall be order for't.

Enter Lucio and Isabella.

Pro. 'Saue your Honour.
Ang. Stay a little while: y'are welcome: what's your | will?
Isab. I am a wofull Sutor to your Honour,
'Please but your Honor heare me.
Ang. Well: what's your suite.
Isab. There is a vice that most I doe abhorre,
And most desire should meet the blow of Iustice;
For which I would not plead, but that I must,
For which I must not plead, but that I am
At warre, twixt will, and will not.
Ang. Well: the matter?
Isab. I haue a brother is condemn'd to die,
I doe beseech you let it be his fault,
And not my brother.
Pro. Heauen giue thee mouing graces.
Ang. Condemne the fault, and not the actor of it,
Why euery fault's condemnd ere it be done:
Mine were the verie Cipher of a Function
To fine the faults, whose fine stands in record,
And let goe by the Actor:
Isab. Oh iust, but seuere Law:
I had a brother then; heauen keepe your honour.
Luc. Giue't not ore so: to him againe, entreat him,
Kneele downe before him, hang vpon his gowne,
You are too cold: if you should need a pin,
You could not with more tame a tongue desire it:
To him, I say.
Isab. Must he needs die?
Ang. Maiden, no remedie.
Isab. Yes: I doe thinke that you might pardon him,
And neither heauen, nor man grieue at the mercy.

Angelo I will not do't.
Isabel But can you if you would?
Angelo Look what I will not, that I cannot do.
Isabel But might you do't, and do the world no wrong,
If so your heart were touch'd with that remorse
As mine is to him?
Angelo He's sentenc'd, 'tis too late.
Lucio [*Aside*] You are too cold.
Isabel Too late? Why, no! I that do speak a word
May call it again. Well, believe this:[17]
No ceremony that to great ones longs,
Not the king's crown, nor the deputed sword,
The marshal's truncheon, nor the judge's robe,
Become them with one half so good a grace
As mercy does.
If he had been as you, and you as he,
You would have slipp'd like him, but he like you
Would not have been so stern.
Angelo Pray you be gone.
Isabel I would to heaven I had your potency,
And you were Isabel. Should it then be thus?
No! I would tell what 'twere to be a judge,
And what a prisoner.
Lucio [*Aside*] Ay, touch him. There's the vein.
Angelo Your brother is a forfeit of the law,
And you but waste your words.
Isabel Alas, alas!
Why, all the souls that were, were forfeit once,
And He that might the vantage best have took
Found out the remedy. How would you be
If He, which is the top of judgement, should
But judge you as you are? O, think on that,
And mercy then will breathe within your lips
Like man new-made.
Angelo Be you content, fair maid,
It is the law, not I, condemn your brother.

Ang. I will not doe't.
Isab. But can you if you would?
Ang. Looke what I will not, that I cannot doe.
Isab. But might you doe't & do the world no wrong
If so your heart were touch'd with that remorse,
As mine is to him?
Ang. Hee's sentenc'd, tis too late.
Luc. You are too cold.
Isab. Too late? why no: I that doe speak a word
May call it againe: well, beleeue this
No ceremony that to great ones longs,
Not the Kings Crowne; nor the deputed sword,
The Marshalls Truncheon, nor the Iudges Robe
Become them with one halfe so good a grace
As mercie does: If he had bin as you, and you as he,
You would haue slipt like him, but he like you
Would not haue beene so sterne.
Ang. Pray you be gone.
Isab. I would to heauen I had your potencie,
And you were *Isabell*: should it then be thus?
No: I would tell what 'twere to be a Iudge,
And what a prisoner.
Luc. I, touch him: there's the vaine.
Ang. Your Brother is a forfeit of the Law,
And you but waste your words.
Isab. Alas, alas:
Why all the soules that were, were forfeit once,
And he that might the vantage best haue tooke,
Found out the remedie: how would you be,
If he, which is the top of Iudgement, should
But iudge you, as you are? Oh, thinke on that,
And mercie then will breathe within your lips
Like man new made.
Ang. Be you content, (faire Maid)
It is the Law, not I, condemne your brother,

Were he my kinsman, brother, or my son,
It should be thus with him: he must die tomorrow.

Isabel Tomorrow? Oh, that's sudden! Spare him, spare him!
He's not prepar'd for death. Even for our kitchens
We kill the fowl of season; shall we serve heaven
With less respect than we do minister
To our gross selves? Good, good my lord, bethink you:
Who is it that hath died for this offence?
There's many have committed it.

Lucio [*Aside*] Ay, well said.

Angelo The law hath not been dead, though it hath slept.
Those many had not dar'd to do that evil
If the first that did th'edict infringe
Had answer'd for his deed. Now 'tis awake,
Takes note of what is done, and like a prophet
Looks in a glass that shows what future evils –
Either now, or by remissness new-conceiv'd,[18]
And so, in progress, to be hatch'd and born –
Are now to have no successive degrees,
But here they live to end.

Isabel Yet show some pity!

Angelo I show it most of all when I show justice;
For then I pity those I do not know,
Which a dismiss'd offence would after gall,
And do him right that, answering one foul wrong,
Lives not to act another. Be satisfied.
Your brother dies tomorrow. Be content.

Isabel So you must be the first that gives this sentence,
And he, that suffers. O, it is excellent
To have a giant's strength, but it is tyrannous
To use it like a giant.

Lucio [*Aside*] That's well said.

Isabel Could great men thunder
As Jove himself does, Jove would ne'er be quiet,

Were he my kinsman, brother, or my sonne,
It should be thus with him: he must die to morrow.
Isab. To morrow? oh, that's sodaine,
Spare him, spare him:
Hee's not prepar'd for death; euen for our kitchins
We kill the fowle of season: shall we serue heauen
With lesse respect then we doe minister
To our grosse-selues? good, good, my Lord, bethink you;
Who is it that hath di'd for this offence?
There's many haue committed it.
Luc. I, well said.
Ang. The Law hath not bin dead, thogh it hath slept
Those many had not dar'd to doe that euill
If the first, that did th'Edict infringe
Had answer'd for his deed: Now 'tis awake,
Takes note of what is done, and like a Prophet
Lookes in a glasse that shewes what future euils
Either now, or by remissenesse, new conceiu'd,
And so in progresse to be hatch'd, and borne,
Are now to haue no successiue degrees,
But here they liue to end.
Isab. Yet shew some pittie.
Ang. I shew it most of all, when I show Iustice;
For then I pittie those I doe not know,
Which a dismis'd offence, would after gaule
And doe him right, that answering one foule wrong
Liues not to act another. Be satisfied;
Your Brother dies to morrow; be content.
Isab. So you must be ye first that giues this sentence,
And hee, that suffers: Oh, it is excellent
To haue a Giants strength: but it is tyrannous
To vse it like a Giant.
Luc. That's well said.
Isab. Could great men thunder
As *Ioue* himselfe do's, *Ioue* would neuer be quiet,

For every pelting petty officer
Would use his heaven for thunder, nothing but thunder!
Merciful heaven,
Thou rather with thy sharp and sulphurous bolt
Splits the unwedgeable and gnarlèd oak
Than the soft myrtle. But man, proud man,
Dress'd in a little brief authority,
Most ignorant of what he's most assur'd –
His glassy essence – like an angry ape
Plays such fantastic tricks before high heaven
As makes the angels weep, who with our spleens
Would all themselves laugh mortal.

Lucio [*Aside*] Oh, to him, to him, wench! He will relent,
He's coming, I perceive't.

Provost [*Aside*] Pray heaven she win him!

Isabel We cannot weigh our brother with ourself.
Great men may jest with saints; 'tis wit in them,
But in the less, foul profanation.

Lucio [*Aside*] Thou'rt i'th' right, girl, more o' that!

Isabel That in the captain's but a choleric word
Which in the soldier is flat blasphemy.

Lucio [*Aside*] Art advised o' that? More on't!

Angelo Why do you put these sayings upon me?

Isabel Because authority, though it err like others,
Hath yet a kind of medicine in itself
That skins the vice o'th' top. Go to your bosom,
Knock there, and ask your heart what it doth know
That's like my brother's fault. If it confess
A natural guiltiness, such as is his,
Let it not sound a thought upon your tongue
Against my brother's life.

Angelo [*Aside*] She speaks, and 'tis such sense
That my sense breeds with it. – Fare you well.

Isabel Gentle my lord, turn back.

Angelo I will bethink me. Come again tomorrow.

For euery pelting petty Officer
Would vse his heauen for thunder;
Nothing but thunder: Mercifull heauen,
Thou rather with thy sharpe and sulpherous bolt
Splits the vn-wedgable and gnarled Oke,
Then the soft Mertill: But man, proud man,
Drest in a little briefe authoritie,
Most ignorant of what he's most assur'd,
(His glassie Essence) like an angry Ape
Plaies such phantastique tricks before high heauen,
As makes the Angels weepe: who with our spleenes,
Would all themselues laugh mortall.

Luc. Oh, to him, to him wench: he will relent,
Hee's comming: I perceiue't.

Pro. Pray heauen she win him.

Isab. We cannot weigh our brother with our selfe,
Great men may iest with Saints: tis wit in them,
But in the lesse fowle prophanation.

Luc. Thou'rt i'th right (Girle) more o'that.

Isab. That in the Captaine's but a chollericke word,
Which in the Souldier is flat blasphemie.

Luc. Art auis'd o'that? more on't.

Ang. Why doe you put these sayings vpon me?

Isab. Because Authoritie, though it erre like others,
Hath yet a kinde of medicine in it selfe
That skins the vice o'th top; goe to your bosome,
Knock there, and aske your heart what it doth know
That's like my brothers fault: if it confesse
A naturall guiltinesse, such as is his,
Let it not sound a thought vpon your tongue
Against my brothers life.

Ang. Shee speakes, and 'tis such sence
That my Sence breeds with it; fare you well.

Isab. Gentle my Lord, turne backe.

Ang. I will bethinke me: come againe to morrow.

Isabel Hark how I'll bribe you: good my lord, turn back.
Angelo How? Bribe me?
Isabel Ay, with such gifts that heaven shall share with you.
Lucio [*Aside*] You had marred all else.
Isabel Not with fond sicles of the tested gold,[19]
Or stones whose rate are either rich or poor
As fancy values them; but with true prayers
That shall be up at heaven and enter there
Ere sunrise – prayers from preservèd souls,
From fasting maids whose minds are dedicate
To nothing temporal.
Angelo Well; come to me tomorrow.
Lucio [*Aside*] Go to. 'Tis well. Away.
Isabel Heaven keep your honour safe!
Angelo [*Aside*] Amen.
For I am that way going to temptation
Where prayers cross.
Isabel At what hour tomorrow
Shall I attend your lordship?
Angelo At any time 'fore noon.
Isabel Save your honour.
[*Exeunt* ISABEL, LUCIO, *and* PROVOST]
Angelo From thee – even from thy virtue!
What's this? What's this? Is this her fault or mine?
The tempter or the tempted, who sins most, ha?
Not she, nor doth she tempt; but it is I
That, lying by the violet in the sun,
Do as the carrion does, not as the flower,
Corrupt with virtuous season. Can it be
That modesty may more betray our sense
Than woman's lightness? Having waste-ground enough,
Shall we desire to raze the sanctuary
And pitch our evils there? Oh fie, fie, fie!
What dost thou, or what art thou, Angelo?
Dost thou desire her foully for those things
That make her good? O, let her brother live!

Isa. Hark, how Ile bribe you: good my Lord turn back.
Ang. How? bribe me?
Is. I, with such gifts that heauen shall share with you.
Luc. You had mar'd all else.
Isab. Not with fond Sickles of the tested-gold,
Or Stones, whose rate are either rich, or poore
As fancie values them: but with true prayers,
That shall be vp at heauen, and enter there
Ere Sunne rise: prayers from preserued soules,
From fasting Maides, whose mindes are dedicate
To nothing temporall.
Ang. Well: come to me to morrow.
Luc. Goe to: 'tis well; away.
Isab. Heauen keepe your honour safe.
Ang. Amen.
For I am that way going to temptation,
Where prayers crosse.
Isab. At what hower to morrow,
Shall I attend your Lordship?
Ang. At any time 'fore-noone.
Isab. 'Saue your Honour.
Aug. From thee: euen from thy vertue.
What's this? what's this? is this her fault, or mine?
The Tempter, or the Tempted, who sins most? ha?
Not she: nor doth she tempt: but it is I,
That, lying by the Violet in the Sunne,
Doe as the Carrion do's, not as the flowre,
Corrupt with vertuous season: Can it be,
That Modesty may more betray our Sence
Then womans lightnesse? hauing waste ground enough,
Shall we desire to raze the Sanctuary
And pitch our euils there? oh fie, fie, fie:
What dost thou? or what art thou *Angelo*?
Dost thou desire her fowly, for those things
That make her good? oh, let her brother liue:

Thieves for their robbery have authority
When judges steal themselves. What, do I love her,
That I desire to hear her speak again,
And feast upon her eyes? What is't I dream on?
O cunning enemy that, to catch a saint,
With saints dost bait thy hook! Most dangerous
Is that temptation that doth goad us on
To sin, in loving virtue! Never could the strumpet,
With all her double vigour – art and nature –
Once stir my temper; but this virtuous maid
Subdues me quite. Ever till now
When men were fond, I smil'd, and wonder'd how.

Exit

2.3

Enter DUKE [*as Friar Lodowick*] *and* PROVOST

Duke Hail to you, Provost – so I think you are.

Provost I am the Provost. What's your will, good friar?

Duke Bound by my charity and my blessèd order,
I come to visit the afflicted spirits
Here in the prison. Do me the common right
To let me see them, and to make me know
The nature of their crimes, that I may minister
To them accordingly.

Provost I would do more than that, if more were needful.

Enter JULIET

Look, here comes one – a gentlewoman of mine,
Who, falling in the flaws of her own youth,
Hath blister'd her report. She is with child,
And he that got it, sentenc'd – a young man
More fit to do another such offence
Than die for this.

Duke When must he die?

Theeues for their robbery haue authority,
When Iudges steale themselues: what, doe I loue her,
That I desire to heare her speake againe?
And feast vpon her eyes? what is't I dreame on?
Oh cunning enemy, that to catch a Saint,
With Saints dost bait thy hooke: most dangerous
Is that temptation, that doth goad vs on
To sinne, in louing vertue: neuer could the Strumpet
With all her double vigor, Art, and Nature
Once stir my temper: but this vertuous Maid
Subdues me quite: Euer till now
When men were fond, I smild, and wondred how. *Exit.*

Scena Tertia.

Enter Duke and Prouost.

Duke. Haile to you, *Prouost*, so I thinke you are.
Pro. I am the Prouost: whats your will, good Frier?
Duke. Bound by my charity, and my blest order,
I come to visite the afflicted spirits
Here in the prison: doe me the common right
To let me see them: and to make me know
The nature of their crimes, that I may minister
To them accordingly.
Pro. I would do more then that, if more were needfull

Enter Iuliet.

Looke here comes one: a Gentlewoman of mine,
Who falling in the flawes of her owne youth,
Hath blisterd her report: She is with childe,
And he that got it, sentenc'd: a yong man,
More fit to doe another such offence,
Then dye for t his.
Duk. When must he dye?

Provost As I do think, tomorrow.
[*To* JULIET] I have provided for you. Stay awhile,
And you shall be conducted.
Duke Repent you, fair one, of the sin you carry?
Juliet I do, and bear the shame most patiently.
Duke I'll teach you how you shall arraign your conscience
And try your penitence if it be sound
Or hollowly put on.
Juliet I'll gladly learn.
Duke Love you the man that wrong'd you?
Juliet Yes, as I love the woman that wrong'd him.
Duke So then it seems your most offenceful act
Was mutually committed?
Juliet Mutually.
Duke Then was your sin of heavier kind than his.
Juliet I do confess it and repent it, father.
Duke 'Tis meet so, daughter, but lest you do repent
As that the sin hath brought you to this shame,
Which sorrow is always toward ourselves, not heaven,
Showing we would not spare heaven, as we love it,
But as we stand in fear –
Juliet I do repent me as it is an evil,
And take the shame with joy.
Duke There rest.
Your partner, as I hear, must die tomorrow,
And I am going with instruction to him.
Grace go with you. *Benedicite*! *Exit*
Juliet Must die tomorrow? O injurious love,[21]
That respites me a life whose very comfort
Is still a dying horror!
Provost 'Tis pity of him. *Exeunt*

Pro. As I do thinke to morrow.
I haue prouided for you, stay a while
And you shall be conducted.
Duk. Repent you (faire one) of the sin you carry?
Iul. I doe; and beare the shame most patiently.
Du. Ile teach you how you shal araign your consciēce
And try your penitence, if it be sound,
Or hollowly put on.
Iul. Ile gladly learne.
Duk. Loue you the man that wrong'd you?
Iul. Yes, as I loue the woman that wrong'd him.
Duk. So then it seemes your most offence full act
Was mutually committed.
Iul. Mutually.
Duk. Then was your sin of heauier kinde then his.
Iul. I doe confesse it, and repent it (Father.)
Duk. 'Tis meet so (daughter) but least you do repent
As that the sin hath brought you to this shame,
Which sorrow is alwaies toward our selues, not heauen,
Showing we would not spare heauen, as we loue it,
But as we stand in feare.
Iul. I doe repent me, as it is an euill,
And take the shame with ioy.
Duke. There rest:
Your partner (as I heare) must die to morrow,
And I am going with instruction to him:
Grace goe with you, *Benedicite*. *Exit.*
Iul. Must die to morrow? oh iniurious Loue
That respits me a life, whose very comfort
Is still a dying horror.
Pro. 'Tis pitty of him. *Exeunt.*

2.4

Enter ANGELO

Angelo When I would pray and think, I think and pray
To several subjects. Heaven hath my empty words
Whilst my invention, hearing not my tongue,
Anchors on Isabel – heaven in my mouth,[22]
As if I did but only chew his name,
And in my heart the strong and swelling evil
Of my conception. The state whereon I studied
Is like a good thing being often read,
Grown sere and tedious.[23] Yea, my gravity,
Wherein – let no man hear me! – I take pride,
Could I with boot change for an idle plume
Which the air beats for vain. O place, O form,
How often dost thou with thy case, thy habit,
Wrench awe from fools, and tie the wiser souls
To thy false seeming! Blood, thou art blood.
Let's write 'Good Angel' on the Devil's horn,
'Tis not the Devil's crest. How now? Who's there?

Enter SERVANT

Servant One Isabel, a sister, desires access to you.
Angelo Teach her the way. [*Exit* SERVANT]
O heavens,
Why does my blood thus muster to my heart,
Making both it unable for itself
And dispossessing all my other parts
Of necessary fitness?
So play the foolish throngs with one that swoons,
Come all to help him, and so stop the air
By which he should revive; and even so
The general subject to a well-wish'd king
Quit their own part, and in obsequious fondness
Crowd to his presence, where their untaught love
Must needs appear offence.

Scena Quarta.

Enter Angelo.

An. When I would pray, & think, I thinke, and pray
To seuerall subiects: heauen hath my empty words,
Whilst my Inuention, hearing not my Tongue,
Anchors on *Isabell*: heauen in my mouth,
As if I did but onely chew his name,
And in my heart the strong and swelling euill
Of my conception: the state whereon I studied
Is like a good thing, being often read
Growne feard, and tedious: yea, my Grauitie
Wherein (let no man heare me) I take pride,
Could I, with boote, change for an idle plume
Which the ayre beats for vaine: oh place, oh forme,
How often dost thou with thy case, thy habit
Wrench awe from fooles, and tye the wiser soules
To thy false seeming? Blood, thou art blood,
Let's write good Angell on the Deuills horne
'Tis not the Deuills Crest: how now? who's there?

Enter Seruant.

Ser. One *Isabell*, a Sister, desires accesse to you.

Ang. Teach her the way: oh, heauens
Why doe's my bloud thus muster to my heart,
Making both it vnable for it selfe,
And dispossessing all my other parts
Of necessary fitnesse?
So play the foolish throngs with one that swounds,
Come all to help him, and so stop the ayre
By which hee should reuiue: and euen so
The generall subiect to a wel-wisht King
Quit their owne part, and in obsequious fondnesse
Crowd to his presence, where their vn-taught loue
Must needs appear offence: how now faire Maid.

Enter ISABEL

How now, fair maid?

Isabel I am come to know your pleasure.

Angelo That you might know it would much better please me
Than to demand what 'tis. Your brother cannot live.

Isabel Even so? Heaven keep your honour.

Angelo Yet may he live a while; and it may be
As long as you or I. Yet he must die.

Isabel Under your sentence?

Angelo Yea.

Isabel When, I beseech you? That, in his reprieve,
Longer or shorter, he may be so fitted
That his soul sicken not.

Angelo Ha? Fie, these filthy vices! It were as good
To pardon him that hath from nature stolen
A man already made, as to remit
Their saucy sweetness that do coin heaven's image
In stamps that are forbid. 'Tis all as easy
Falsely to take away a life true-made
As to put mettle in restrainèd means [24]
To make a false one.

Isabel 'Tis set down so in heaven, but not in earth.

Angelo Say you so? Then I shall pose you quickly.
Which had you rather: that the most just law
Now took your brother's life; or, to redeem him, [25]
Give up your body to such sweet uncleanness
As she that he hath stain'd?

Isabel Sir, believe this:
I had rather give my body than my soul.

Angelo I talk not of your soul. Our compell'd sins
Stand more for number than for account.

Isabel How say you?

Angelo Nay, I'll not warrant that, for I can speak
Against the thing I say. Answer to this:
I – now the voice of the recorded law –

Enter Isabella.

Isab. I am come to know your pleasure. (me,
An. That you might know it, wold much better please
Then to demand what 'tis: your Brother cannot liue.
Isab. Euen so: heauen keepe your Honor.
Ang. Yet may he liue a while: and it may be
As long as you, or I: yet he must die.
Isab. Vnder your Sentence?
Ang. Yea.
Isab. When, I beseech you: that in his Reprieue
(Longer, or shorter) he may be so fitted
That his soule sicken not.
Ang. Ha? fie, these filthy vices: It were as good
To pardon him, that hath from nature stolne
A man already made, as to remit
Their sawcie sweetnes, that do coyne heauens Image
In stamps that are forbid: 'tis all as easie,
Falsely to take away a life true made,
As to put mettle in restrained meanes
To make a false one.
Isab. 'Tis set downe so in heauen, but not in earth.
Ang. Say you so: then I shall poze you quickly.
Which had you rather, that the most iust Law
Now tooke your brothers life, and to redeeme him
Giue vp your body to such sweet vncleannesse
As she that he hath staind?
Isab. Sir, beleeue this.
I had rather giue my body, then my soule.
Ang. I talke not of your soule: our compel'd sins
Stand more for number, then for accompt.
Isab. How say you?
Ang. Nay Ile not warrant that: for I can speake
Against the thing I say: Answere to this,
I (now the voyce of the recorded Law)

Pronounce a sentence on your brother's life;
Might there not be a charity in sin
To save this brother's life?

Isabel Please you to do't,
I'll take it as a peril to my soul
It is no sin at all but charity.

Angelo Pleas'd you to do't, at peril of your soul,
Were equal poise of sin and charity.

Isabel That I do beg his life, if it be sin,
Heaven let me bear it. You granting of my suit,
If that be sin, I'll make it my morn-prayer
To have it added to the faults of mine,
And nothing of your answer.

Angelo Nay, but hear me;
Your sense pursues not mine. Either you are ignorant
Or seem so, crafty – and that's not good.

Isabel Let me be ignorant, and in nothing good [26]
But graciously to know I am no better.

Angelo Thus wisdom wishes to appear most bright
When it doth tax itself; as these black masks
Proclaim an enshield beauty ten times louder [27]
Than beauty could, display'd. But mark me.
To be receivèd plain, I'll speak more gross:
Your brother is to die.

Isabel So.

Angelo And his offence is so, as it appears,
Accountant to the law upon that pain.

Isabel True.

Angelo Admit no other way to save his life –
As I subscribe not that, nor any other,
But in the loss of question – that you, his sister,
Finding yourself desir'd of such a person
Whose credit with the judge, or own great place,
Could fetch your brother from the manacles

Pronounce a sentence on your Brothers life,
Might there not be a charitie in sinne,
To saue this Brothers life?

Isab. Please you to doo't,
Ile take it as a perill to my soule,
It is no sinne at all, but charitie.

Ang. Pleas'd you to doo't, at perill of your soule
Were equall poize of sinne, and charitie.

Isab. That I do beg his life, if it be sinne
Heauen let me beare it: you granting of my suit,
If that be sin, Ile make it my Morne-praier,
To haue it added to the faults of mine,
And nothing of your answere.

Ang. Nay, but heare me,
Your sence pursues not mine: either you are ignorant,
Or seeme so crafty; and that's not good.

Isab. Let be ignorant, and in nothing good,
But graciously to know I am no better.

Ang. Thus wisdome wishes to appeare most bright,
When it doth taxe it selfe: As these blacke Masques
Proclaime an en-shield beauty ten times louder
Then beauty could displaied: But marke me,
To be receiued plaine, Ile speake more grosse:
Your Brother is to dye.

Isab. So.

Ang. And his offence is so, as it appeares,
Accountant to the Law, vpon that paine.

Isab. True.

Ang. Admit no other way to saue his life
(As I subscribe not that, nor any other,
But in the losse of question) that you, his Sister,
Finding your selfe desir'd of such a person,
Whose creadit with the Iudge, or owne great place,
Could fetch your Brother from the Manacles

Of the all-binding law;[28] and that there were
No earthly mean to save him, but that either
You must lay down the treasures of your body
To this suppos'd, or else to let him suffer:
What would you do?

Isabel As much for my poor brother as myself.
That is, were I under the terms of death,
Th'impression of keen whips I'd wear as rubies,
And strip myself to death as to a bed
That longing have been sick for, ere I'd yield
My body up to shame.[29]

Angelo Then must your brother die.

Isabel And 'twere the cheaper way:
Better it were a brother died at once
Than that a sister, by redeeming him,
Should die for ever.

Angelo Were not you then as cruel as the sentence
That you have slander'd so?

Isabel Ignomy in ransom and free pardon
Are of two houses: lawful mercy
Is nothing kin to foul redemption.

Angelo You seem'd of late to make the law a tyrant,
And rather prov'd the sliding of your brother
A merriment than a vice.

Isabel O pardon me, my lord. It oft falls out,
To have what we would have, we speak not what we mean.
I something do excuse the thing I hate
For his advantage that I dearly love.

Angelo We are all frail.

Isabel Else let my brother die,
If not a feudary but only he
Owe and succeed thy weakness.

Angelo Nay, women are frail too.

Isabel Ay, as the glasses where they view themselves,

Of the all-building-Law: and that there were
No earthly meane to saue him, but that either
You must lay downe the treasures of your body,
To this supposed, or else to let him suffer:
What would you doe?
Isab. As much for my poore Brother, as my selfe;
That is: were I vnder the tearmes of death,
Th'impression of keene whips, I'ld weare as Rubies,
And strip my selfe to death, as to a bed,
That longing haue bin sicke for, ere I'ld yeeld
My body vp to shame.
Ang. Then must your brother die.
Isa. And 'twer the cheaper way:
Better it were a brother dide at once,
Then that a sister, by redeeming him
Should die for euer.
Ang. Were not you then as cruell as the Sentence,
That you haue slander'd so?
Isa. Ignomie in ransome, and free pardon
Are of two houses: lawfull mercie,
Is nothing kin to fowle redemption.
Ang. You seem'd of late to make the Law a tirant,
And rather prou'd the sliding of your brother
A merriment, then a vice.
Isa. Oh pardon me my Lord, it oft fals out
To haue, what we would haue,
We speake not what vve meane:
I something do excuse the thing I hate,
For his aduantage that I dearely loue.
Ang. We are all fraile.
Isa. Else let my brother die,
If not a fedarie but onely he
Owe, and succeed thy weaknesse.
Aug. Nay, women are fraile too.
Isa. I, as the glasses where they view themselues,

Which are as easy broke as they make forms.
Women? Help, heaven! Men their creation mar
In profiting by them. Nay, call us ten times frail,
For we are soft as our complexions are,
And credulous to false prints.

Angelo I think it well,
And from this testimony of your own sex –
Since I suppose we are made to be no stronger
Than faults may shake our frames – let me be bold.
I do arrest your words. Be that you are,
That is, a woman. If you be more, you're none.
If you be one – as you are well express'd
By all external warrants – show it now
By putting on the destin'd livery.

Isabel I have no tongue but one. Gentle my lord,
Let me entreat you, speak the former language.

Angelo Plainly conceive I love you.

Isabel My brother did love Juliet,
And you tell me that he shall die for't.

Angelo He shall not, Isabel, if you give me love.

Isabel I know your virtue hath a licence in't,
Which seems a little fouler than it is
To pluck on others.

Angelo Believe me, on mine honour,
My words express my purpose.

Isabel Ha? Little honour, to be much believ'd,
And most pernicious purpose! Seeming, seeming!
I will proclaim thee, Angelo, look for't.
Sign me a present pardon for my brother,
Or with an outstretch'd throat I'll tell the world aloud
What man thou art.

Angelo Who will believe thee, Isabel?
My unsoil'd name, th'austereness of my life,
My vouch against you, and my place i'th' state,
Will so your accusation overweigh

Which are as easie broke as they make formes:
Women? Helpe heauen; men their creation marre
In profiting by them: Nay, call vs ten times fraile,
For we are soft, as our complexions are,
And credulous to false prints.
Ang. I thinke it well:
And from this testimonie of your owne sex
(Since I suppose we are made to be no stronger
Then faults may shake our frames) let me be bold;
I do arrest your words. Be that you are,
That is a woman; if you be more, you'r none.
If you be one (as you are well exprest
By all externall warrants) shew it now,
By putting on the destin'd Liuerie.
Isa. I haue no tongue but one; gentle my Lord,
Let me entreate you speake the former language.
Ang. Plainlie conceiue I loue you.
Isa. My brother did loue *Iuliet*,
And you tell me that he shall die for't.
Ang. He shall not *Isabell* if you giue me loue.
Isa. I know your vertue hath a licence in't,
Which seemes a little fouler then it is,
To plucke on others.
Ang. Beleeue me on mine Honor,
My words expresse my purpose.
Isa. Ha? Little honor, to be much beleeu'd,
And most pernitious purpose: Seeming, seeming.
I will proclaime thee *Angelo*, looke for't.
Signe me a present pardon for my brother,
Or with an out-stretcht throate Ile tell the world aloud
What man thou art.
Ang. Who will beleeue thee *Isabell*?
My vnsoild name, th'austeerenesse of my life,
My vouch against you, and my place i'th State,
Will so your accusation ouer-weigh,

That you shall stifle in your own report
And smell of calumny. I have begun,
And now I give my sensual race the rein.
Fit thy consent to my sharp appetite,
Lay by all nicety and prolixious blushes
That banish what they sue for, redeem thy brother
By yielding up thy body to my will,
Or else he must not only die the death
But thy unkindness shall his death draw out
To lingering sufferance. Answer me tomorrow,
Or, by the affection that now guides me most,
I'll prove a tyrant to him. As for you,
Say what you can, my false o'erweighs your true. *Exit*

Isabel To whom should I complain? Did I tell this,
Who would believe me? O perilous mouths
That bear in them one and the selfsame tongue,
Either of condemnation or approof,
Bidding the law make curtsy to their will,
Hooking both right and wrong to th'appetite,
To follow as it draws! I'll to my brother.
Though he hath fallen by prompture of the blood,
Yet hath he in him such a mind of honour
That had he twenty heads to tender down
On twenty bloody blocks, he'd yield them up
Before his sister should her body stoop
To such abhorr'd pollution.
Then Isabel live chaste, and brother die:
'More than our brother is our chastity.'
I'll tell him yet of Angelo's request,
And fit his mind to death, for his soul's rest. *Exit*

That you shall stifle in your owne reporr,
And smell of calumnie. I haue begun,
And now I giue my sensuall race, the reine,
Fit thy consent to my sharpe appetite,
Lay by all nicetie, and prolixious blushes
That banish what they sue for: Redeeme thy brother,
By yeelding vp thy bodie to my will,
Or else he must not onelie die the death,
But thy vnkindnesse shall his death draw out
To lingring sufferance: Answer me to morrow,
Or by the affection that now guides me most,
Ile proue a Tirant to him. As for you,
Say what you can; my false, ore-weighs your true. *Exit*

Isa. To whom should I complaine? Did I tell this,
Who would beleeue me? O perilous mouthes
That beare in them, one and the selfesame tongue,
Either of condemnation, or approofe,
Bidding the Law make curtsie to their will,
Hooking both right and wrong to th'appetite,
To follow as it drawes. Ile to my brother,
Though he hath falne by prompture of the blood,
Yet hath he in him such a minde of Honor,
That had he twentie heads to tender downe
On twentie bloodie blockes, heel'd yeeld them vp,
Before his sister should her bodie stoope
To such abhord pollution.
Then *Isabell* liue chaste, and brother die;
"More then our Brother, is our Chastitie.
Ile tell him yet of *Angelo*'s request,
And fit his minde to death, for his soules rest. *Exit.*

3.1

Enter DUKE [*as Friar Lodowick*], CLAUDIO, *and* PROVOST

Duke So then you hope of pardon from Lord Angelo?

Claudio The miserable have no other medicine
But only hope.
I have hope to live, and am prepar'd to die.

Duke Be absolute for death: either death or life
Shall thereby be the sweeter. Reason thus with life:
If I do lose thee, I do lose a thing
That none but fools would keep. A breath thou art,
Servile to all the skyey influences
That dost this habitation where thou keep'st
Hourly afflict. Merely, thou art Death's fool,
For him thou labour'st by thy flight to shun,
And yet runn'st toward him still. Thou art not noble,
For all th'accommodations that thou bear'st
Are nurs'd by baseness. Thou'rt by no means valiant,
For thou dost fear the soft and tender fork
Of a poor worm. Thy best of rest is sleep,
And that thou oft provok'st, yet grossly fear'st
Thy death, which is no more. Thou art not thyself,
For thou exists on many a thousand grains
That issue out of dust. Happy thou art not,
For what thou hast not, still thou striv'st to get,
And what thou hast, forget'st. Thou art not certain,
For thy complexion shifts to strange effects
After the moon. If thou art rich, thou'rt poor,
For like an ass whose back with ingots bows
Thou bear'st thy heavy riches but a journey,
And death unloads thee. Friend hast thou none,
For thine own bowels which do call thee sire,
The mere effusion of thy proper loins,
Do curse the gout, serpigo, and the rheum

Actus Tertius. Scena Prima.

Enter Duke, Claudio, and Prouost.

Du. So then you hope of pardon from Lord *Angelo*?
Cla. The miserable haue no other medicine
But onely hope: I'haue hope to liue, and am prepar'd to die.
Duke. Be absolute for death: either death or life
Shall thereby be the sweeter. Reason thus with life:
If I do loose thee, I do loose a thing
That none but fooles would keepe: a breath thou art,
Seruile to all the skyie-influences,
That dost this habitation where thou keepst
Hourely afflict: Meerely, thou art deaths foole,
For him thou labourst by thy flight to shun,
And yet runst toward him still. Thou art not noble,
For all th'accommodations that thou bearst,
Are nurst by basenesse: Thou'rt by no meanes valiant,
For thou dost feare the soft and tender forke
Of a poore worme: thy best of rest is sleepe,
And that thou oft prouoakst, yet grosselie fearst
Thy death, which is no more. Thou art not thy selfe,
For thou exists on manie a thousand graines
That issue out of dust. Happie thou art not,
For what thou hast not, still thou striu'st to get,
And what thou hast forgetst. Thou art not certaine,
For thy complexion shifts to strange effects,
After the Moone: If thou art rich, thou'rt poore,
For like an Asse, whose backe with Ingots bowes;
Thou bearst thy heauie riches but a iournie,
And death vnloads thee; Friend hast thou none.
For thine owne bowels which do call thee, fire
The meere effusion of thy proper loines
Do curse the Gowt, Sapego, and the Rheume

For ending thee no sooner. Thou hast nor youth nor age,
But as it were an after-dinner's sleep,
Dreaming on both: for all thy blessèd youth
Becomes as agèd, and doth beg the alms
Of palsied eld;[31] and when thou art old and rich,
Thou hast neither heat, affection, limb, nor beauty
To make thy riches pleasant. What's yet in this
That bears the name of life? Yet in this life
Lie hid more thousand deaths; yet death we fear
That makes these odds all even.

Claudio I humbly thank you.
To sue to live, I find I seek to die,
And seeking death, find life. Let it come on.

Isabel [*Within*]
What ho, peace here, grace, and good company![32]

Provost Who's there? Come in, the wish deserves a welcome.

Duke Dear sir, ere long I'll visit you again.

Claudio Most holy sir, I thank you.

Enter ISABEL

Isabel My business is a word or two with Claudio.

Provost And very welcome. – Look, signor, here's your sister.

Duke Provost, a word with you.

Provost As many as you please.

Duke Bring me to hear them speak where I may be
concealed.[33]

[DUKE *and* PROVOST *withdraw*]

Claudio Now, sister, what's the comfort?

Isabel Why,
As all comforts are: most good, most good indeed.
Lord Angelo, having affairs to heaven,
Intends you for his swift ambassador,
Where you shall be an everlasting lieger.
Therefore your best appointment make with speed;
Tomorrow you set on.

For ending thee no sooner. Thou hast nor youth, nor age
But as it were an after-dinners sleepe
Dreaming on both, for all thy blessed youth
Becomes as aged, and doth begge the almes
Of palsied-Eld: and when thou art old, and rich
Thou hast neither heate, affection, limbe, nor beautie
To make thy riches pleasant: what's yet in this
That beares the name of life? Yet in this life
Lie hid moe thousand deaths; yet death we feare
That makes these oddes, all euen.

Cla. I humblie thanke you.
To sue to liue, I finde I seeke to die,
And seeking death, finde life: Let it come on.

Enter Isabella.

Isab. What hoa? Peace heere; Grace, and good companie.

Pro. Who's there? Come in, the wish deserues a welcome.

Duke. Deere sir, ere long Ile visit you againe.

Cla. Most holie Sir, I thanke you.

Isa. My businesse is a word or two with *Claudio*.

Pro. And verie welcom: looke Signior, here's your sister.

Duke. Prouost, a word with you.

Pro. As manie as you please.

Duke. Bring them to heare me speak, where I may be conceal'd.

Cla. Now sister, what's the comfort?

Isa. Why,
As all comforts are: most good, most good indeede,
Lord *Angelo* hauing affaires to heauen
Intends you for his swift Ambassador,
Where you shall be an euerlasting Leiger;
Therefore your best appointment make with speed,
To Morrow you set on.

Claudio Is there no remedy?
Isabel None but such remedy as, to save a head,
To cleave a heart in twain.
Claudio But is there any?
Isabel Yes, brother, you may live:
There is a devilish mercy in the judge,
If you'll implore it, that will free your life,
But fetter you till death.
Claudio Perpetual durance?
Isabel Ay, just. Perpetual durance: a restraint
Through all the world's vastidity you had,[34]
To a determin'd scope.
Claudio But in what nature?
Isabel In such a one as, you consenting to't,
Would bark your honour from that trunk you bear,
And leave you naked.
Claudio Let me know the point.
Isabel O, I do fear thee, Claudio, and I quake
Lest thou a feverous life shouldst entertain,
And six or seven winters more respect
Than a perpetual honour. Dar'st thou die?
The sense of death is most in apprehension,
And the poor beetle that we tread upon
In corporal sufferance finds a pang as great
As when a giant dies.
Claudio Why give you me this shame?
Think you I can a resolution fetch
From flowery tenderness? If I must die,
I will encounter darkness as a bride,
And hug it in my mine arms.
Isabel There spake my brother; there my father's grave
Did utter forth a voice. Yes, thou must die.
Thou art too noble to conserve a life
In base appliances. This outward-sainted Deputy,
Whose settled visage and deliberate word

Clau. Is there no remedie?
Isa. None, but such remedie, as to saue a head
To cleaue a heart in twaine:
Clau. But is there anie?
Isa. Yes brother, you may liue;
There is a diuellish mercie in the Iudge,
If you'l implore it, that will free your life,
But fetter you till death.
Cla. Perpetuall durance?
Isa. I iust, perpetuall durance, a restraint
Through all the worlds vastiditie you had
To a determin'd scope.
Clau. But in what nature?
Isa. In such a one, as you consenting too't,
Would barke your honor from that trunke you beare,
And leaue you naked.
Clau. Let me know the point.
Isa. Oh, I do feare thee *Claudio*, and I quake,
Least thou a feauorous life shouldst entertaine,
And six or seuen winters more respect
Then a perpetuall Honor. Dar'st thou die?
The sence of death is most in apprehension,
And the poore Beetle that we treade vpon
In corporall sufferance, finds a pang as great,
As when a Giant dies.
Cla. Why giue you me this shame?
Thinke you I can a resolution fetch
From flowrie tendernesse? If I must die,
I will encounter darknesse as a bride,
And hugge it in my mine armes.
Isa. There spake my brother: there my fathers graue
Did vtter forth a voice. Yes, thou must die:
Thou art too noble, to conserue a life
In base appliances. This outward sainted Deputie,
Whose setled visage, and deliberate word

Nips youth i'th' head, and follies doth enew[35]
As falcon doth the fowl, is yet a devil.
His filth within being cast, he would appear
A pond as deep as hell.

Claudio The princely Angelo?[36]

Isabel O, 'tis the cunning livery of hell
The damned'st body to invest and cover
In princely guards! Dost thou think, Claudio,
If I would yield him my virginity
Thou mightst be freed?

Claudio O heavens, it cannot be!

Isabel Yes, he would give't thee, from this rank offence
So to offend him still. This night's the time
That I should do what I abhor to name,
Or else thou diest tomorrow.

Claudio Thou shalt not do't.

Isabel O, were it but my life,
I'd throw it down for your deliverance
As frankly as a pin.

Claudio Thanks, dear Isabel.

Isabel Be ready, Claudio, for your death tomorrow.

Claudio Yes. Has he affections in him
That thus can make him bite the law by th' nose
When he would force it? Sure, it is no sin,
Or of the deadly seven it is the least.

Isabel Which is the least?

Claudio If it were damnable, he being so wise,
Why would he for the momentary trick
Be perdurably fin'd? O Isabel!

Isabel What says my brother?

Claudio Death is a fearful thing.

Isabel And shamèd life a hateful.

Claudio Ay, but to die, and go we know not where;
To lie in cold obstruction, and to rot;
This sensible warm motion to become

Nips youth i'th head, and follies doth emmew
As Falcon doth the Fowle, is yet a diuell:
His filth within being cast, he would appeare
A pond, as deepe as hell.

Cla. The prenzie, *Angelo*?

Isa. Oh 'tis the cunning Liuerie of hell,
The damnest bodie to inuest, and couer
In prenzie gardes; dost thou thinke *Claudio*,
If I would yeeld him my virginitie
Thou might'st be freed?

Cla. Oh heauens, it cannot be.

Isa. Yes, he would giu't thee; from this rank offence
So to offend him still. This night's the time
That I should do what I abhorre to name,
Or else thou diest to morrow.

Clau. Thou shalt not do't.

Isa. O, were it but my life,
I'de throw it downe for your deliuerance
As frankely as a pin.

Clau. Thankes deere *Isabell*.

Isa. Be readie *Claudio*, for your death to morrow.

Clau. Yes. Has he affections in him,
That thus can make him bite the Law by th'nose,
When he would force it? Sure it is no sinne,
Or of the deadly seuen it is the least.

Isa. Which is the least?

Cla. If it were damnable, he being so wise,
Why would he for the momentarie tricke
Be perdurablie fin'de? Oh *Isabell*.

Isa. What saies my brother?

Cla. Death is a fearefull thing.

Isa. And shamed life, a hatefull.

Cla. I, but to die, and go we know not where,
To lie in cold obstruction, and to rot,
This sensible warme motion, to become

A kneaded clod, and the delighted spirit[37]
To bathe in fiery floods, or to reside
In thrilling region of thick-ribbèd ice,
To be imprison'd in the viewless winds,
And blown with restless violence round about
The pendent world, or to be worse than worst
Of those that lawless and incertain thought
Imagine howling – 'tis too horrible!
The weariest and most loathèd worldly life
That age, ache, penury, and imprisonment
Can lay on nature is a paradise
To what we fear of death.

Isabel Alas, alas!

Claudio Sweet sister, let me live.
What sin you do to save a brother's life,
Nature dispenses with the deed so far
That it becomes a virtue.

Isabel Oh, you beast!
O faithless coward, O dishonest wretch!
Wilt thou be made a man out of my vice?
Is't not a kind of incest to take life
From thine own sister's shame? What should I think?
Heaven shield my mother play'd my father fair,
For such a warpèd slip of wilderness
Ne'er issued from his blood! Take my defiance:
Die, perish. Might but my bending down
Reprieve thee from thy fate, it should proceed.
I'll pray a thousand prayers for thy death,
No word to save thee.

Claudio Nay, hear me, Isabel!

Isabel Oh, fie, fie, fie!
Thy sin's not accidental, but a trade.
Mercy to thee would prove itself a bawd.
'Tis best that thou diest quickly.

Claudio O hear me, Isabella!

A kneaded clod; And the delighted spirit
To bath in fierie floods, or to recide
In thrilling Region of thicke-ribbed Ice,
To be imprison'd in the viewlesse windes
And blowne with restlesse violence round about
The pendant world: or to be worse then worst
Of those, that lawlesse and incertaine thought,
Imagine howling, 'tis too horrible.
The weariest, and most loathed worldly life
That Age, Ache, periury, and imprisonment
Can lay on nature, is a Paradise
To what we feare of death.
Isa. Alas, alas.
Cla. Sweet Sister, let me liue.
What sinne you do, to saue a brothers life,
Nature dispenses with the deede so farre,
That it becomes a vertue.
Isa. Oh you beast,
Oh faithlesse Coward, oh dishonest wretch,
Wilt thou be made a man, out of my vice?
Is't not a kinde of Incest, to take life
From thine owne sisters shame? What should I thinke,
Heauen shield my Mother plaid my Father faire:
For such a warped slip of wildernesse
Nere issu'd from his blood. Take my defiance,
Die, perish: Might but my bending downe
Repreeue thee from thy fate, it should proceede.
Ile pray a thousand praiers for thy death,
No word to saue thee.
Cla. Nay heare me *Isabell.*
Isa. Oh fie, fie, fie?
Thy sinn's not accidentall, but a Trade;
Mercy to thee would proue it selfe a Bawd,
'Tis best that thou diest quickly.
Cla. Oh heare me *Isabella.*

Duke [*Coming forward*]
Vouchsafe a word, young sister, but one word.

Isabel What is your will?

Duke Might you dispense with your leisure, I would by and by have some speech with you. The satisfaction I would require is likewise your own benefit.

Isabel I have no superfluous leisure; my stay must be stolen out of other affairs – but I will attend you a while.

Duke [*To* CLAUDIO] Son, I have overheard what hath passed between you and your sister. Angelo had never the purpose to corrupt her; only he hath made an assay of her virtue, to practise his judgement with the disposition of natures. She, having the truth of honour in her, hath made him that gracious denial which he is most glad to receive. I am confessor to Angelo, and I know this to be true. Therefore prepare yourself to death. Do not satisfy your resolution with hopes that are fallible. Tomorrow you must die. Go to your knees, and make ready.

Claudio Let me ask my sister pardon. I am so out of love with life that I will sue to be rid of it.

Duke Hold you there. Farewell. – Provost, a word with you.

Provost [*Coming forward*] What's your will, father?

Duke That now you are come, you will be gone. Leave me a while with the maid. My mind promises, with my habit, no loss shall touch her by my company.

Provost In good time. *Exit* [*with* CLAUDIO]

Duke The hand that hath made you fair hath made you good. The goodness that is cheap in beauty makes beauty brief in goodness; but grace, being the soul of your complexion, shall keep the body of it ever fair. The assault that Angelo hath made to you, fortune hath conveyed to my understanding, and but that frailty hath examples for his falling, I should wonder at Angelo. How will you do to content this substitute, and to save your brother?

Duk. Vouchsafe a word, yong sister, but one word.

Isa. What is your Will.

Duk. Might you dispense with your leysure, I would by and by haue some speech with you: the satisfaction I would require, is likewise your owne benefit.

Isa. I haue no superfluous leysure, my stay must be stolen out of other affaires: but I will attend you a while.

Duke. Son, I haue ouer-heard what hath past between you & your sister. *Angelo* had neuer the purpose to corrupt her; onely he hath made an assay of her vertue, to practise his iudgement with the disposition of natures. She (hauing the truth of honour in her) hath made him that gracious deniall, which he is most glad to receiue: I am Confessor to *Angelo*, and I know this to be true, therfore prepare your selfe to death: do not satisfie your resolution with hopes that are fallible, to morrow you must die, goe to your knees, and make ready.

Cla. Let me ask my sister pardon, I am so out of loue with life, that I will sue to be rid of it.

Duke. Hold you there: farewell: *Prouost*, a word with you.

Pro. What's your will (father?)

Duk. That now you are come, you wil be gone: leaue me a while with the Maid, my minde promises with my habit, no losse shall touch her by my company.

Pro. In good time. *Exit.*

Duk. The hand that hath made you faire, hath made you good: the goodnes that is cheape in beauty, makes beauty briefe in goodnes; but grace being the soule of your complexion, shall keepe the body of it euer faire: the assault that *Angelo* hath made to you, Fortune hath conuaid to my vnderstanding; and but that frailty hath examples for his falling, I should wonder at *Angelo*: how will you doe to content this Substitute, and to saue your Brother?

Isabel I am now going to resolve him. I had rather my brother die by the law than my son should be unlawfully born. But O, how much is the good Duke deceived in Angelo! If ever he return, and I can speak to him, I will open my lips in vain or discover his government.

Duke That shall not be much amiss. Yet, as the matter now stands, he will avoid your accusation: he made trial of you only. Therefore fasten your ear on my advisings, to the love I have in doing good. A remedy presents itself. I do make myself believe that you may most uprighteously do a poor wronged lady a merited benefit, redeem your brother from the angry law, do no stain to your own gracious person, and much please the absent Duke – if peradventure he shall ever return to have hearing of this business.

Isabel Let me hear you speak farther. I have spirit to do anything that appears not foul in the truth of my spirit.

Duke Virtue is bold, and goodness never fearful. Have you not heard speak of Mariana, the sister of Frederick, the great soldier who miscarried at sea?

Isabel I have heard of the lady, and good words went with her name.

Duke She should this Angelo have married – was affianced to her oath, and the nuptial appointed; between which time of the contract and limit of the solemnity, her brother Frederick was wrecked at sea, having in that perished vessel the dowry of his sister. But mark how heavily this befell to the poor gentlewoman: there she lost a noble and renowned brother, in his love toward her ever most kind and natural; with him, the portion and sinew of her fortune, her marriage dowry; with both, her combinate husband, this well-seeming Angelo.

Isab. I am now going to resolue him: I had rather my brother die by the Law, then my sonne should be vnlawfullie borne. But (oh) how much is the good Duke deceiu'd in *Angelo*: if euer he returne, and I can speake to him, I will open my lips in vaine, or discouer his gouernment.

Duke. That shall not be much amisse: yet, as the matter now stands, he will auoid your accusation: he made triall of you onelie. Therefore fasten your eare on my aduisings, to the loue I haue in doing good; a remedie presents it selfe. I doe make my selfe beleeue that you may most vprighteously do a poor wronged Lady a merited benefit; redeem your brother from theangry Law; doe no staine to your owne gracious person, and much please the absent Duke, if peraduenture he shall euer returne to haue hearing of this businesse.

Isab. Let me heare you speake farther; I haue spirit to do any thing that appeares not fowle in the truth of my spirit.

Duke. Vertue is bold, and goodnes neuer fearefull: Haue you not heard speake of *Mariana* the sister of *Fredericke* the great Souldier, who miscarried at Sea?

Isa. I haue heard of the Lady, and good words went with her name.

Duke. Shee should this *Angelo* haue married: was affianced to her oath, and the nuptiall appointed: between which time of the contract, and limit of the solemnitie, her brother *Fredericke* was wrackt at Sea, hauing in that perished vessell, the dowry of his sister: but marke how heauily this befell to the poore Gentlewoman, there she lost a noble and renowned brother, in his loue toward her, euer most kinde and naturall: with him the portion and sinew of her fortune, her marriage dowry: with both, her combynate-husband, this well-seeming *Angelo*.

Isabel Can this be so? Did Angelo so leave her?

Duke Left her in her tears, and dried not one of them with his comfort; swallowed his vows whole, pretending in her discoveries of dishonour; in few, bestowed her on her own lamentation, which she yet wears for his sake; and he, a marble to her tears, is washed with them, but relents not.

Isabel What a merit were it in death to take this poor maid from the world! What corruption in this life, that it will let this man live! But how out of this can she avail?

Duke It is a rupture that you may easily heal – and the cure of it not only saves your brother, but keeps you from dishonour in doing it.

Isabel Show me how, good father.

Duke This fore-named maid hath yet in her the continuance of her first affection. His unjust unkindness, that in all reason should have quenched her love, hath, like an impediment in the current, made it more violent and unruly. Go you to Angelo, answer his requiring with a plausible obedience, agree with his demands to the point – only refer yourself to this advantage: first, that your stay with him may not be long, that the time may have all shadow and silence in it, and the place answer to convenience.[38] This being granted in course, and now follows all: we shall advise this wronged maid to stead up your appointment, go in your place. If the encounter acknowledge itself hereafter, it may compel him to her recompense – and here by this is your brother saved, your honour untainted, the poor Mariana advantaged, and the corrupt Deputy scaled.[39] The maid will I frame and make fit for his attempt. If you think well to carry this as you may, the doubleness of the benefit defends the deceit from reproof. What think you of it?

Isab. Can this be so? did *Angelo* so leaue her?

Duke. Left her in her teares, & dried not one of them with his comfort: swallowed his vowes whole, pretending in her, discoueries of dishonor: in few, bestow'd her on her owne lamentation, which she yet weares for his sake: and he, a marble to her teares, is washed with them, but relents not.

Isab. What a merit were it in death to take this poore maid from the world? what corruption in this life, that it will let this man liue? But how out of this can shee auaile?

Duke. It is a rupture that you may easily heale: and the cure of it not onely saues your brother, but keepes you from dishonor in doing it.

Isab. Shew me how (good Father.)

Duk. This fore-named Maid hath yet in her the continuance of her first affection: his vniust vnkindenesse (that in all reason should haue quenched her loue) hath (like an impediment in the Current) made it more violent and vnruly: Goe you to *Angelo*, answere his requiring with a plausible obedience, agree with his demands to the point: onely referre your selfe to this aduantage; first, that your stay with him may not be long: that the time may haue all shadow, and silence in it: and the place answere to conuenience: this being granted in course, and now followes all: wee shall aduise this wronged maid to steed vp your appointment, goe in your place: if the encounter acknowledge it selfe heereafter, it may compell him to her recompence; and heere, by this is your brother saued, your honor vntainted, the poore *Mariana* aduantaged, and the corrupt Deputy scaled. The Maid will I frame, and make fit for his attempt: if you thinke well to carry this as you may, the doublenes of the benefit defends the deceit from reproofe. What thinke you of it?

Isabel The image of it gives me content already, and I trust it will grow to a most prosperous perfection.

Duke It lies much in your holding up. Haste you speedily to Angelo. If for this night he entreat you to his bed, give him promise of satisfaction. I will presently to Saint Luke's: there at the moated grange resides this dejected Mariana; at that place call upon me, and dispatch with Angelo, that it may be quickly.

Isabel I thank you for this comfort. Fare you well, good father. *Exit*

Enter ELBOW, CLOWN, *and officers* [40]

Elbow Nay, if there be no remedy for it but that you will needs buy and sell men and women like beasts, we shall have all the world drink brown and white bastard.

Duke O heavens, what stuff is here!

Clown 'Twas never merry world since, of two usuries, the merriest was put down and the worser allowed, by order of law, a furred gown to keep him warm – and furred with fox on lamb-skins too, to signify that craft, being richer than innocency, stands for the facing.[41]

Elbow Come your way, sir. – Bless you, good father friar.

Duke And you, good brother father. What offence hath this man made you, sir?

Elbow Marry, sir, he hath offended the law, and, sir, we take him to be a thief too, sir, for we have found upon him, sir, a strange pick-lock, which we have sent to the Deputy.

Duke [*To* CLOWN] Fie, sirrah, a bawd, a wicked bawd!
The evil that thou causest to be done,
That is thy means to live. Do thou but think
What 'tis to cram a maw or clothe a back
From such a filthy vice. Say to thyself,
'From their abominable and beastly touches
I drink, I eat, array myself, and live.'[42]

Isab. The image of it giues me content already, and I trust it will grow to a most prosperous perfection.

Duk. It lies much in your holding vp: haste you speedily to *Angelo*, if for this night he intreat you to his bed, giue him promise of satisfaction: I will presently to S. *Lukes*, there at the moated-Grange recides this deiected *Mariana*; at that place call vpon me, and dispatch with *Angelo*, that it may be quickly.

Isab. I thank you for this comfort: fare youwell good father. *Exit.*

Enter Elbow, Clowne, Officers.

Elb. Nay, if there be no remedy for it, but that you will needes buy and sell men and women like beasts, we shall haue all the world drinke browne & white bastard.

Duk. Oh heauens, what stuffe is heere.

Clow. Twas neuer merry world since of two vsuries the merriest was put downe, and the worser allow'd by order of Law; a fur'd gowne to keepe him warme; and furd with Foxe and Lamb-skins too, to signifie, that craft being richer then Innocency, stands for the facing.

Elb. Come your way sir: 'blesse you good Father Frier.

Duk. And you good Brother Father; what offence hath this man made you, Sir?

Elb. Marry Sir, he hath offended the Law; and Sir, we take him to be a Theefe too Sir: for wee haue found vpon him Sir, a strange Pick-lock, which we haue sent to the Deputie.

Duke. Fie, sirrah, a Bawd, a wicked bawd,
The euill that thou causest to be done,
That is thy meanes to liue. Do thou but thinke
What 'tis to cram a maw, or cloath a backe
From such a filthie vice: say to thy selfe,
From their abhominable and beastly touches
I drinke, I eate away my selfe, and liue:

Canst thou believe thy living is a life,
So stinkingly depending? Go mend, go mend.

Clown Indeed, it does stink in some sort, sir. But yet, sir I would prove –

Duke Nay, if the Devil have given thee proofs for sin,
Thou wilt prove his. – Take him to prison, officer.
Correction and instruction must both work
Ere this rude beast will profit.

Elbow He must before the Deputy, sir; he has given him warning. The Deputy cannot abide a whoremaster. If he be a whoremonger, and comes before him, he were as good go a mile on his errand.

Duke That we are all, as some would seem to be,
From our faults, as faults from seeming, free![43]

Enter LUCIO

Elbow His neck will come to your waist: a cord, sir.

Clown I spy comfort, I cry bail! Here's a gentleman, and a friend of mine.

Lucio How now, noble Pompey? What, at the wheels of Caesar? Art thou led in triumph? What, is there none of Pygmalion's images newly made woman to be had now, for putting the hand in the pocket and extracting clutched?[44] What reply, ha? What sayst thou to this tune, matter, and method? Is't not drowned i'th' last rain? Ha? What sayst thou, trot? Is the world as it was, man? Which is the way? Is it sad, and few words? Or how? The trick of it?

Duke Still thus, and thus; still worse!

Lucio How doth my dear morsel thy mistress? Procures she still, ha?

Clown Troth, sir, she hath eaten up all her beef, and she is herself in the tub.

Lucio Why, 'tis good; it is the right of it; it must be so. Ever your fresh whore and your powdered bawd: an

Canst thou beleeue thy liuing is a life,
So stinkingly depending? Go mend, go mend.

Clo. Indeed, it do's stinke in some sort, Sir:
But yet Sir I would proue.

Duke. Nay, if the diuell haue giuen thee proofs for sin
Thou wilt proue his. Take him to prison Officer:
Correction, and Instruction must both worke
Ere this rude beast will profit.

Elb. He must before the Deputy Sir, he ha's giuen him warning: the Deputy cannot abide a Whore-master: if he be a Whore-monger, and comes before him, he were as good go a mile on his errand.

Duke. That we are all, as some would seeme to bee
From our faults, as faults from seeming free.

Enter Lucio.

Elb. His necke will come to your wast, a Cord sir.

Clo. I spy comfort, I cry baile: Here's a Gentleman, and a friend of mine.

Luc. How now noble *Pompey*? What, at the wheels of *Cæsar*? Art thou led in triumph? What is there none of *Pigmalions* Images newly made woman to bee had now, for putting the hand in the pocket, and extracting clutch'd? What reply? Ha? What saist thou to this Tune, Matter, and Method? Is't not drown'd i'th last raine? Ha? What saist thou Trot? Is the world as it was Man? Which is the vvay? Is it sad, and few words? Or how? The tricke of it?

Duke. Still thus, and thus: still vvorse?

Luc. How doth my deere Morsell, thy Mistris? Procures she still? Ha?

Clo. Troth sir, shee hath eaten vp all her beefe, and she is her selfe in the tub.

Luc. Why 'tis good: It is the right of it: it must be so. Euer your fresh Whore, and your pouder'd Baud, an unshunned consequence – it must be so. Art going to prison, Pompey?

Clown Yes, faith, sir.

Lucio Why, 'tis not amiss, Pompey. Farewell. Go say I sent thee thither. For debt, Pompey? Or how?

Elbow For being a bawd, for being a bawd.

Lucio Well then, imprison him. If imprisonment be the due of a bawd, why, 'tis his right. Bawd is he, doubtless, and of antiquity too: bawd-born. Farewell, good Pompey. Commend me to the prison, Pompey. You will turn good husband now, Pompey: you will keep the house.

Clown I hope, sir, your good worship will be my bail?

Lucio No, indeed will I not, Pompey; it is not the wear. I will pray, Pompey, to increase your bondage. If you take it not patiently, why, your mettle is the more. Adieu, trusty Pompey. – Bless you, friar.

Duke And you.

Lucio Does Bridget paint still, Pompey, ha?

Elbow Come your ways, sir, come.

Clown You will not bail me then, sir?

Lucio Then, Pompey, nor now. – What news abroad, friar? What news?

Elbow Come your ways, sir, come.

Lucio Go to kennel, Pompey, go.

[*Exeunt* ELBOW, POMPEY, *and officers*]

What news, friar, of the Duke?

Duke I know none. Can you tell me of any?

Lucio Some say he is with the Emperor of Russia; other some, he is in Rome. But where is he, think you?

Duke I know not where; but wheresoever, I wish him well.

Lucio It was a mad fantastical trick of him to steal from the state, and usurp the beggary he was never born to.

vnshun'd consequence, it must be so. Art going to prison *Pompey*?

Clo. Yes faith sir.

Luc. Why 'tis not amisse *Pompey*: farewell: goe say I sent thee thether: for debt *Pompey*? Or how?

Elb. For being a baud, for being a baud.

Luc. Well, then imprison him: If imprisonment be the due of a baud, why 'tis his right. Baud is he doubtlesse, and of antiquity too: Baud borne. Farwell good *Pompey*: Commend me to the prison *Pompey*, you will turne good husband now *Pompey*, you vvill keepe the house.

Clo. I hope Sir, your good Worship wil be my baile?

Luc. No indeed vvil I not *Pompey*, it is not the wear: I will pray (*Pompey*) to encrease your bondage if you take it not patiently: Why, your mettle is the more: Adieu trustie *Pompey*.
Blesse you Friar.

Duke. And you.

Luc. Do's *Bridget* paint still, *Pompey*? Ha?

Elb. Come your waies sir, come.

Clo. You will not baile me then Sir?

Luc. Then *Pompey*, nor now: what newes abroad *Frier*? What newes?

Elb. Come your waies sir, come.

Luc. Goe to kennell (*Pompey*) goe:
What newes *Frier* of the Duke?

Duke. I know none: can you tell me of any?

Luc. Some say he is with the Emperor of *Russia*: other some, he is in *Rome*: but where is he thinke you?

Duke. I know not where: but wheresoeuer, I wish him well.

Luc. It was a mad fantasticall tricke of him to steale from the State, and vsurpe the beggerie hee was neuer

Lord Angelo dukes it well in his absence: he puts transgression to't.

Duke He does well in't.

Lucio A little more lenity to lechery would do no harm in him. Something too crabbed that way, friar.

Duke It is too general a vice, and severity must cure it.

Lucio Yes, in good sooth, the vice is of a great kindred, it is well allied – but it is impossible to extirp it quite, friar, till eating and drinking be put down. They say this Angelo was not made by man and woman after this downright way of creation. Is it true, think you?

Duke How should he be made, then?

Lucio Some report, a sea-maid spawned him; some, that he was begot between two stockfishes. But it is certain that when he makes water, his urine is congealed ice – that I know to be true; and he is no motion generative – that's infallible.[45]

Duke You are pleasant, sir, and speak apace.

Lucio Why, what a ruthless thing is this in him, for the rebellion of a codpiece to take away the life of a man! Would the Duke that is absent have done this? Ere he would have hanged a man for the getting a hundred bastards, he would have paid for the nursing a thousand. He had some feeling of the sport, he knew the service, and that instructed him to mercy.

Duke I never heard the absent Duke much detected for women. He was not inclined that way.

Lucio Oh, sir, you are deceived.

Duke 'Tis not possible.

Lucio Who, not the Duke? Yes, your beggar of fifty; and his use was to put a ducat in her clack-dish. The Duke had crotchets in him. He would be drunk too, that let me inform you.

Duke You do him wrong, surely.

borne to: Lord *Angelo* Dukes it well in his absence: he puts transgression too't.

Duke. He do's well in't.

Luc. A little more lenitie to Lecherie would doe no harme in him: Something too crabbed that way, *Frier*.

Duk. It is too general a vice, and seueritie must cure it.

Luc. Yes in good sooth, the vice is of a great kindred; it is vvell allied, but it is impossible to extirpe it quite, Frier, till eating and drinking be put downe. They say this *Angelo* vvas not made by Man and Woman, after this downe-right vvay of Creation: is it true, thinke you?

Duke. How should he be made then?

Luc. Some report, a Sea-maid spawn'd him. Some, that he vvas begot betweene two Stocke-fishes. But it is certaine, that when he makes water, his Vrine is congeal'd ice, that I know to bee true: and he is a motion generatiue, that's infallible.

Duke. You are pleasant sir, and speake apace.

Luc. Why, what a ruthlesse thing is this in him, for the rebellion of a Cod-peece, to take away the life of a man? Would the Duke that is absent haue done this? Ere he vvould haue hang'd a man for the getting a hundred Bastards, he vvould haue paide for the Nursing a thousand. He had some feeling of the sport, hee knew the seruice, and that instructed him to mercie.

Duke. I neuer heard the absent Duke much detected for Women, he was not enclin'd that vvay.

Luc. Oh Sir, you are deceiu'd.

Duke. 'Tis not possible.

Luc. Who, not the Duke? Yes, your beggar of fifty: and his vse was, to put a ducket in her Clack-dish; the Duke had Crochets in him. Hee would be drunke too, that let me informe you.

Duke. You do him wrong, surely.

Lucio Sir, I was an inward of his. A shy fellow was the Duke, and I believe I know the cause of his withdrawing.

Duke What, I prithee, might be the cause?

Lucio No, pardon: 'tis a secret must be locked within the teeth and the lips. But this I can let you understand: the greater file of the subject held the Duke to be wise.

Duke Wise? Why, no question but he was.

Lucio A very superficial, ignorant, unweighing fellow.

Duke Either this is envy in you, folly, or mistaking. The very stream of his life, and the business he hath helmed, must upon a warranted need give him a better proclamation. Let him be but testimonied in his own bringings-forth, and he shall appear to the envious a scholar, a statesman, and a soldier. Therefore you speak unskilfully; or, if your knowledge be more, it is much darkened in your malice.

Lucio Sir, I know him, and I love him.

Duke Love talks with better knowledge, and knowledge with dearer love.[46]

Lucio Come, sir, I know what I know.

Duke I can hardly believe that, since you know not what you speak. But if ever the Duke return – as our prayers are he may – let me desire you to make your answer before him. If it be honest you have spoke, you have courage to maintain it. I am bound to call upon you, and I pray you your name.

Lucio Sir, my name is Lucio, well known to the Duke.

Duke He shall know you better, sir, if I may live to report you.

Lucio I fear you not.

Duke Oh, you hope the Duke will return no more? Or you imagine me too unhurtful an opposite? But indeed I can do you little harm. You'll forswear this again.

Luc. Sir, I vvas an inward of his: a shie fellow vvas the Duke, and I beleeue I know the cause of his vvithdrawing.

Duke. What (I prethee) might be the cause?

Luc. No, pardon: 'Tis a secret must bee lockt within the teeth and the lippes: but this I can let you vnderstand, the greater file of the subiect held the Duke to be vvise.

Duke. Wise? Why no question but he was.

Luc. A very superficiall, ignorant, vnweighing fellow

Duke. Either this is Enuie in you, Folly, or mistaking: The very streame of his life, and the businesse he hath helmed, must vppon a warranted neede, giue him a better proclamation. Let him be but testimonied in his owne bringings forth, and hee shall appeare to the enuious, a Scholler, a Statesman, and a Soldier: therefore you speake vnskilfully: or, if your knowledge bee more, it is much darkned in your malice.

Luc. Sir, I know him, and I loue him.

Duke. Loue talkes with better knowledge, & knowledge with deare loue.

Luc. Come Sir, I know what I know.

Duke. I can hardly beleeue that, since you know not what you speake. But if euer the Duke returne (as our praiers are he may) let mee desire you to make your answer before him: if it bee honest you haue spoke, you haue courage to maintaine it; I am bound to call vppon you, and I pray you your name?

Luc. Sir my name is *Lucio*, wel known to the Duke.

Duke. He shall know you better Sir, if I may liue to report you.

Luc. I feare you not.

Duke. O, you hope the Duke will returne no more: or you imagine me to vnhurtfull an opposite: but indeed I can doe you little harme: You'll for-sweare this againe?

Lucio I'll be hanged first! Thou art deceived in me, friar. But no more of this. Canst thou tell if Claudio die tomorrow or no?

Duke Why should he die, sir?

Lucio Why? For filling a bottle with a tun-dish. I would the Duke we talk of were returned again. This ungenitured agent will unpeople the province with continency. Sparrows must not build in his house-eaves, because they are lecherous. The Duke yet would have dark deeds darkly answered; he would never bring them to light. Would he were returned! Marry, this Claudio is condemned for untrussing. Farewell, good friar, I prithee pray for me. The Duke (I say to thee again) would eat mutton on Fridays. He's now past it, yet (and I say to thee) he would mouth with a beggar, though she smelt brown bread and garlic. Say that I said so. Farewell. *Exit*

Duke No might nor greatness in mortality
Can censure 'scape. Back-wounding calumny
The whitest virtue strikes. What king so strong
Can tie the gall up in the slanderous tongue?[47]
But who comes here?

Enter ESCALUS, PROVOST, *and* BAWD [*with officers*]

Escalus Go, away with her to prison.

Bawd Good my lord, be good to me! Your honour is accounted a merciful man. Good my lord!

Escalus Double and treble admonition, and still forfeit in the same kind? This would make mercy swear and play the tyrant.

Provost A bawd of eleven years' continuance, may it please your honour.

Bawd My lord, this is one Lucio's information against me. Mistress Kate Keepdown was with child by him in the Duke's time; he promised her marriage. His child is a year-and-a-quarter old come Philip-and-Jacob – I have

Luc. Ile be hang'd first: Thou art deceiu'd in mee Friar. But no more of this: Canst thou tell if *Claudio* die to morrow, or no?

Duke. Why should he die Sir?

Luc. Why? For filling a bottle with a Tunne-dish: I would the Duke we talke of were return'd againe: this vngenitur'd Agent will vn-people the Prouince with Continencie. Sparrowes must not build in his house-eeues, because they are lecherous: The Duke yet would haue darke deeds darkelie answered, hee would neuer bring them to light: would hee were return'd. Marrie this *Claudio* is condemned for vntrussing. Farwell good Friar, I prethee pray for me: The Duke (I say to thee againe) would eate Mutton on Fridaies. He's now past it, yet (and I say to thee) hee would mouth with a beggar, though she smelt browne-bread and Garlicke: say that I said so: Farewell. *Exit.*

Duke. No might, nor greatnesse in mortality
Can censure scape: Back-wounding calumnie
The whitest vertue strikes. What King so strong,
Can tie the gall vp in the slanderous tong?
But who comes heere?

Enter Escalus, Prouost, and Bawd.

Esc. Go, away with her to prison.

Bawd. Good my Lord be good to mee, your Honor is accounted a mercifull man: good my Lord.

Esc. Double, and trebble admonition, and still forfeite in the same kinde? This would make mercy sweare and play the Tirant.

Pro. A Bawd of eleuen yeares continuance, may it please your Honor.

Bawd. My Lord, this is one *Lucio*'s information against me, Mistris *Kate Keepe-downe* was with childe by him in the Dukes time, he promis'd her marriage: his Childe is a yeere and a quarter olde come *Philip* and *Ia-*

kept it myself – and see how he goes about to abuse me.

Escalus That fellow is a fellow of much licence. Let him be called before us. Away with her to prison. – Go to, no more words. [*Exeunt officers with* BAWD]
Provost, my brother Angelo will not be altered; Claudio must die tomorrow. Let him be furnished with divines, and have all charitable preparation. If my brother wrought by my pity, it should not be so with him.

Provost So please you, this friar hath been with him, and advised him for th'entertainment of death.

Escalus Good even, good father.

Duke Bliss and goodness on you.

Escalus Of whence are you?

Duke Not of this country, though my chance is now
To use it for my time. I am a brother
Of gracious order, late come from the See
In special business from his Holiness.

Escalus What news abroad i'th' world?

Duke None, but that there is so great a fever on goodness that the dissolution of it must cure it. Novelty is only in request, and, as it is, as dangerous to be aged in any kind of course as it is virtuous to be constant in any undertaking.[48] There is scarce truth enough alive to make societies secure, but security enough to make fellowships accursed. Much upon this riddle runs the wisdom of the world. This news is old enough, yet it is every day's news. I pray you, sir, of what disposition was the Duke?

Escalus One that above all other strifes contended especially to know himself.

Duke What pleasure was he given to?

Escalus Rather rejoicing to see another merry, than merry at anything which professed to make him rejoice. A gentleman of all temperance. But leave we him to his

cob: I haue kept it my selfe; and see how hee goes about to abuse me.

Esc. That fellow is a fellow of much License: Let him be call'd before vs, Away with her to prison: Goe too, no more words. Prouost, my Brother *Angelo* will not be alter'd, *Claudio* must die to morrow: Let him be furnish'd with Diuines, and haue all charitable preparation. If my brother wrought by my pitie, it should not be so with him.

Pro. So please you, this Friar hath beene with him, and aduis'd him for th'entertainment of death.

Esc. Good'euen, good Father.

Duke. Blisse, and goodnesse on you.

Esc. Of whence are you?

Duke. Not of this Countrie, though my chance is now
To vse it for my time: I am a brother
Of gracious Order, late come from the Sea,
In speciall businesse from his Holinesse.

Esc. What newes abroad i'th World?

Duke. None, but that there is so great a Feauor on goodnesse, that the dissolution of it must cure it. Noueltie is onely in request, and as it is as dangerous to be aged in any kinde of course, as it is vertuous to be constant in any vndertaking. There is scarse truth enough aliue to make Societies secure, but Securitie enough to make Fellowships accurst: Much vpon this riddle runs the wisedome of the world: This newes is old enough, yet it is euerie daies newes. I pray you Sir, of what disposition was the Duke?

Esc. One, that aboue all other strifes,
Contended especially to know himselfe.

Duke. What pleasure was he giuen to?

Esc. Rather reioycing to see another merry, then merrrie at anie thing which profest to make him reioice. A Gentleman of all temperance. But leaue wee him to events, with a prayer they may prove prosperous, and let me desire to know how you find Claudio prepared. I am made to understand that you have lent him visitation.

Duke He professes to have received no sinister measure from his judge, but most willingly humbles himself to the determination of justice. Yet had he framed to himself, by the instruction of his frailty, many deceiving promises of life, which I, by my good leisure, have discredited to him, and now is he resolved to die.

Escalus You have paid the heavens your function, and the prisoner the very debt of your calling. I have laboured for the poor gentleman to the extremest shore of my modesty, but my brother-justice have I found so severe that he hath forced me to tell him he is indeed Justice.

Duke If his own life answer the straitness of his proceeding, it shall become him well; wherein if he chance to fail, he hath sentenced himself.

Escalus I am going to visit the prisoner. Fare you well.

Duke Peace be with you.

[*Exeunt* PROVOST *and* ESCALUS]

He who the sword of heaven will bear [49]
Should be as holy as severe;
Pattern in himself to know,
Grace to stand, and virtue, go;
More nor less to others paying
Than by self-offences weighing.
Shame to him whose cruel striking
Kills for faults of his own liking.
Twice treble shame on Angelo,
To weed my vice, and let his grow.
O, what may Man within him hide,
Though Angel on the outward side?
How may likeness made in crimes,

his euents, with a praier they may proue prosperous, & let me desire to know, how you finde *Claudio* prepar'd? I am made to vnderstand, that you haue lent him visitation.

Duke. He professes to haue receiued no sinister measure from his Iudge, but most willingly humbles himselfe to the determination of Iustice: yet had he framed to himselfe (by the instruction of his frailty) manie deceyuing promises of life, which I (by my good leisure) haue discredited to him, and now is he resolu'd to die.

Esc. You haue paid the heauens your Function, and the prisoner the verie debt of your Calling. I haue labour'd for the poore Gentleman, to the extremest shore of my modestie, but my brother-Iustice haue I found so seuere, that he hath forc'd me to tell him, hee is indeede Iustice.

Duke. If his own life,
Answere the straitnesse of his proceeding,
It shall become him well: wherein if he chance to faile he hath sentenc'd himselfe.

Esc. I am going to visit the prisoner, Fare you well.

Duke. Peace be with you.
He who the sword of Heauen will beare,
Should be as holy, as seueare:
Patterne in himselfe to know,
Grace to stand, and Vertue go:
More, nor lesse to others paying,
Then by selfe-offences weighing.
Shame to him, whose cruell striking,
Kils for faults of his owne liking:
Twice trebble shame on *Angelo*,
To vveede my vice, and let his grow.
Oh, what may Man within him hide,
Though Angel on the outward side?
How may likenesse made in crimes,

Making practice on the times,
To draw with idle spiders' strings
Most ponderous and substantial things?
Craft against vice I must apply.
With Angelo tonight shall lie
His old betrothèd but despis'd.
So disguise shall by th' disguis'd
Pay with falsehood false exacting,
And perform an old contracting. *Exit*

4.1

Enter MARIANA, *and* BOY *singing*

Boy (*Sings*)
Take, O take those lips away,[50]
That so sweetly were forsworn;
And those eyes, the break of day,
Lights that do mislead the morn;
But my kisses bring again, bring again,
Seals of love, but seal'd in vain, seal'd in vain.
Enter DUKE [*as Friar Lodowick*]

Mariana Break off thy song, and haste thee quick away.
Here comes a man of comfort, whose advice
Hath often still'd my brawling discontent. [*Exit* BOY]
I cry you mercy, sir, and well could wish
You had not found me here so musical.
Let me excuse me, and believe me so,
My mirth it much displeas'd, but pleas'd my woe.

Duke 'Tis good; though music oft hath such a charm
To make bad good, and good provoke to harm.
I pray you tell me, hath anybody enquired for me here

Making practise on the Times,
To draw with ydle Spiders strings
Most ponderous and substantiall things?
Craft against vice, I must applie.
With *Angelo* to night shall lye
His old betroathed (but despised:)
So disguise shall by th'disguised
Pay with falshood, falfe exacting,
And performe an olde contracting. *Exit*

Actus Quartus. Scœna Prima.

Enter Mariana, and Boy singing.

Song. *Take, oh take those lips away,*
that so sweetly were forsworne,
And those eyes: the breake of day
lights that doe mislead the Morne;
But my kisses bring againe, bring againe,
Seales of loue, but seal'd in vaine, seal'd in vaine.

Enter Duke.

Mar. Breake off thy song, and haste thee quick away,
Here comes a man of comfort, whose aduice
Hath often still'd my brawling discontent.
I cry you mercie, Sir, and well could wish
You had not found me here so musicall.
Let me excuse me, and beleeue me so,
My mirth it much displeas'd, but pleas'd my woe.

Duk. 'Tis good; though Musick oft hath such a charme
To make bad, good; and good prouoake to harme.
I pray you tell me, hath any body enquir'd for mee here

today? Much upon this time have I promised here to meet.

Mariana You have not been enquired after. I have sat here all day.

Enter ISABEL

Duke I do constantly believe you. The time is come even now. I shall crave your forbearance a little; maybe I will call upon you anon for some advantage to yourself.

Mariana I am always bound to you. *Exit*

Duke Very well met, and welcome.
What is the news from this good Deputy?

Isabel He hath a garden circummur'd with brick,
Whose western side is with a vineyard back'd,
And to that vineyard is a planchèd gate
That makes his opening with this bigger key.
This other doth command a little door
Which from the vineyard to the garden leads;
There have I made my promise,
Upon the heavy middle of the night,
To call upon him.

Duke But shall you on your knowledge find this way?

Isabel I have ta'en a due and wary note upon't.
With whispering and most guilty diligence,
In action all of precept, he did show me
The way twice o'er.

Duke Are there no other tokens
Between you 'greed, concerning her observance?

Isabel No, none, but only a repair i'th' dark,
And that I have possess'd him my most stay
Can be but brief – for I have made him know
I have a servant comes with me along
That stays upon me, whose persuasion is
I come about my brother.

Duke 'Tis well borne up.
I have not yet made known to Mariana

to day; much vpon this time haue I promis'd here to meete.

Mar. You haue not bin enquir'd after: I haue sat here all day.

Enter Isabell.

Duk. I doe constantly beleeue you: the time is come euen now. I shall craue your forbearance alittle, may be I will call vpon you anone for some aduantage to your selfe.

Mar. I am alwayes bound to you. *Exit.*

Duk. Very well met, and well come:
What is the newes from this good Deputie?

Isab. He hath a Garden circummur'd with Bricke,
Whose westerne side is with a Vineyard back't;
And to that Vineyard is a planched gate,
That makes his opening with this bigger Key:
This other doth command a little doore,
Which from the Vineyard to the Garden leades,
There haue I made my promise, vpon the
Heauy midle of the night, to call vpon him.

Duk. But shall you on your knowledge find this way?

Isab. I haue t'ane a due, and wary note vpon't,
With whispering, and most guiltie diligence,
In action all of precept, he did show me
The way twice ore.

Duk. Are there no other tokens
Betweene you 'greed, concerning her obseruance?

Isab. No: none but onely a repaire ith' darke,
And that I haue possest him, my most stay
Can be but briefe: for I haue made him know,
I haue a Seruant comes with me along
That staies vpon me; whose perswasion is,
I come about my Brother.

Duk. 'Tis well borne vp.
I haue not yet made knowne to *Mariana*

A word of this. – What ho, within! Come forth.

Enter MARIANA

I pray you be acquainted with this maid;
She comes to do you good.

Isabel I do desire the like.

Duke Do you persuade yourself that I respect you?

Mariana Good friar, I know you do, and have found it.[51]

Duke Take, then, this your companion by the hand,
Who hath a story ready for your ear.
I shall attend your leisure – but make haste:
The vaporous night approaches.

Mariana [*To* ISABEL] Will't please you walk aside?

Exeunt [MARIANA *and* ISABEL]

Duke O place and greatness! Millions of false eyes
Are stuck upon thee; volumes of report
Run with these false, and most contrarious quest [52]
Upon thy doings; thousand escapes of wit
Make thee the father of their idle dream,
And rack thee in their fancies.

Enter MARIANA *and* ISABEL

Welcome. How agreed?

Isabel She'll take the enterprise upon her, father,
If you advise it.

Duke It is not my consent,
But my entreaty too.

Isabel Little have you to say
When you depart from him but, soft and low,
'Remember now my brother.'

Mariana Fear me not.

Duke Nor, gentle daughter, fear you not at all.
He is your husband on a pre-contract:
To bring you thus together 'tis no sin,
Sith that the justice of your title to him
Doth flourish the deceit. Come, let us go;
Our corn's to reap, for yet our tithe's to sow. *Exeunt*

Enter Mariana.

A word of this: what hoa, within; come forth,
I pray you be acquainted with this Maid,
She comes to doe you good.

Isab. I doe desire the like.

Duk. Do you perswade your selfe that I respect you?

Mar. Good Frier, I know you do, and haue found it.

Duke. Take then this your companion by the hand
Who hath a storie readie for your eare:
I shall attend your leisure, but make haste
The vaporous night approaches.

Mar. Wilt please you walke aside. *Exit.*

Duke. Oh Place, and greatnes: millions of false eies
Are stucke vpon thee: volumes of report
Run with these false, and most contrarious Quest
Vpon thy doings: thousand escapes of wit
Make thee the father of their idle dreame,
And racke thee in their fancies. Welcome, how agreed?

Enter Mariana and Isabella.

Isab. Shee'll take the enterprize vpon her father,
If you aduise it.

Duke. It is not my consent,
But my entreaty too.

Isa. Little haue you to say
When you depart from him, but soft and low,
Remember now my brother.

Mar. Feare me not.

Duk. Nor gentle daughter, feare you not at all:
He is your husband on a pre-contract:
To bring you thus together 'tis no sinne,
Sith that the Iustice of your title to him
Doth flourish the deceit. Come, let vs goe,
Our Corne's to reape, for yet our Tithes to sow. *Exeunt.*

4.2

Enter PROVOST *and* CLOWN

Provost Come hither, sirrah. Can you cut off a man's head?

Clown If the man be a bachelor, sir, I can; but if he be a married man, he's his wife's head, and I can never cut off a woman's head.

Provost Come, sir, leave me your snatches, and yield me a direct answer. Tomorrow morning are to die Claudio and Barnardine. Here is in our prison a common executioner, who in his office lacks a helper. If you will take it on you to assist him, it shall redeem you from your gyves; if not, you shall have your full time of imprisonment, and your deliverance with an unpitied whipping, for you have been a notorious bawd.

Clown Sir, I have been an unlawful bawd time out of mind, but yet I will be content to be a lawful hangman. I would be glad to receive some instruction from my fellow partner.

Provost What ho, Abhorson! Where's Abhorson there?

Enter ABHORSON

Abhorson Do you call, sir?

Provost Sirrah, here's a fellow will help you tomorrow in your execution. If you think it meet, compound with him by the year, and let him abide here with you; if not, use him for the present, and dismiss him. He cannot plead his estimation with you: he hath been a bawd.

Abhorson A bawd, sir? Fie upon him! He will discredit our mystery.

Provost Go to, sir, you weigh equally: a feather will turn the scale. *Exit*

Clown Pray, sir, by your good favour – for surely, sir, a good favour you have, but that you have a hanging look –

Scena Secunda.

Enter Prouost and Clowne.

Pro. Come hither sirha; can you cut off a mans head?

Clo. If the man be a Bachelor Sir, I can:
But if he be a married man, he's his wiues head,
And I can neuer cut off a womans head.

Pro. Come sir, leaue me your snatches, and yeeld mee a direct answere. To morrow morning are to die *Claudio* and *Barnardine*: heere is in our prison a common executioner, who in his office lacks a helper, if you will take it on you to assist him, it shall redeeme you from your Gyues: if not, you shall haue your full time of imprisonment, and your deliuerance with an vnpittied whipping; for you haue beene a notorious bawd.

Clo. Sir, I haue beene an vnlawfull bawd, time out of minde, but yet I will bee content to be a lawfull hangman: I would bee glad to receiue some instruction from my fellow partner.

Pro. What hoa, *Abhorson*: where's *Abhorson* there?

Enter Abhorson.

Abh. Doe you call sir?

Pro. Sirha, here's a fellow will helpe you to morrow in your execution: if you thinke it meet, compound with him by the yeere, and let him abide here with you, if not, vse him for the present, and dismisse him, hee cannot plead his estimation with you: he hath beene a Bawd.

Abh. A Bawd Sir? fie vpon him, he will discredit our mysterie.

Pro. Goe too Sir, you waigh equallie: a feather will turne the Scale. *Exit.*

Clo. Pray sir, by your good fauor: for surely sir, a good fauor you haue, but that you haue a hanging look:

do you call, sir, your occupation a 'mystery'?

Abhorson Ay, sir, a mystery.

Clown Painting, sir, I have heard say, is a mystery; and your whores, sir, being members of my occupation, using painting, do prove my occupation a mystery. But what mystery there should be in hanging, if I should be hanged I cannot imagine.

Abhorson Sir, it is a mystery.

Clown Proof.

Abhorson Every true man's apparel fits your thief.

Clown If it be too little for your thief, your true man thinks it big enough. If it be too big for your thief, your thief thinks it little enough. So every true man's apparel fits your thief.[53]

Enter PROVOST

Provost Are you agreed?

Clown Sir, I will serve him, for I do find your hangman is a more penitent trade than your bawd: he doth oftener ask forgiveness.

Provost You, sirrah, provide your block and your axe tomorrow, four o'clock.

Abhorson Come on, bawd, I will instruct thee in my trade. Follow.

Clown I do desire to learn, sir, and I hope, if you have occasion to use me for your own turn, you shall find me yare.[54] For truly, sir, for your kindness I owe you a good turn.

Provost Call hither Barnardine and Claudio.

Exeunt [ABHORSON *and* CLOWN]

Th'one has my pity, not a jot the other,
Being a murderer, though he were my brother.

Enter CLAUDIO

Look, here's the warrant, Claudio, for thy death.
'Tis now dead midnight, and by eight tomorrow
Thou must be made immortal. Where's Barnardine?

Claudio As fast lock'd up in sleep as guiltless labour

Doe you call sir, your occupation a Mysterie?

Abh. I Sir, a Misterie.

Clo. Painting Sir, I haue heard say, is a Misterie; and your Whores sir, being members of my occupation, vsing painting, do proue my Occupation, a Misterie: but what Misterie there should be in hanging, if I should be hang'd, I cannot imagine.

Abh. Sir, it is a Misterie.

Clo. Proofe.

Abh. Euerie true mans apparrell fits your Theefe.

Clo. If it be too little for your theefe, your true man thinkes it bigge enough. If it bee too bigge for your Theefe, your Theefe thinkes it little enough: So euerie true mans apparrell fits your Theefe.

Enter Prouost.

Pro. Are you agreed?

Clo. Sir, I will serue him: For I do finde your Hangman is a more penitent Trade then your Bawd: he doth oftner aske forgiuenesse.

Pro. You sirrah, prouide your blocke and your Axe to morrow, foure a clocke.

Abh. Come on (Bawd) I will instruct thee in my Trade: follow.

Clo. I do desire to learne sir: and I hope, if you haue occasion to vse me for your owne turne, you shall finde me y'are. For truly sir, for your kindnesse, I owe you a good turne. *Exit*

Pro. Call hether *Barnardine* and *Claudio*:
Th'one has my pitie; not a iot the other,
Being a Murtherer, though he were my brother.

Enter Claudio.

Looke, here's the Warrant *Claudio*, for thy death,
'Tis now dead midnight, and by eight to morrow
Thou must be made immortall. Where's *Barnardine*?

Cla. As fast lock'd vp in sleepe, as guiltlesse labour,

When it lies starkly in the traveller's bones.
He will not wake.

Provost Who can do good on him?
Well, go, prepare yourself. [*Knocking within*]
But hark, what noise?
Heaven give your spirits comfort!
[*Exit* CLAUDIO. *Knocking within*]
By and by! –
I hope it is some pardon or reprieve
For the most gentle Claudio.

Enter DUKE [*as Friar Lodowick*]

Welcome, father.

Duke The best and wholesom'st spirits of the night
Envelop you, good Provost. Who call'd here of late?

Provost None since the curfew rung.

Duke Not Isabel?

Provost No.

Duke They will then, ere't be long.

Provost What comfort is for Claudio?

Duke There's some in hope.

Provost It is a bitter deputy.

Duke Not so, not so: his life is parallel'd
Even with the stroke and line of his great justice.
He doth with holy abstinence subdue
That in himself which he spurs on his power
To qualify in others. Were he meal'd with that
Which he corrects, then were he tyrannous,
But this being so, he's just.
[*Knocking within. Exit* PROVOST]
Now are they come.
This is a gentle provost: seldom-when
The steelèd jailer is the friend of men. [*Knocking*]
How now, what noise? That spirit's possess'd with haste
That wounds th'unsisting postern with these strokes.[55]

[*Enter* PROVOST]

When it lies starkely in the Trauellers bones,
He will not wake.

Pro. Who can do good on him?
Well, go, prepare your selfe. But harke, what noise?
Heauen giue your spirits comfort: by, and by,
I hope it is some pardon, or repreeue
For the most gentle *Claudio*. Welcome Father.

Enter Duke.

Duke. The best, and wholsomst spirits of the night,
Inuellop you, good Prouost: who call'd heere of late?

Pro. None since the Curphew rung.

Duke. Not *Isabell*?

Pro. No.

Duke. They will then er't be long.

Pro. What comfort is for *Claudio*?

Duke. There's some in hope.

Pro. It is a bitter Deputie.

Duke. Not so, not so: his life is paralel'd
Euen with the stroke and line of his great Iustice:
He doth with holie abstinence subdue
That in himselfe, which he spurres on his powre
To qualifie in others: were he meal'd with that
Which he corrects, then were he tirrannous,
But this being so, he's iust. Now are they come.
This is a gentle Prouost, sildome when
The steeled Gaoler is the friend of men:
How now? what noise? That spirit's possest with hast,
That wounds th'vnsisting Posterne with these strokes.

Provost There he must stay until the officer
Arise to let him in. He is call'd up.

Duke Have you no countermand for Claudio yet
But he must die tomorrow?

Provost None, sir, none.

Duke As near the dawning, Provost, as it is,
You shall hear more ere morning.

Provost Happily
You something know, yet I believe there comes
No countermand. No such example have we.
Besides, upon the very siege of justice
Lord Angelo hath to the public ear
Profess'd the contrary.

Enter a MESSENGER

This is his lordship's man.

Duke And here comes Claudio's pardon.[56]

Messenger My lord hath sent you this note, and by me this further charge: that you swerve not from the smallest article of it, neither in time, matter, or other circumstance. Good morrow, for, as I take it, it is almost day.

Provost I shall obey him. [*Exit* MESSENGER]

Duke [*Aside*] This is his pardon, purchas'd by such sin
For which the pardoner himself is in.
Hence hath offence his quick celerity
When it is borne in high authority.
When vice makes mercy, mercy's so extended
That for the fault's love is th'offender friended.
– Now, sir, what news?

Provost I told you. Lord Angelo, belike thinking me remiss in mine office, awakens me with this unwonted putting on, methinks strangely, for he hath not used it before.

Duke Pray you, let's hear.

Pro. There he must stay vntil the Officer
Arise to let him in: he is call'd vp.
Duke. Haue you no countermand for *Claudio* yet?
But he must die to morrow?
Pro. None Sir, none.
Duke. As neere the dawning Prouost, as it is,
You shall heare more ere Morning.
Pro. Happely
You something know: yet I beleeue there comes
No countermand: no such example haue we:
Besides, vpon the verie siege of Iustice,
Lord *Angelo* hath to the publike eare
Profest the contrarie.

Enter a Messenger.

Duke. This is his Lords man.
Pro. And heere comes *Claudio*'s pardon.
Mess. My Lord hath sent you this note,
And by mee this further charge;
That you swerue not from the smallest Article of it,
Neither in time, matter, or other circumstance.
Good morrow: for as I take it, it is almost day.
Pro. I shall obey him.
Duke. This is his Pardon purchas'd by such sin,
For which the Pardoner himselfe is in:
Hence hath offence his quicke celeritie,
When it is borne in high Authority.
When Vice makes Mercie; Mercie's so extended,
That for the faults loue, is th'offender friended.
Now Sir, what newes?
Pro. I told you:
Lord *Angelo* (be-like) thinking me remisse
In mine Office, awakens mee
With this vnwonted putting on, methinks strangely:
For he hath not vs'd it before.
Duk. Pray you let's heare.

Provost [*Reads*] (*the letter*) 'Whatsoever you may hear to the contrary, let Claudio be executed by four of the clock, and in the afternoon Barnardine. For my better satisfaction, let me have Claudio's head sent me by five. Let this be duly performed with a thought that more depends on it than we must yet deliver. Thus fail not to do your office, as you will answer it at your peril.'
What say you to this, sir?

Duke What is that Barnardine who is to be executed in th'afternoon?

Provost A Bohemian born, but here nursed up and bred; one that is a prisoner nine years old.

Duke How came it that the absent Duke had not either delivered him to his liberty or executed him? I have heard it was ever his manner to do so.

Provost His friends still wrought reprieves for him, and indeed his fact, till now in the government of Lord Angelo, came not to an undoubtful proof.

Duke It is now apparent?

Provost Most manifest, and not denied by himself.

Duke Hath he borne himself penitently in prison? How seems he to be touched?

Provost A man that apprehends death no more dreadfully but as a drunken sleep: careless, reckless, and fearless of what's past, present, or to come; insensible of mortality, and desperately mortal.

Duke He wants advice.

Provost He will hear none. He hath evermore had the liberty of the prison: give him leave to escape hence, he would not. Drunk many times a day, if not many days entirely drunk. We have very oft awaked him, as if to carry him to execution, and showed him a seeming warrant for it; it hath not moved him at all.

Duke More of him anon. There is written in your brow,

The Letter.

Whatsoeuer you may heare to the contrary, let Claudio be executed by foure of the clocke, and in the afternoone Bernardine: For my better satisfaction, let mee haue Claudios head sent me by fiue. Let this be duely performed with a thought that more depends on it, then we must yet deliuer. Thus faile not to doe your Office, as you will answere it at your perill.

What say you to this Sir?

Duke. What is that *Barnardine*, who is to be executed in th'afternoone?

Pro. A Bohemian borne: But here nurst vp & bred, One that is a prisoner nine yeeres old.

Duke. How came it, that the absent Duke had not either deliuer'd him to his libertie, or executed him? I haue heard it was euer his manner to do so.

Pro. His friends still wrought Repreeues for him: And indeed his fact till now in the gouernment of Lord *Angelo*, came not to an vndoubtfull proofe.

Duke. It is now apparant?

Pro. Most manifest, and not denied by himselfe.

Duke. Hath he borne himselfe penitently in prison? Howe seemes he to be touch'd?

Pro. A man that apprehends death no more dreadfully, but as a drunken sleepe, carelesse, wreaklesse, and fearelesse of what's past, present, or to come: insensible of mortality, and desperately mortall.

Duke. He wants aduice.

Pro. He wil heare none: he hath euermore had the liberty of the prison: giue him leaue to escape hence, hee would not. Drunke many times a day, if not many daies entirely drunke. We haue verie oft awak'd him, as if to carrie him to execution, and shew'd him a seeming warrant for it, it hath not moued him at all.

Duke. More of him anon: There is written in your

Provost, honesty and constancy. If I read it not truly, my ancient skill beguiles me; but in the boldness of my cunning, I will lay myself in hazard. Claudio, whom here you have warrant to execute, is no greater forfeit to the law than Angelo who hath sentenced him. To make you understand this in a manifested effect, I crave but four days' respite, for the which you are to do me both a present and a dangerous courtesy.

Provost Pray, sir, in what?

Duke In the delaying death.

Provost Alack, how may I do it, having the hour limited, and an express command, under penalty, to deliver his head in the view of Angelo? I may make my case as Claudio's to cross this in the smallest.

Duke By the vow of mine order I warrant you. If my instructions may be your guide, let this Barnardine be this morning executed, and his head borne to Angelo.

Provost Angelo hath seen them both, and will discover the favour.

Duke Oh, death's a great disguiser, and you may add to it: shave the head, and tie the beard, and say it was the desire of the penitent to be so bared before his death – you know the course is common. If anything fall to you upon this more than thanks and good fortune, by the saint whom I profess I will plead against it with my life.

Provost Pardon me, good father, it is against my oath.

Duke Were you sworn to the Duke or to the Deputy?

Provost To him, and to his substitutes.

Duke You will think you have made no offence if the Duke avouch the justice of your dealing?

Provost But what likelihood is in that?

brow Prouost, honesty and constancie; if I reade it not truly, my ancient skill beguiles me: but in the boldnes of my cunning, I will lay my selfe in hazard: *Claudio*, whom heere you haue warrant to execute, is no greater forfeit to the Law, then *Angelo* who hath sentenc'd him. To make you vnderstand this in a manifested effect, I craue but foure daies respit: for the which, you are to do me both a present, and a dangerous courtesie.

Pro. Pray Sir, in what?

Duke. In the delaying death.

Pro. Alacke, how may I do it? Hauing the houre limited, and an expresse command, vnder penaltie, to deliuer his head in the view of *Angelo*? I may make my case as *Claudio*'s, to crosse this in the smallest.

Duke. By the vow of mine Order, I warrant you,
If my instructions may be your guide,
Let this *Barnardine* be this morning executed,
And his head borne to *Angelo*.

Pro. *Angelo* hath seene them both,
And will discouer the fauour.

Duke. Oh, death's a great disguiser, and you may adde to it; Shaue the head, and tie the beard, and say it was the desire of the penitent to be so bar'de before his death: you know the course is common. If any thing fall to you vpon this, more then thankes and good fortune, by the Saint whom I professe, I will plead against it with my life.

Pro. Pardon me, good Father, it is against my oath.

Duke. Were you sworne to the Duke, or to the Deputie?

Pro. To him, and to his Substitutes.

Duke. You will thinke you haue made no offence, if the Duke auouch the iustice of your dealing?

Pro. But what likelihood is in that?

Duke Not a resemblance, but a certainty. Yet since I see you fearful, that neither my coat, integrity, nor persuasion can with ease attempt you, I will go further than I meant, to pluck all fears out of you. [*Handing him a letter*] Look you, sir: here is the hand and seal of the Duke. You know the character, I doubt not, and the signet is not strange to you?

Provost I know them both.

Duke The contents of this is the return of the Duke. You shall anon over-read it at your pleasure, where you shall find within these two days he will be here. This is a thing that Angelo knows not, for he this very day receives letters of strange tenor, perchance of the Duke's death, perchance entering into some monastery, but by chance nothing of what is writ. Look, th'unfolding star calls up the shepherd. Put not yourself into amazement how these things should be: all difficulties are but easy when they are known. Call your executioner, and off with Barnardine's head. I will give him a present shrift, and advise him for a better place. Yet you are amazed, but this shall absolutely resolve you. Come away, it is almost clear dawn. *Exeunt*

4.3

Enter CLOWN

Clown I am as well acquainted here as I was in our house of profession. One would think it were Mistress Overdone's own house, for here be many of her old customers. First, here's young Master Rash: he's in for a commodity of brown paper and old ginger, nine-score and seventeen pounds, of which he made five marks ready money – marry, then ginger was not

Duke. Not a resemblance, but a certainty; yet since I see you fearfull, that neither my coate, integrity, nor perswasion, can with ease attempt you, I wil go further then I meant, to plucke all feares out of you. Looke you Sir, heere is the hand and Seale of the Duke: you know the Charracter I doubt not, and the Signet is not strange to you?

Pro. I know them both.

Duke. The Contents of this, is the returne of the Duke; you shall anon ouer-reade it at your pleasure: where you shall finde within these two daies, he wil be heere. This is a thing that *Angelo* knowes not, for hee this very day receiues letters of strange tenor, perchance of the Dukes death, perchance entering into some Monasterie, but by chance nothing of what is writ. Looke, th'vnfolding Starre calles vp the Shepheard; put not your selfe into amazement, how these things should be; all difficulties are but easie vvhen they are knowne. Call your executioner, and off wlth *Barnardines* head: I will giue him a present shrift, and aduise him for a better place. Yet you are amaz'd, but this shall absolutely resolue you: Come away, it is almost cleere dawne. *Exit.*

Scena Tertia.

Enter Clowne.

Clo. I am as well acquainted heere, as I was in our house of profession: one would thinke it vvere Mistris *Ouer-dons* owne house, for heere be manie of her olde Customers. First, here's yong Mr *Rash*, hee's in for a commoditie of browne paper, and olde Ginger, nine score and seuenteene pounds, of which hee made fiue Markes readie money: marrie then, Ginger was not much in request, for the old women were all dead. Then is there here one Master Caper, at the suit of Master Threepile the mercer, for some four suits of peach-coloured satin – which now peaches him a beggar. Then have we here young Dizzy,[57] and young Master Deepvow, and Master Copperspur, and Master Starvelackey (the rapier-and-dagger man), and young Dropheir (that killed lusty Pudding), and Master Forthlight (the tilter), and brave Master Shoetie (the great traveller), and wild Halfcan (that stabbed Pots) – and I think forty more: all great doers in our trade, and are now 'for the Lord's sake'.

Enter ABHORSON

Abhorson Sirrah, bring Barnardine hither.

Clown Master Barnardine, you must rise and be hanged, Master Barnardine!

Abhorson What ho, Barnardine!

Barnardine (*Within*) A pox o' your throats! Who makes that noise there? What are you?

Clown Your friends, sir, the hangman. You must be so good, sir, to rise and be put to death.

Barnardine (*Within*) Away, you rogue, away! I am sleepy.

Abhorson Tell him he must awake, and that quickly too.

Clown Pray, Master Barnardine, awake till you are executed, and sleep afterwards.

Abhorson Go in to him, and fetch him out.

Clown He is coming, sir, he is coming. I hear his straw rustle.

Enter BARNARDINE

Abhorson Is the axe upon the block, sirrah?

Clown Very ready, sir.

Barnardine How now, Abhorson, what's the news with you?

Abhorson Truly, sir, I would desire you to clap into your prayers,

much in request, for the olde Women vvere all dead. Then is there heere one Mr *Caper*, at the suite of Master *Three-Pile* the Mercer, for some foure suites of Peach–colour'd Satten, which now peaches him a beggar. Then haue vve heere, yong *Dizie*, and yong Mr *Deepe-vow*, and Mr *Copperspurre*, and Mr *Starue-Lackey* the Rapier and dagger man, and yong *Drop-heire* that kild lustie *Pudding*, and Mr *Forthlight* the Tilter, and braue Mr *Shootie* the great Traueller, and wilde *Halfe-Canne* that stabb'd Pots, and I thinke fortie more, all great doers in our Trade, and are now for the Lords sake.

Enter Abhorson.

Abh. Sirrah, bring *Barnardine* hether.

Clo. Mr *Barnardine*, you must rise and be hang'd,
Mr *Barnardine*.

Abh. What hoa *Barnardine*.

Barnardine within.

Bar. A pox o'your throats: who makes that noyse there? What are you?

Clo. Your friends Sir, the Hangman:
You must be so good Sir to rise, and be put to death.

Bar. Away you Rogue, away, I am sleepie.

Abh. Tell him he must awake,
And that quickly too.

Clo: Pray Master *Barnardine*, awake till you areexecuted, and sleepe afterwards.

Ab. Go in to him, and fetch him out.

Clo. He is comming Sir, he is comming: I heare his Straw russle.

Enter Barnardine.

Abh. Is the Axe vpon the blocke, sirrah?

Clo. Verie readie Sir.

Bar. How now *Abhorson*?
What's the newes vvith you?

Abh. Truly Sir, I would desire you to clap into your

for look you, the warrant's come.

Barnardine You rogue! I have been drinking all night, I am not fitted for't.

Clown Oh, the better, sir: for he that drinks all night and is hanged betimes in the morning, may sleep the sounder all the next day.

Enter DUKE [*as Friar Lodowick*]

Abhorson Look you, sir, here comes your ghostly father. Do we jest now, think you?

Duke Sir, induced by my charity, and hearing how hastily you are to depart, I am come to advise you, comfort you, and pray with you.

Barnardine Friar, not I. I have been drinking hard all night, and I will have more time to prepare me, or they shall beat out my brains with billets. I will not consent to die this day, that's certain.

Duke Oh, sir, you must. And therefore I beseech you
Look forward on the journey you shall go.

Barnardine I swear I will not die today for any man's persuasion.

Duke But hear you –

Barnardine Not a word! If you have anything to say to me, come to my ward, for thence will not I today. *Exit*

Enter PROVOST

Duke Unfit to live or die? O gravel heart!
After him, fellows, bring him to the block.[58]

Exeunt [ABHORSON *and* CLOWN]

Provost Now, sir, how do you find the prisoner?

Duke A creature unprepar'd, unmeet for death,
And to transport him in the mind he is
Were damnable.

Provost Here in the prison, father,
There died this morning of a cruel fever
One Ragozine, a most notorious pirate –
A man of Claudio's years, his beard and head

prayers: for looke you, the Warrants come.

Bar. You Rogue, I haue bin drinking all night, I am not fitted for't.

Clo. Oh, the better Sir: for he that drinkes all night, and is hanged betimes in the morning, may sleepe the sounder all the next day.

Enter Duke.

Abh. Looke you Sir, heere comes your ghostly Father: do we iest now thinke you?

Duke. Sir, induced by my charitie, and hearing how hastily you are to depart, I am come to aduise you, Comfort you, and pray with you.

Bar. Friar, not I: I haue bin drinking hard all night, and I will haue more time to prepare mee, or they shall beat out my braines with billets: I will not consent to die this day, that's certaine.

Duke. Oh sir, you must: and therefore I beseech you Looke forward on the iournie you shall go.

Bar. I sweare I will not die to day for anie mans perswasion.

Duke. But heare you:

Bar. Not a word: if you haue anie thing to say to me, come to my Ward: for thence will not I to day.

Exit

Enter Prouost.

Duke. Vnfit to liue, or die: oh grauell heart.
After him (Fellowes) bring him to the blocke.

Pro. Now Sir, how do you finde the prisoner?

Duke. A creature vnpre-par'd, vnmeet for death,
And to transport him in the minde he is,
Were damnable.

Pro. Heere in the prison, Father.
There died this morning of a cruell Feauor,
One *Ragozine*, a most notorious Pirate,
A man of *Claudio*'s yeares: his beard, and head

Just of his colour. What if we do omit
This reprobate till he were well inclin'd,
And satisfy the Deputy with the visage
Of Ragozine, more like to Claudio?

Duke Oh, 'tis an accident that heaven provides!
Dispatch it presently; the hour draws on
Prefix'd by Angelo. See this be done,
And sent according to command, whiles I
Persuade this rude wretch willingly to die.

Provost This shall be done, good father, presently;
But Barnardine must die this afternoon,
And how shall we continue Claudio,
To save me from the danger that might come
If he were known alive?

Duke Let this be done:
Put them in secret holds, both Barnardine
And Claudio.
Ere twice the sun hath made his journal greeting
To yonder generation,[59] you shall find
Your safety manifested.

Provost I am your free dependant.

Duke Quick, dispatch, and send the head to Angelo.

Exit PROVOST

Now will I write letters to Angelo –
The Provost, he shall bear them – whose contents
Shall witness to him I am near at home,
And that by great injunctions I am bound
To enter publicly. Him I'll desire
To meet me at the consecrated fount
A league below the city; and from thence,
By cold gradation and well-balanc'd form,
We shall proceed with Angelo.

Enter PROVOST [*with a severed head*]

Provost Here is the head. I'll carry it myself.

Duke Convenient is it. Make a swift return,
For I would commune with you of such things

Iust of his colour. What if we do omit
This Reprobate, til he were wel enclin'd,
And satisfie the Deputie with the visage
Of *Ragozine*, more like to *Claudio*?
Duke. Oh, 'tis an accident that heauen prouides:
Dispatch it presently, the houre drawes on
Prefixt by *Angelo*: See this be done,
And sent according to command, whiles I
Perswade this rude wretch willingly to die.
Pro. This shall be done (good Father) presently:
But *Barnardine* must die this afternoone,
And how shall we continue *Claudio*,
To saue me from the danger that might come,
If he were knowne aliue?
Duke. Let this be done,
Put them in secret holds, both *Barnardine* and *Claudio*,
Ere twice the Sun hath made his iournall greeting
To yond generation, you shal finde
Your safetie manifested.
Pro. I am your free dependant. *Exit.*
Duke. Quicke, dispatch, and send the head to *Angelo*
Now wil I write Letters to *Angelo*,
(The Prouost he shal beare them) whose contents
Shal witnesse to him I am neere at home:
And that by great Iniunctions I am bound
To enter publikely: him Ile desire
To meet me at the consecrated Fount,
A League below the Citie: and from thence,
By cold gradation, and weale-ballanc'd forme.
We shal proceed with *Angelo*.

Enter Prouost.

Pro. Heere is the head, Ile carrie it my selfe.
Duke. Conuenient is it: Make a swift returne,
For I would commune with you of such things,

That want no ear but yours.

Provost I'll make all speed. *Exit*

Isabel (*Within*) Peace, ho, be here!

Duke The tongue of Isabel! She's come to know
If yet her brother's pardon be come hither.
But I will keep her ignorant of her good,
To make her heavenly comforts of despair
When it is least expected.

Enter ISABEL

Isabel Ho, by your leave!

Duke Good morning to you, fair and gracious daughter.

Isabel The better given me by so holy a man.
Hath yet the Deputy sent my brother's pardon?

Duke He hath releas'd him, Isabel, from the world.
His head is off, and sent to Angelo.

Isabel Nay, but it is not so!

Duke It is no other.
Show your wisdom, daughter, in your close patience.

Isabel Oh, I will to him and pluck out his eyes!

Duke You shall not be admitted to his sight.

Isabel Unhappy Claudio, wretched Isabel,
Injurious world, most damnèd Angelo!

Duke This nor hurts him, nor profits you a jot.
Forbear it therefore; give your cause to heaven.
Mark what I say, which you shall find
By every syllable a faithful verity.
The Duke comes home tomorrow – nay, dry your eyes.
One of our convent, and his confessor,
Gives me this instance. Already he hath carried
Notice to Escalus and Angelo,
Who do prepare to meet him at the gates,
There to give up their power. If you can pace your wisdom
In that good path that I would wish it go,

That want no eare but yours.

Pro. Ile make all speede. *Exit*

Isabell within.

Isa. Peace hoa, be heere.

Duke. The tongue of *Isabell*. She's come to know,
If yet her brothers pardon be come hither:
But I will keepe her ignorant of her good,
To make her heauenly comforts of dispaire,
When it is least expected.

Enter Isabella.

Isa. Hoa, by your leaue.

Duke. Good morning to you, faire, and gracious daughter.

Isa. The better giuen me by so holy a man,
Hath yet the Deputie sent my brothers pardon?

Duke. He hath releasd him, *Isabell*, from the world,
His head is off, and sent to *Angelo*.

Isa. Nay, but it is not so.

Duke. It is no other,
Shew your wisedome daughter in your close patience.

Isa. Oh, I wil to him, and plucke out his eies.

Duk. You shal not be admitted to his sight.

Isa. Vnhappie *Claudio*, wretched *Isabell*,
Iniurious world, most damned *Angelo*.

Duke. This nor hurts him, nor profits you a iot,
Forbeare it therefore, giue your cause to heauen,
Marke what I say, which you shal finde
By euery sillable a faithful veritie.
The Duke comes home to morrow: nay drie your eyes,
One of our Couent, and his Confessor
Giues me this instance: Already he hath carried
Notice to *Escalus* and *Angelo*,
Who do prepare to meete him at the gates, (dome,
There to giue vp their powre: If you can pace your wis-
In that good path that I would wish it go,

And you shall have your bosom on this wretch,
Grace of the Duke, revenges to your heart,
And general honour.

Isabel I am directed by you.

Duke This letter then to Friar Peter give;
'Tis that he sent me of the Duke's return.
Say by this token I desire his company
At Mariana's house tonight. Her cause, and yours,
I'll perfect him withal, and he shall bring you
Before the Duke, and to the head of Angelo
Accuse him home and home. For my poor self,
I am combinèd by a sacred vow,
And shall be absent. Wend you with this letter.
Command these fretting waters from your eyes
With a light heart. Trust not my holy order
If I pervert your course. Who's here?

Enter LUCIO

Lucio Good even.
Friar, where's the Provost?

Duke Not within, sir.

Lucio O pretty Isabella, I am pale at mine heart to see thine eyes so red. Thou must be patient. I am fain to dine and sup with water and bran. I dare not for my head fill my belly; one fruitful meal would set me to't. But they say the Duke will be here tomorrow. By my troth, Isabel, I loved thy brother; if the old fantastical Duke of dark corners had been at home, he had lived.

[*Exit* ISABEL]

Duke Sir, the Duke is marvellous little beholding to your reports, but the best is, he lives not in them.

Lucio Friar, thou knowest not the Duke so well as I do. He's a better woodman than thou tak'st him for.

Duke Well; you'll answer this one day. Fare ye well.

Lucio Nay, tarry, I'll go along with thee. I can tell thee pretty tales of the Duke.

And you shal haue your bosome on this wretch,
Grace of the Duke, reuenges to your heart,
And general Honor.

Isa. I am directed by you.

Duk. This Letter then to Friar *Peter* giue,
'Tis that he sent me of the Dukes returne:
Say, by this token, I desire his companie
At *Mariana*'s house to night. Her cause, and yours
Ile perfect him withall, and he shal bring you
Before the Duke; and to the head of *Angelo*
Accuse him home and home. For my poore selfe,
I am combined by a sacred Vow,
And shall be absent. Wend you with this Letter:
Command these fretting waters from your eies
With a light heart; trust not my holie Order
If I peruert your course: whose heere?

Enter Lucio.

Luc. Good 'euen;
Frier, where's the Prouost?

Duke. Not within Sir.

Luc. Oh prettie *Isabella*, I am pale at mine heart, to see thine eyes so red: thou must be patient; I am faine to dine and sup with water and bran: I dare not for my head fill my belly. One fruitful Meale would set mee too't: but they say the Duke will be heere to Morrow. By my troth *Isabell* I lou'd thy brother, if the olde fantastical Duke of darke corners had bene at home, he had liued.

Duke. Sir, the Duke is marueilous little beholding to your reports, but the best is, he liues not in them.

Luc. Friar, thou knowest not the Duke so wel as I do: he's a better woodman then thou tak'st him for.

Duke. Well: you'l answer this one day. Fare ye well.

Luc. Nay tarrie, Ile go along with thee,
I can tel thee pretty tales of the Duke.

Duke You have told me too many of him already, sir, if they be true; if not true, none were enough.

Lucio I was once before him for getting a wench with child.

Duke Did you such a thing?

Lucio Yes, marry did I – but I was fain to forswear it. They would else have married me to the rotten medlar.

Duke Sir, your company is fairer than honest. Rest you well.

Lucio By my troth, I'll go with thee to the lane's end. If bawdy talk offend you, we'll have very little of it. Nay, friar, I am a kind of burr: I shall stick. *Exeunt*

4.4

Enter ANGELO *and* ESCALUS

Escalus Every letter he hath writ hath disvouched other.

Angelo In most uneven and distracted manner. His actions show much like to madness; pray heaven his wisdom be not tainted. And why meet him at the gates and reliver our authorities there?[60]

Escalus I guess not.

Angelo And why should we proclaim it in an hour before his entering, that if any crave redress of injustice, they should exhibit their petitions in the street?

Escalus He shows his reason for that: to have a dispatch of complaints, and to deliver us from devices hereafter, which shall then have no power to stand against us.

Angelo Well; I beseech you let it be proclaimed betimes i'th' morn. I'll call you at your house. Give notice to such men of sort and suit as are to meet him.

Escalus I shall, sir. Fare you well.

Angelo Good night. *Exit* ESCALUS

Duke. You haue told me too many of him already sir if they be true: if not true, none were enough.

Lucio. I was once before him for getting a Wench with childe.

Duke. Did you such a thing?

Luc. Yes marrie did I; but I was faine to forswear it, They would else haue married me to the rotten Medler.

Duke. Sir your company is fairer then honest, rest you well.

Lucio. By my troth Ile go with thee to the lanes end: if baudy talke offend you, we'el haue very litle of it: nay Friar, I am a kind of Burre, I shal sticke. *Exeunt*

Scena Quarta.

Enter Angelo & Escalus.

Esc. Euery Letter he hath writ, hath disuouch'd other.

An. In most vneuen and distracted manner, his actions show much like to madnesse, pray heauen his wisedome bee not tainted: and why meet him at the gates and reliuer ou rauthorities there?

Esc. I ghesse not.

Ang. And why should wee proclaime it in an howre before his entring, that if any craue redresse of iniustice, they should exhibit their petitions in the street?

Esc. He showes his reason for that: to haue a dispatch of Complaints, and to deliuer vs from deuices heereafter, which shall then haue no power to stand against vs.

Ang. Well: I beseech you let it bee proclaim'd betimes i'th' morne, Ile call you at your house: giue notice to such men of sort and suite as are to meete him.

Esc. I shall sir: fareyouwell. *Exit.*

Ang. Good night.

This deed unshapes me quite; makes me unpregnant
And dull to all proceedings. A deflower'd maid –
And by an eminent body that enforc'd
The law against it! But that her tender shame
Will not proclaim against her maiden loss,
How might she tongue me! Yet reason dares her no,
For my authority bears of a credent bulk,[61]
That no particular scandal once can touch
But it confounds the breather. He should have liv'd,
Save that his riotous youth with dangerous sense
Might in the times to come have ta'en revenge
By so receiving a dishonour'd life
With ransom of such shame. Would yet he had liv'd!
Alack, when once our grace we have forgot,
Nothing goes right: we would, and we would not.

Exit

4.5

Enter DUKE [*as himself*] *and Friar* PETER

Duke These letters at fit time deliver me.
The Provost knows our purpose and our plot.
The matter being afoot, keep your instruction
And hold you ever to our special drift,
Though sometimes you do blench from this to that
As cause doth minister. Go call at Flavius' house,[62]
And tell him where I stay. Give the like notice
To Valencius, Rowland, and to Crassus,
And bid them bring the trumpets to the gate.
But send me Flavius first.

Peter It shall be speeded well. [*Exit*]

Enter Varrius

Duke I thank thee, Varrius, thou hast made good haste.
Come, we will walk. There's other of our friends
Will greet us here anon. My gentle Varrius. *Exeunt*

This deede vnshapes me quite, makes me vnpregnant
And dull to all proceedings. A deflowred maid,
And by an eminent body, that enforc'd
The Law against it? But that her tender shame
Will not proclaime against her maiden losse,
How might she tongue me? yet reason dares her no,
For my Authority beares of a credent bulke,
That no particular scandall once can touch
But it confounds the breather. He should haue liu'd,
Saue that his riotous youth with dangerous sense
Might in the times to come haue ta'ne reuenge
By so receiuing a dishonor'd life
With ransome of such shame: would yet he had liued.
Alack, when once our grace we haue forgot,
Nothing goes right, we would, and we would not. *Exit.*

Scena Quinta.

Enter Duke and Frier Peter.

Duke. These Letters at fit time deliuer me.
The Prouost knowes our purpose and our plot,
The matter being a foote, keepe your instruction
And hold you euer to our speciall drift,
Though sometimes you doe blench from this to that
As cause doth minister: Goe call at *Flauia*'s house,
And tell him where I stay: giue the like notice
To *Valencius*, *Rowland*, and to *Crassus*,
And bid them bring the Trumpets to the gate:
But send me *Flauius* first.

Peter. It shall be speeded well.

Enter Varrius.

Duke. I thanke thee *Varrius*, thou hast made good hast,
Come, we will walke: There's other of our friends
Will greet vs heere anon: my gentle *Uarrius*. *Exeunt.*

4.6

Enter ISABEL *and* MARIANA

Isabel To speak so indirectly I am loath.
I would say the truth, but to accuse him so,
That is your part. Yet I am advis'd to do it,
He says, to veil full purpose.

Mariana Be rul'd by him.

Isabel Besides, he tells me that if peradventure
He speak against me on the adverse side,
I should not think it strange, for 'tis a physic
That's bitter to sweet end.

Enter Friar PETER

Mariana I would Friar Peter –

Isabel O peace, the friar is come.

Peter Come, I have found you out a stand most fit
Where you may have such vantage on the Duke
He shall not pass you. Twice have the trumpets sounded.
The generous and gravest citizens
Have hent the gates, and very near upon
The Duke is entering. Therefore hence, away. *Exeunt*

5.1

Enter at several doors DUKE [*as himself*], *Varrius, lords,*
ANGELO, ESCALUS, LUCIO, [*officers,*] *and citizens*

Duke My very worthy cousin, fairly met.
Our old and faithful friend, we are glad to see you.

Angelo & Escalus Happy return be to your royal grace.

Duke Many and hearty thankings to you both.

Scena Sexta.

Enter Isabella and Mariana.

Isab. To speak so indirectly I am loath,
I would say the truth, but to accuse him so
That is your part, yet I am aduis'd to doe it,
He saies, to vaile full purpose.

Mar. Be rul'd by him.

Isab. Besides he tells me, that if peraduenture
He speake against me on the aduerse side,
I should not thinke it strange, for 'tis a physicke
That's bitter, to sweet end.

Enter Peter.

Mar. I would *Frier Peter*

Isab. Oh peace, the *Frier* is come.

Peter. Come I haue found you out a stand most fit,
Where you may haue such vantage on the *Duke*
He shall not passe you:
Twice haue the Trumpets sounded.
The generous, and grauest Citizens
Haue hent the gates, and very neere vpon
The *Duke* is entring:
Therefore hence away. *Exeunt.*

Acta Quintus. Scœna Prima.

Enter Duke, Uarrius, Lords, Angelo, Esculus, Lucio, Citizens at seuerall doores.

Duk. My very worthy Cosen, fairely met,
Our old, and faithfull friend, we are glad to see you.

Ang.Esc. Happy returne be to your royall grace.

Duk. Many and harty thankings to you both:

We have made enquiry of you, and we hear
Such goodness of your justice that our soul
Cannot but yield you forth to public thanks,
Forerunning more requital.

Angelo You make my bonds still greater.

Duke O, your desert speaks loud, and I should wrong it
To lock it in the wards of covert bosom,
When it deserves, with characters of brass,
A forted residence 'gainst the tooth of time
And razure of oblivion. Give me your hand,[63]
And let the subject see, to make them know
That outward courtesies would fain proclaim
Favours that keep within. Come, Escalus,
You must walk by us on our other hand;
And good supporters are you.

Enter Friar PETER *and* ISABEL

Peter Now is your time. Speak loud, and kneel before him.

Isabel Justice, O royal Duke! Vail your regard
Upon a wrong'd – I would fain have said a maid.
O worthy Prince, dishonour not your eye
By throwing it on any other object
Till you have heard me in my true complaint,
And given me justice! Justice! Justice! Justice!

Duke Relate your wrongs. In what? By whom? Be brief.
Here is Lord Angelo shall give you justice.
Reveal yourself to him.

Isabel O worthy Duke,
You bid me seek redemption of the Devil.
Hear me yourself: for that which I must speak
Must either punish me, not being believ'd,
Or wring redress from you. Hear me! O hear me here!

Angelo My lord, her wits, I fear me, are not firm.

We haue made enquiry of you, and we heare
Such goodnesse of your Iustice, that our soule
Cannot but yeeld you forth to publique thankes
Forerunning more requitall.

Ang. You make my bonds still greater.

Duk. Oh your desert speaks loud, & I should wrong it
To locke it in the wards of couert bosome
When it deserues with characters of brasse
A forted residence 'gainst the tooth of time,
And razure of obliuion: Giue we your hand
And let the Subiect see, to make them know
That outward curtesies would faine proclaime
Fauours that keepe within: Come *Escalus*,
You must walke by vs, on our other hand:
And good supporters are you.

Enter Peter and Isabella.

Peter. Now is your time
Speake loud, and kneele before him.

Isab. Iustice, O royall *Duke*, vaile your regard
Vpon a wrong'd (I would faine haue said a Maid)
Oh worthy Prince, dishonor not your eye
By throwing it on any other obiect,
Till you haue heard me, in my true complaint,
And giuen me Iustice, Iustice, Iustice, Iustice.

Duk. Relate your wrongs;
In what, by whom? be briefe:
Here is Lord *Angelo* shall giue you Iustice,
Reueale your selfe to him.

Isab. Oh worthy *Duke*,
You bid me seeke redemption of the diuell,
Heare me your selfe: for that which I must speake
Must either punish me, not being beleeu'd,
Or wring redresse from you:
Heare me: oh heare me, heere.

Ang. My Lord, her wits I feare me are not firme:

She hath been a suitor to me for her brother,
Cut off by course of justice –

Isabel By course of justice!

Angelo And she will speak most bitterly and strange.

Isabel Most strange, but yet most truly will I speak.
That Angelo's forsworn, is it not strange?
That Angelo's a murderer, is't not strange?
That Angelo is an adulterous thief,
An hypocrite, a virgin-violator,
Is it not strange, and strange?

Duke Nay, it is ten times strange.

Isabel It is not truer he is Angelo
Than this is all as true as it is strange;
Nay, it is ten times true, for truth is truth
To th'end of reckoning.

Duke Away with her. Poor soul,
She speaks this in th'infirmity of sense.

Isabel O Prince, I conjure thee, as thou believ'st
There is another comfort than this world,
That thou neglect me not with that opinion
That I am touch'd with madness. Make not impossible
That which but seems unlike. 'Tis not impossible
But one, the wicked'st caitiff on the ground,
May seem as shy, as grave, as just, as absolute,
As Angelo; even so may Angelo
In all his dressings, characts, titles, forms,
Be an arch-villain. Believe it, royal Prince,
If he be less, he's nothing, but he's more,
Had I more name for badness.

Duke By mine honesty,
If she be mad, as I believe no other,
Her madness hath the oddest frame of sense,
Such a dependency of thing on thing,
As e'er I heard in madness.

Isabel O gracious Duke,

She hath bin a suitor to me, for her Brother
Cut off by course of Iustice.
Isab. By course of Iustice.
Aug. And she will speake most bitterly, and strange.
Isab. Most strange: but yet most truely wil I speake,
That *Angelo's* forsworne, is it not strange?
That *Angelo's* a murtherer, is't not strange?
That *Angelo* is an adulterous thiefe,
An hypocrite, a virgin violator,
Is it not strange? and strange?
Duke. Nay it is ten times strange?
Isa. It is not truer he is *Angelo*,
Then this is all as true, as it is strange;
Nay, it is ten times true, for truth is truth
To th'end of reckning.
Duke. Away with her: poore soule
She speakes this, in th'infirmity of sence.
Isa. Oh Prince, I coniure thee, as thou beleeu'st
There is another comfort, then this world,
That thou neglect me not, with that opinion
That I am touch'd with madnesse: make not impossible
That which but seemes vnlike, 'tis not impossible
But one, the wickedst caitiffe on the ground
May seeme as shie, as graue, as iust, as absolute:
As *Angelo*, euen so may *Angelo*
In all his dressings, caracts, titles, formes,
Be an arch-villaine: Beleeue it, royall Prince
If he be lesse, he's nothing, but he's more,
Had I more name for badnesse.
Duke. By mine honesty
If she be mad, as I beleeue no other,
Her madnesse hath the oddest frame of sense,
Such a dependancy of thing, on thing,
As ere I heard in madnesse.
Isab. Oh gracious *Duke*

Harp not on that, nor do not banish reason
For inequality, but let your reason serve
To make the truth appear where it seems hid,
And hide the false seems true.

Duke Many that are not mad
Have, sure, more lack of reason. What would you say?

Isabel I am the sister of one Claudio,
Condemn'd upon the act of fornication
To lose his head, condemn'd by Angelo.
I – in probation of a sisterhood –
Was sent to by my brother; one Lucio
As then the messenger –

Lucio That's I, an't like your grace.
I came to her from Claudio, and desir'd her
To try her gracious fortune with Lord Angelo
For her poor brother's pardon.

Isabel That's he indeed.

Duke [*To* LUCIO] You were not bid to speak.

Lucio No, my good lord,
Nor wish'd to hold my peace.

Duke I wish you now, then.
Pray you take note of it, and when you have
A business for yourself, pray heaven you then
Be perfect.

Lucio I warrant your honour.

Duke The warrant's for yourself: take heed to't.

Isabel This gentleman told somewhat of my tale.

Lucio Right.

Duke It may be right, but you are i' the wrong
To speak before your time. – Proceed.

Isabel I went
To this pernicious caitiff Deputy –

Duke That's somewhat madly spoken.

Isabel Pardon it,

Harpe not on that; nor do not banish reason
For inequality, but let your reason serue
To make the truth appeare, where it seemes hid,
And hide the false seemes true.
Duk. Many that are not mad
Haue sure more lacke of reason:
What would you say?
Isab. I am the Sister of one *Claudio*,
Condemnd vpon the Act of Fornication
To loose his head, condemn'd by *Angelo*,
I, (in probation of a Sisterhood)
Was sent to by my Brother; one *Lucio*
As then the Messenger.
Luc. That's I, and't like your Grace:
I came to her from *Claudio*, and desir'd her,
To try her gracious fortune with Lord *Angelo*,
For her poore Brothers pardon.
Isab. That's he indeede.
Duk. You were not bid to speake.
Luc. No, my good Lord,
Nor wish'd to hold my peace.
Duk. I wish you now then,
Pray you take note of it: and when you haue
A businesse for your selfe: pray heauen you then
Be perfect.
Luc. I warrant your honor.
Duk. The warrant's for your selfe: take heede to't.
Isab. This Gentleman told somewhat of my Tale.
Luc. Right.
Duk. It may be right, but you are i'the wrong
To speake before your time: proceed,
Isab. I went
To this pernicious Caitiffe Deputie.
Duk. That's somewhat madly spoken.
Isab: Pardon it,

The phrase is to the matter.

Duke Mended again. The matter; proceed.

Isabel In brief, to set the needless process by –
How I persuaded, how I pray'd, and kneel'd,
How he refell'd me, and how I replied
(For this was of much length) – the vile conclusion
I now begin with grief and shame to utter.
He would not but by gift of my chaste body
To his concupiscible intemperate lust,
Release my brother; and after much debatement,
My sisterly remorse confutes mine honour,
And I did yield to him. But the next morn betimes,
His purpose surfeiting, he sends a warrant
For my poor brother's head.

Duke This is most likely!

Isabel O that it were as like as it is true!

Duke By heaven, fond wretch, thou know'st not what thou speak'st,
Or else thou art suborn'd against his honour
In hateful practice. First, his integrity
Stands without blemish. Next, it imports no reason
That with such vehemency he should pursue
Faults proper to himself. If he had so offended,
He would have weigh'd thy brother by himself,
And not have cut him off. Someone hath set you on.
Confess the truth, and say by whose advice
Thou cam'st here to complain.

Isabel And is this all?
Then O you blessèd ministers above,
Keep me in patience, and with ripen'd time
Unfold the evil which is here wrapp'd up
In countenance! Heaven shield your grace from woe,
As I, thus wrong'd, hence unbelievèd go.

Duke I know you'd fain be gone. An officer!
To prison with her! Shall we thus permit
A blasting and a scandalous breath to fall

The phrase is to the matter.
Duke. Mended againe: the matter: proceed.
Isab. In briefe, to set the needlesse processe by:
How I perswaded, how I praid, and kneel'd,
How he refeld me, and how I replide
(For this was of much length) the vild conclusion
I now begin with griefe, and shame to vtter.
He would not, but by gift of my chaste body
To his concupiscible intemperate lust
Release my brother; and after much debatement,
My sisterly remorse, confutes mine honour,
And I did yeeld to him: But the next morne betimes,
His purpose surfetting, he sends a warrant
For my poore brothers head.
Duke. This is most likely.
Isab. Oh that it were as like as it is true. (speak'st,
Duk. By heauen (fond wretch) ỷ knowst not what thou
Or else thou art suborn'd against his honor
In hatefull practise: first his Integritie
Stands without blemish: next it imports no reason,
That with such vehemency he should pursue
Faults proper to himselfe: if he had so offended
He would haue waigh'd thy brother by himselfe,
And not haue cut him off: some one hath set you on:
Confesse the truth, and say by whose aduice
Thou cam'st heere to complaine.
Isab. And is this all?
Then oh you blessed Ministers aboue
Keepe me in patience, and with ripened time
Vnfold the euill, which is heere wrapt vp
In countenance: heauen shield your Grace from woe,
As I thus wrong'd, hence vnbeleeued goe.
Duke. I know you'ld faine be gone: An Officer:
To prison with her: Shall we thus permit
A blasting and a scandalous breath to fall,

On him so near us? This needs must be a practice.
Who knew of your intent and coming hither?

Isabel One that I would were here: Friar Lodowick.

Duke A ghostly father, belike. – Who knows that Lodowick?

Lucio My lord, I know him. 'Tis a meddling friar.
I do not like the man. Had he been lay, my lord,
For certain words he spake against your grace
In your retirement, I had swing'd him soundly.

Duke Words against me? This' a good friar belike!
And to set on this wretched woman here
Against our substitute! Let this friar be found.

Lucio But yesternight, my lord, she and that friar,
I saw them at the prison: a saucy friar,
A very scurvy fellow.

Peter Bless'd be your royal grace!
I have stood by, my lord, and I have heard
Your royal ear abus'd. First hath this woman
Most wrongfully accus'd your substitute,
Who is as free from touch or soil with her
As she from one ungot.

Duke We did believe no less.
Know you that Friar Lodowick that she speaks of?

Peter I know him for a man divine and holy,
Not scurvy, nor a temporary meddler,
As he's reported by this gentleman;
And on my trust, a man that never yet
Did, as he vouches, misreport your grace.

Lucio My lord, most villainously, believe it.

Peter Well, he in time may come to clear himself;
But at this instant he is sick, my lord,
Of a strange fever. Upon his mere request,
Being come to knowledge that there was complaint
Intended 'gainst Lord Angelo, came I hither
To speak as from his mouth what he doth know

On him so neere vs? This needs must be a practise;
Who knew of your intent and comming hither?
Isa. One that I would were heere, *Frier Lodowick*.
Duk. A ghostly Father, belike:
Who knowes that *Lodowicke*?
Luc. My Lord, I know him, 'tis a medling Fryer,
I doe not like the man: had he been Lay my Lord,
For certaine words he spake against your Grace
In your retirment, I had swing'd him soundly.
Duke. Words against mee? this 'a good Fryer belike
And to set on this wretched woman here
Against our Substitute: Let this Fryer be found.
Luc. But yesternight my Lord, she and that Fryer
I saw them at the prison: a sawcy Fryar,
A very scuruy fellow.
Peter. Blessed be your Royall Grace:
I haue stood by my Lord, and I haue heard
Your royall eare abus'd: first hath this woman
Most wrongfully accus'd your Substitute,
Who is as free from touch, or soyle with her
As she from one vngot.
Duke. We did beleeue no lesse.
Know you that Frier *Lodowick* that she speakes of?
Peter. I know him for a man diuine and holy,
Not scuruy, nor a temporary medler
As he's reported by this Gentleman:
And on my trust, a man that neuer yet
Did (as he vouches) mis-report your Grace.
Luc. My Lord, most villanously, beleeue it.
Peter. Well: he in time may come to cleere himselfe;
But at this instant he is sicke, my Lord:
Of a strange Feauor: vpon his meere request
Beiug come to knowledge, that there was complaint
Intended 'gainst Lord *Angelo*, came I hether
To speake as from his mouth, what he doth know

Is true and false, and what he with his oath
And all probation will make up full clear
Whensoever he's convented. First, for this woman,
To justify this worthy nobleman
So vulgarly and personally accus'd,
Her shall you hear disprovèd to her eyes,
Till she herself confess it. [*Exit* ISABEL *under guard*][64]

Duke Good friar, let's hear it.
Do you not smile at this, Lord Angelo?
O heaven, the vanity of wretched fools!
Give us some seats. Come, cousin Angelo,
In this I'll be impartial. Be you judge
Of your own cause.

Enter MARIANA [*veiled*]

Is this the witness, friar?
First let her show her face, and after speak.[65]

Mariana Pardon, my lord, I will not show my face
Until my husband bid me.

Duke What, are you married?

Mariana No, my lord.

Duke Are you a maid?

Mariana No, my lord.

Duke A widow then?

Mariana Neither, my lord.

Duke Why, you are nothing then: neither maid, widow, nor wife?

Lucio My lord, she may be a punk, for many of them are neither maid, widow, nor wife.

Duke Silence that fellow. I would he had some cause to prattle for himself.

Lucio Well, my lord.

Mariana My lord, I do confess I ne'er was married,
And I confess besides I am no maid:
I have known my husband, yet my husband

Is true, and false: And what he with his oath
And all probation will make vp full cleare
Whensoeuer he's conuented: First for this woman,
To iustifie this worthy Noble man
So vulgarly and personally accus'd,
Her shall you heare disproued to her eyes,
Till she her selfe confesse it.
Duk. Good Frier, let's heare it:
Doe you not smile at this, Lord *Angelo*?
Oh heauen, the vanity of wretched fooles.
Giue vs some seates. Come cosen *Angelo*,
In this I'll be impartiall: be you Iudge
Of your owne Cause: Is this the Witnes Frier?

Enter Mariana.

First, let her shew your face, and after, speake.
Mar. Pardon my Lord, I will not shew my face
Vntill my husband bid me.
Duke. What, are you married?
Mar. No my Lord.
Duke. Are you a Maid?
Mar. No my Lord.
Duk. A Widow then?
Mar. Neither, my Lord.
Duk. Why you are nothing then: neither Maid, Widow, nor Wife?
Luc. My Lord, she may be a Puncke: for many of them, are neither Maid, Widow, nor Wife.
Duk. Silence that fellow: I would he had some cause to prattle for himselfe.
Luc. Well my Lord.
Mar. My Lord, I doe confesse I nere was married,
And I confesse besides, I am no Maid,
I haue known my husband, yet my husband

Knows not that ever he knew me.

Lucio He was drunk then, my lord, it can be no better.

Duke For the benefit of silence, would thou wert so too.

Lucio Well, my lord.

Duke This is no witness for Lord Angelo.

Mariana Now I come to't, my lord.
She that accuses him of fornication
In self-same manner doth accuse my husband,
And charges him, my lord, with such a time
When I'll depose I had him in mine arms
With all th'effect of love.

Angelo Charges she more than me?

Mariana Not that I know.

Duke No? You say your husband.

Mariana Why, just, my lord, and that is Angelo,
Who thinks he knows that he ne'er knew my body,
But knows, he thinks, that he knows Isabel's.

Angelo This is a strange abuse. Let's see thy face.

Mariana [*Unveiling*] My husband bids me; now I will unmask.
This is that face, thou cruel Angelo,
Which once thou swor'st was worth the looking on.
This is the hand which with a vow'd contract
Was fast belock'd in thine. This is the body
That took away the match from Isabel,
And did supply thee at thy garden-house
In her imagin'd person.

Duke Know you this woman?

Lucio Carnally, she says.

Duke Sirrah, no more!

Lucio Enough, my lord.

Angelo My lord, I must confess I know this woman,
And five years since there was some speech of marriage
Betwixt myself and her, which was broke off,
Partly for that her promisèd proportions
Came short of composition, but in chief

Knowes not, that euer he knew me.

Luc. He was drunk then, my Lord, it can be no better.

Duk. For the benefit of silence, would thou wert so to.

Luc. Well, my Lord.

Duk. This is no witnesse for Lord *Angelo*.

Mar. Now I come to't, my Lord.
Shee that accuses him of Fornication,
In selfe-same manner, doth accuse my husband,
And charges him, my Lord, with such a time,
When I'le depose I had him in mine Armes
With all th'effect of Loue.

Ang. Charges she moe then me?

Mar. Not that I know.

Duk. No? you say your husband.

Mar. Why iust, my Lord, and that is *Angelo*,
Who thinkes he knowes, that he nere knew my body,
But knows, he thinkes, that he knowes *Isabels*.

Ang. This is a strange abuse: Let's see thy face.

Mar. My husband bids me, now I will vnmaske.
This is that face, thou cruell *Angelo*
Which once thou sworst, was worth the looking on:
This is the hand, which with a vowd contract
Was fast belockt in thine: This is the body
That tooke away the match from *Isabell*,
And did supply thee at thy garden-house
In her Imagin'd person.

Duke. Know you this woman?

Luc. Carnallie she saies.

Duk Sirha, no more.

Luc. Enoug my Lord.

Ang. My Lord, I must confesse, I know this woman,
And fiue yeres since there was some speech of marriage
Betwixt my selfe, and her: which was broke off,
Partly for that her promis'd proportions
Came short of Composition: But in chiefe

For that her reputation was disvalued
In levity. Since which time of five years
I never spake with her, saw her, nor heard from her,
Upon my faith and honour.

Mariana Noble Prince,
As there comes light from heaven, and words from breath,
As there is sense in truth, and truth in virtue,
I am affianc'd this man's wife, as strongly
As words could make up vows. And, my good lord,
But Tuesday night last gone, in's garden-house,
He knew me as a wife. As this is true,
Let me in safety raise me from my knees,
Or else for ever be confixèd here
A marble monument.

Angelo I did but smile till now.
Now, good my lord, give me the scope of justice.
My patience here is touch'd. I do perceive
These poor informal women are no more
But instruments of some more mightier member
That sets them on. Let me have way, my lord,
To find this practice out.

Duke Ay, with my heart,
And punish them to your height of pleasure.
Thou foolish friar, and thou pernicious woman,
Compact with her that's gone, think'st thou thy oaths,
Though they would swear down each particular saint,
Were testimonies against his worth and credit
That's seal'd in approbation? You, Lord Escalus,
Sit with my cousin, lend him your kind pains
To find out this abuse, whence 'tis deriv'd.
There is another friar that set them on;
Let him be sent for.

Peter Would he were here, my lord, for he indeed
Hath set the women on to this complaint.
Your Provost knows the place where he abides,

For that her reputation was dis-valued
In leuitie: Since which time of fiue yeres
I neuer spake with her, saw her, nor heard from her
Vpon my faith, and honor.
Mar. Noble Prince,
As there comes light from heauen, and words frō breath,
As there is sence in truth, and truth in vertue,
I am affianced this mans wife, as strongly
As words could make vp vowes: And my good Lord,
But Tuesday night last gon, in's garden house,
He knew me as a wife. As this is true,
Let me in safety raise me from my knees,
Or else for euer be confixed here
A Marble Monument.
Ang. I did but smile till now,
Now, good my Lord, giue me the scope of Iustice,
My patience here is touch'd: I doe perceiue
These poore informall women, are no more
But instruments of some more mightier member
That sets them on. Let me haue way, my Lord
To finde this practise out.
Duke. I, with my heart,
And punish them to your height of pleasure.
Thou foolish Frier, and thou pernicious woman
Compact with her that's gone: thinkst thou, thy oathes,
Though they would swear downe each particular Saint,
Were testimonies against his worth, and credit
That's seald in approbation? you, Lord *Escalus*
Sit with my Cozen, lend him your kinde paines
To finde out this abuse, whence 'tis deriu'd.
There is another Frier that set them on,
Let him be sent for.
Peter. Would he were here, my Lord, for he indeed
Hath set the women on to this Complaint;
Your Prouost knowes the place where he abides,

And he may fetch him.

Duke Go, do it instantly.

[*Exit one or more*][66]

And you, my noble and well-warranted cousin,
Whom it concerns to hear this matter forth,
Do with your injuries as seems you best
In any chastisement. I for a while will leave you;
But stir not you till you have well determin'd
Upon these slanderers.

Escalus My lord, we'll do it throughly.

Exit DUKE

Signor Lucio, did not you say you knew that Friar Lodowick to be a dishonest person?

Lucio '*Cucullus non facit monachum.*' Honest in nothing but in his clothes, and one that hath spoke most villainous speeches of the Duke.

Escalus We shall entreat you to abide here till he come, and enforce them against him. We shall find this friar a notable fellow.

Lucio As any in Vienna, on my word.

Escalus Call that same Isabel here once again, I would speak with her. [*Exit one or more*]
Pray you, my lord, give me leave to question. You shall see how I'll handle her.

Lucio Not better than he, by her own report.

Escalus Say you?

Lucio Marry, sir, I think if you handled her privately, she would sooner confess. Perchance publicly she'll be ashamed.

Enter DUKE [*as Friar Lodowick, with the*] PROVOST, *and* ISABEL [*guarded*]

Escalus I will go darkly to work with her.

Lucio That's the way – for women are light at midnight.

Escalus Come on, mistress, here's a gentlewoman denies all that you have said.

Lucio My lord, here comes the rascal I spoke of, here with the Provost.

And he may fetch him.

Duke. Goe, doe it instantly:
And you, my noble and well-warranted Cosen
Whom it concernes to heare this matter forth,
Doe with your iniuries as seemes you best
In any chastisement; I for a while
Will leaue you; but stir not you till you haue
Well determin'd vpon these Slanderers. *Exit.*

Esc. My Lord, wee'll doe it throughly: Signior *Lucio*, did not you say you knew that Frier *Lodowick* to be a dishonest person?

Luc. Cucullus non facit Monachum, honest in nothing but in his Clothes, and one that hath spoke most villanous speeches of the Duke.

Esc. We shall intreat you to abide heere till he come, and inforce them against him: we shall finde this Frier a notable fellow.

Luc. As any in *Vienna*, on my word.

Esc. Call that same *Isabell* here once againe, I would speake with her: pray you, my Lord, giue mee leaue to question, you shall see how Ile handle her.

Luc. Not better then he, by her owne report.

Esc. Say you?

Luc. Marry sir, I thinke, if you handled her priuately She would sooner confesse, perchance publikely she'll be asham'd.

Enter Duke, Prouost, Isabella.

Esc. I will goe darkely to worke with her.

Luc. That's the way: for women are light at midnight.

Esc. Come on Mistris, here's a Gentlewoman,
Denies all that you haue said.

Luc. My Lord, here comes the rascall I spoke of,
Here, with the *Prouost*.

Escalus In very good time. Speak not you to him till we call upon you.

Lucio Mum.

Escalus Come, sir, did you set these women on to slander Lord Angelo? They have confessed you did.

Duke 'Tis false.

Escalus How? Know you where you are?

Duke Respect to your great place, and let the Devil
Be sometime honour'd for his burning throne.
Where is the Duke? 'Tis he should hear me speak.

Escalus The Duke's in us, and we will hear you speak.
Look you speak justly.

Duke Boldly, at least. But O, poor souls,
Come you to seek the lamb here of the fox?
Good night to your redress. Is the Duke gone?
Then is your cause gone too. The Duke's unjust
Thus to retort your manifest appeal,
And put your trial in the villain's mouth
Which here you come to accuse.

Lucio This is the rascal. This is he I spoke of.

Escalus Why, thou unreverend and unhallow'd friar!
Is't not enough thou hast suborn'd these women
To accuse this worthy man, but in foul mouth,
And in the witness of his proper ear,
To call him villain – and then to glance from him
To th' Duke himself, to tax him with injustice?
Take him hence. To th' rack with him! We'll touse you
Joint by joint, but we will know his purpose.
What? 'Unjust'!

Duke Be not so hot. The Duke
Dare no more stretch this finger of mine than he
Dare rack his own. His subject am I not,
Nor here provincial. My business in this state
Made me a looker-on here in Vienna,
Where I have seen corruption boil and bubble

Esc. In very good time: speake not you to him, till we call vpon you.

Luc. Mum.

Esc. Come Sir, did you set these women on to slander Lord *Angelo*? they haue confes'd you did.

Duk. 'Tis false.

Esc. How? Know you where you are?

Duk. Respect to your great place; and let the diuell
Be sometime honour'd, for his burning throne.
Where is the *Duke*? 'tis he should heare me speake.

Esc. The *Duke's* in vs: and we will heare you speake,
Looke you speake iustly.

Duk. Boldly, at least. But oh poore soules,
Come you to seeke the Lamb here of the Fox;
Good night to your redress: Is the *Duke* gone?
Then is your cause gone too: The *Duke's* vniust,
Thus to retort your manifest Appeale,
And put your triall in the villaines mouth,
Which here you come to accuse.

Luc. This is the rascall: this is he I spoke of.

Esc. Why thou vnreuerend, and vnhallowed Fryer:
Is't not enough thou hast suborn'd these women,
To accuse this worthy man? but in foule mouth,
And in the witnesse of his proper eare,
To call him villaine; and then to glance from him,
To th'*Duke* himselfe, to taxe him with Iniustice?
Take him hence; to th' racke with him: we'll towze you
Ioynt by ioynt, but we will know his purpose:
What? vniust?

Duk. Be not so hot: the *Duke* dare
No more stretch this finger of mine, then he
Dare racke his owne: his Subiect am I not,
Nor here Prouinciall: My businesse in this State
Made me a looker on here in *Vienna*,
Where I haue seene corruption boyle and bubble,

Till it o'errun the stew; laws for all faults,
But faults so countenanc'd that the strong statutes
Stand like the forfeits in a barber's shop,
As much in mock as mark.

Escalus Slander to th' state!
Away with him to prison.

Angelo What can you vouch against him, Signor Lucio?
Is this the man that you did tell us of?

Lucio 'Tis he, my lord. – Come hither, goodman Baldpate. Do you know me?

Duke I remember you, sir, by the sound of your voice. I met you at the prison, in the absence of the Duke.

Lucio Oh, did you so? And do you remember what you said of the Duke?

Duke Most notedly, sir.

Lucio Do you so, sir? And was the Duke a fleshmonger, a fool, and a coward, as you then reported him to be?

Duke You must, sir, change persons with me ere you make that my report. You indeed spoke so of him, and much more, much worse.

Lucio Oh, thou damnable fellow! Did not I pluck thee by the nose for thy speeches?

Duke I protest I love the Duke as I love myself.

Angelo Hark how the villain would close now, after his treasonable abuses!

Escalus Such a fellow is not to be talked withal. Away with him to prison. Where is the Provost? Away with him to prison. Lay bolts enough upon him, let him speak no more. Away with those giglets too, and with the other confederate companion.

[*The* PROVOST *approaches the* DUKE]

Duke Stay, sir, stay a while.

Angelo What, resists he? Help him, Lucio.

Lucio Come, sir! Come, sir! Come, sir! Foh, sir! Why, you bald-pated lying rascal! You must be hooded, must

Till it ore-run the Stew: Lawes, for all faults,
But faults so countenanc'd, that the strong Statutes
Stand like the forfeites in a Barbers shop,
As much in mocke, as marke.

Esc. Slander to th' State:
Away with him to prison.

Ang. What can you vouch against him Signior *Lucio*? Is this the man that you did tell vs of?

Luc. 'Tis he, my Lord: come hither goodman bald-pate, doe you know me?

Duk. I remember you Sir, by the sound of your voice, I met you at the Prison, in the absence of the *Duke*.

Luc. Oh, did you so? and do you remember what you said of the *Duke*.

Duk. Most notedly Sir.

Luc. Do you so Sir: And was the *Duke* a flesh-monger, a foole, and a coward, as you then reported him to be?

Duk. You must (Sir) change persons with me, ere you make that my report: you indeede spoke so of him, and much more, much worse.

Luc. Oh thou damnable fellow: did not I plucke thee by the nose, for thy speeches?

Duk. I protest, I loue the *Duke*, as I loue my selfe.

Ang. Harke how the villaine would close now, after his treasonable abuses.

Esc. Such a fellow is not to be talk'd withall: Away with him to prison: Where is the *Prouost*? away with him to prison: lay bolts enough vpon him: let him speak no more: away with those Giglets too, and with the other confederate companion.

Duk. Stay Sir, stay a while.

Ang. What, resists he? helpe him *Lucio*.

Luc. Come sir, come sir, come sir: foh sir, why you bald-pated lying rascall: you must be hooded must you?

you? Show your knave's visage, with a pox to you!
Show your sheep-biting face, and be hanged an hour!
Will't not off?

[LUCIO *pulls off the friar's hood from the* DUKE*'s head*]

Duke Thou art the first knave that e'er mad'st a Duke.
First, Provost, let me bail these gentle three.
[*To* LUCIO] Sneak not away, sir, for the friar and you
Must have a word anon. – Lay hold on him.

Lucio [*Aside*] This may prove worse than hanging.

Duke [*To* ESCALUS]
What you have spoke, I pardon. Sit you down.
We'll borrow place of him.
[*To* ANGELO] Sir, by your leave.
Hast thou or word, or wit, or impudence,
That yet can do thee office? If thou hast,
Rely upon it till my tale be heard,
And hold no longer out.

Angelo O my dread lord,
I should be guiltier than my guiltiness
To think I can be undiscernible
When I perceive your grace, like power divine,
Hath look'd upon my passes. Then, good Prince,
No longer session hold upon my shame,
But let my trial be mine own confession.
Immediate sentence, then, and sequent death
Is all the grace I beg.

Duke Come hither, Mariana. –
Say, wast thou e'er contracted to this woman?

Angelo I was, my lord.

Duke Go, take her hence, and marry her instantly. –
Do you the office, friar; which consummate,
Return him here again. – Go with him, Provost.

Exeunt [ANGELO, MARIANA, *Friar* PETER, *and* PROVOST]

Escalus My lord, I am more amaz'd at his dishonour
Than at the strangeness of it.

show your knaues visage with a poxe to you: show your sheepe-biting face, and be hang'd an houre: will't not off?

Duk. Thou art the first knaue, that ere made'st a *Duke.*
First *Prouost*, let me bayle these gentle three:
Sneake not away Sir, for the Fryer, and you,
Must haue a word anon: lay hold on him.

Luc. This may proue worse then hanging.

Duk. What you haue spoke, I pardon: sit you downe,
We'll borrow place of him; Sir, by your leaue:
Ha'st thou or word, or wit, or impudence,
That yet can doe thee office? If thou ha'st
Rely vpon it, till my tale be heard,
And hold no longer out.

Ang. Oh, my dread Lord,
I should be guiltier then my guiltinesse,
To thinke I can be vndiscerneable,
When I perceiue your grace, like powre diuine,
Hath look'd vpon my passes. Then good Prince,
No longer Session hold vpon my shame,
But let my Triall, be mine owne Confession:
Immediate sentence then, and sequent death,
Is all the grace I beg.

Duk. Come hither *Mariana*,
Say: was't thou ere contracted to this woman?

Ang. I was my Lord.

Duk. Goe take her hence, and marry her instantly.
Doe you the office (*Fryer*) which consummate,
Returne him here againe: goe with him *Prouost*. *Exit.*

Esc. My Lord, I am more amaz'd at his dishonor,
Then at the strangenesse of it.

Duke Come hither, Isabel.
Your friar is now your prince. As I was then,
Advertising and holy to your business,
Not changing heart with habit, I am still
Attorney'd at your service.

Isabel O give me pardon
That I, your vassal, have employ'd and pain'd
Your unknown sovereignty.

Duke You are pardon'd, Isabel.
And now, dear maid, be you as free to us.
Your brother's death, I know, sits at your heart,
And you may marvel why I obscur'd myself,
Labouring to save his life, and would not rather
Make rash remonstrance of my hidden power
Than let him so be lost. O most kind maid,
It was the swift celerity of his death,
Which I did think with slower foot came on,
That brain'd my purpose. But peace be with him.
That life is better life, past fearing death,
Than that which lives to fear. Make it your comfort,
So happy is your brother.

Isabel I do, my lord.

Enter ANGELO, MARIANA, *Friar* PETER, *and* PROVOST

Duke For this new-married man approaching here,
Whose salt imagination yet hath wrong'd
Your well-defended honour, you must pardon
For Mariana's sake; but as he adjudg'd your brother,
Being criminal in double violation
Of sacred chastity and of promise-breach
Thereon dependent for your brother's life,
The very mercy of the law cries out
Most audible, even from his proper tongue,
'An Angelo for Claudio, death for death:
Haste still pays haste, and leisure answers leisure;
Like doth quit like, and Measure still for Measure.'

Duk. Come hither *Isabell*,
Your *Frier* is now your Prince: As I was then
Aduertysing, and holy to your businesse,
(Not changing heart with habit) I am still,
Atturnied at your seruice.
Isab. Oh giue me pardon
That I, your vassaile, haue imploid, and pain'd
Your vnknowne Soueraigntie.
Duk. You are pardon'd *Isabell*:
And now, deere Maide, be you as free to vs.
Your Brothers death I know sits at your heart:
And you may maruaile, why I obscur'd my selfe,
Labouring to saue his life: and would not rather
Make rash remonstrance of my hidden powre,
Then let him so be lost: oh most kinde Maid,
It was the swift celeritie of his death,
Which I did thinke, with slower foot came on,
That brain'd my purpose: but peace be with him,
That life is better life past fearing death,
Then that which liues to feare: make it your comfort,
So happy is your Brother.
Enter Angelo, Maria, Peter, Prouost.
Isab. I doe my Lord.
Duk. For this new-maried man, approaching here,
Whose salt imagination yet hath wrong'd
Your well defended honor: you must pardon
For *Mariana*'s sake: But as he adiudg'd your Brother,
Being criminall, in double violation
Of sacred Chastitie, and of promise-breach,
Thereon dependant for your Brothers life,
The very mercy of the Law cries out
Most audible, euen from his proper tongue.
An *Angelo* for *Claudio*, death for death:
Haste still paies haste, and leasure, answers leasure;
Like doth quit like, and *Measure* still for *Measure*:

Then, Angelo, thy fault's thus manifested,
Which, though thou wouldst deny, denies thee vantage.
We do condemn thee to the very block
Where Claudio stoop'd to death, and with like haste.
Away with him.

Mariana O my most gracious lord,
I hope you will not mock me with a husband?

Duke It is your husband mock'd you with a husband.
Consenting to the safeguard of your honour,
I thought your marriage fit; else imputation,
For that he knew you, might reproach your life,
And choke your good to come. For his possessions,
Although by confutation they are ours,[67]
We do instate and widow you with all,
To buy you a better husband.

Mariana O my dear lord,
I crave no other, nor no better man.

Duke Never crave him, we are definitive.

Mariana Gentle my liege – [*She kneels*]

Duke You do but lose your labour.
– Away with him to death.
[*To* LUCIO] Now, sir, to you.

Mariana O my good lord! Sweet Isabel, take my part:
Lend me your knees, and all my life to come
I'll lend you all my life to do you service.

Duke Against all sense you do impòrtune her.
Should she kneel down in mercy of this fact,
Her brother's ghost his pavèd bed would break,
And take her hence in horror.

Mariana Isabel!
Sweet Isabel, do yet but kneel by me;
Hold up your hands, say nothing; I'll speak all.
They say best men are moulded out of faults,
And for the most become much more the better
For being a little bad. So may my husband.

Then *Angelo*, thy fault's thus manifested;
Which though thou would'st deny, denies thee vantage.
We doe condemne thee to the very Blocke
Where *Claudio* stoop'd to death, and with like haste.
Away with him.
Mar. Oh my most gracious Lord,
I hope you will not mocke me with a husband?
Duk. It is your husband mock't you with a husband,
Consenting to the safe-guard of your honor,
I thought your marriage fit: else Imputation,
For that he knew you, might reproach your life,
And choake your good to come: For his Possessions,
Although by confutation they are ours;
We doe en-state, and widow you with all,
To buy you a better husband.
Mar. Oh my deere Lord,
I craue no other, nor no better man.
Duke. Neuer craue him, we are definitiue.
Mar. Gentle my Liege.
Duke. You doe but loose your labour.
Away with him to death: Now Sir, to you.
Mar. Oh my good Lord, sweet *Isabell*, take my part,
Lend me your knees, and all my life to come,
I'll lend you all my life to doe you seruice.
Duke. Against all sence you doe importune her,
Should she kneele downe, in mercie of this fact,
Her Brothers ghost, his paued bed would breake,
And take her hence in horror.
Mar. *Isabell*:
Sweet *Isabel*, doe yet but kneele by me,
Hold vp your hands, say nothing: I'll speake all.
They say best men are moulded out of faults,
And for the most, become much more the better
For being a little bad: So may my husband.

O Isabel, will you not lend a knee?

Duke He dies for Claudio's death.

Isabel [*Kneeling*] Most bounteous sir,
Look, if it please you, on this man condemn'd
As if my brother liv'd. I partly think
A due sincerity govern'd his deeds
Till he did look on me. Since it is so,
Let him not die. My brother had but justice,
In that he did the thing for which he died.
For Angelo,
His act did not o'ertake his bad intent,
And must be buried but as an intent
That perish'd by the way. Thoughts are no subjects,
Intents but merely thoughts.

Mariana Merely, my lord.

Duke Your suit's unprofitable. Stand up, I say. [*They rise*]
I have bethought me of another fault.
Provost, how came it Claudio was beheaded
At an unusual hour?

Provost It was commanded so.

Duke Had you a special warrant for the deed?

Provost No, my good lord, it was by private message.

Duke For which I do discharge you of your office.
Give up your keys.

Provost Pardon me, noble lord.
I thought it was a fault, but knew it not,
Yet did repent me after more advice,
For testimony whereof, one in the prison
That should by private order else have died
I have reserv'd alive.

Duke What's he?

Provost His name is Barnardine.

Duke I would thou hadst done so by Claudio.
Go fetch him hither, let me look upon him.
[*Exit* PROVOST]

Escalus I am sorry one so learnèd and so wise

Oh *Isabel*: will you not lend a knee?
Duke. He dies for *Claudio's* death.
Isab. Most bounteous Sir.
Looke if it please you, on this man condemn'd,
As if my Brother liu'd: I partly thinke,
A due sinceritie gouerned his deedes,
Till he did looke on me: Since it is so,
Let him not die: my Brother had but Iustice,
In that he did the thing for which he dide.
For *Angelo*, his Act did not ore-take his bad intent,
And must be buried but as an intent
That perish'd by the way: thoughts are no subiects
Intents, but meerely thoughts.
Mar. Meerely my Lord.
Duk. Your suite's vnprofitable: stand vp I say:
I haue bethought me of another fault.
Prouost, how came it *Claudio* was beheaded
At an vnusuall howre?
Pro. It was commanded so.
Duke. Had you a speciall warrant for the deed?
Pro. No my good Lord: it was by priuate message.
Duk. For which I doe discharge you of your office,
Giue vp your keyes.
Pro. Pardon me, noble Lord,
I thought it was a fault, but knew it not,
Yet did repent me after more aduice,
For testimony whereof, one in the prison
That should by priuate order else haue dide,
I haue reseru'd aliue.
Duk. What's he?
Pro. His name is *Barnardine*.
Duke. I would thou hadst done so by *Claudio*:
Goe fetch him hither, let me looke vpon him.
Esc. I am sorry, one so learned, and so wise

As you, Lord Angelo, have still appear'd,
Should slip so grossly, both in the heat of blood
And lack of temper'd judgement afterward.

Angelo I am sorry that such sorrow I procure,
And so deep sticks it in my penitent heart
That I crave death more willingly than mercy.
'Tis my deserving, and I do entreat it.

Enter BARNARDINE [*led by the*] PROVOST, CLAUDIO [*muffled*], *and* JULIET

Duke Which is that Barnardine?

Provost This, my lord.

Duke There was a friar told me of this man.
Sirrah, thou art said to have a stubborn soul
That apprehends no further than this world,
And squar'st thy life according. Thou'rt condemn'd;
But, for those earthly faults, I quit them all,
And pray thee take this mercy to provide
For better times to come. Friar, advise him,
I leave him to your hand. – What muffled fellow's that?

Provost This is another prisoner that I sav'd,
Who should have died when Claudio lost his head,
As like almost to Claudio as himself.

[*The* PROVOST *unmuffles* CLAUDIO]

Duke [*To* ISABEL] If he be like your brother, for his sake
Is he pardon'd, and for your lovely sake
Give me your hand, and say you will be mine;
He is my brother too – but fitter time for that.
By this Lord Angelo perceives he's safe;
Methinks I see a quickening in his eye.
Well, Angelo, your evil quits you well.
Look that you love your wife, her worth worth yours.
I find an apt remission in myself,
And yet here's one in place I cannot pardon.
[*To* LUCIO]
You, sirrah, that knew me for a fool, a coward,
One all of luxury, an ass, a madman –

As you, Lord *Angelo*, haue stil appear'd,
Should slip so grosselie, both in the heat of bloud
And lacke of temper'd iudgement afterward.
Ang. I am sorrie, that such sorrow I procure,
And so deepe sticks it in my penitent heart,
That I craue death more willingly then mercy,
'Tis my deseruing, and I doe entreat it.
Enter Barnardine and Prouost, Claudio, Iulietta.
Duke. Which is that *Barnardine*?
Pro. This my Lord.
Duke. There was a Friar told me of this man.
Sirha, thou art said to haue a stubborne soule
That apprehends no further then this world,
And squar'st thy life according: Thou'rt condemn'd,
But for those earthly faults, I quit them all,
And pray thee take this mercie to prouide
For better times to come: Frier aduise him,
I leaue him to your hand. What muffeld fellow's that?
Pro. This is another prisoner that I sau'd,
Who should haue di'd when *Claudio* lost his head,
As like almost to *Claudio*, as himselfe.
Duke. If he be like your brother, for his sake
Is he pardon'd, and for your louelie sake
Giue me your hand, and say you will be mine,
He is my brother too: But fitter time for that:
By this Lord *Angelo* perceiues he's safe,
Methinkes I see a quickning in his eye:
Well *Angelo*, your euill quits you well.
Looke that you loue your wife: her worth, worth yours
I finde an apt remission in my selfe:
And yet heere's one in place I cannot pardon,
You sirha, that knew me for a foole, a Coward,
One all of Luxurie, an asse, a mad man:

Wherein have I so deserv'd of you
That you extol me thus?

Lucio Faith, my lord, I spoke it but according to the trick. If you will hang me for it, you may; but I had rather it would please you I might be whipped.

Duke Whipp'd first, sir, and hang'd after.
Proclaim it, Provost, round about the city:
If any woman wrong'd by this lewd fellow –
As I have heard him swear himself there's one
Whom he begot with child – let her appear,
And he shall marry her. The nuptial finish'd,
Let him be whipp'd and hang'd.

Lucio I beseech your highness, do not marry me to a whore! Your highness said even now I made you a duke; good my lord, do not recompense me in making me a cuckold.

Duke Upon mine honour, thou shalt marry her.
Thy slanders I forgive, and therewithal
Remit thy other forfeits. – Take him to prison,
And see our pleasure herein executed.

Lucio Marrying a punk, my lord, is pressing to death, whipping, and hanging!

Duke Slandering a prince deserves it.
She, Claudio, that you wrong'd, look you restore.
Joy to you, Mariana. Love her, Angelo:
I have confess'd her, and I know her virtue.
Thanks, good friend Escalus, for thy much goodness:
There's more behind that is more gratulate.
Thanks, Provost, for thy care and secrecy:
We shall employ thee in a worthier place.
Forgive him, Angelo, that brought you home
The head of Ragozine for Claudio's:
Th'offence pardons itself. Dear Isabel,
I have a motion much imports your good,
Whereto, if you'll a willing ear incline,

Wherein haue I so deseru'd of you
That you extoll me thus?

Luc. 'Faith my Lord, I spoke it but according to the trick: if you will hang me for it you may: but I had rather it would please you, I might be whipt.

Duke. Whipt first, sir, and hang'd after.
Proclaime it Prouost round about the Citie,
If any woman wrong'd by this lewd fellow
(As I haue heard him sweare himselfe there's one
whom he begot with childe) let her appeare,
And he shall marry her: the nuptiall finish'd,
Let him be whipt and hang'd.

Luc. I beseech your Highnesse doe not marry me to a Whore: your Highnesse said euen now I made you a Duke, good my Lord do not recompence me, in making me a Cuckold.

Duke. Vpon mine honor thou shalt marrie her.
Thy slanders I forgiue, and therewithall
Remit thy other forfeits: take him to prison,
And see our pleasure herein executed.

Luc. Marrying a punke my Lord, is pressing to death, Whipping and hanging.

Duke. Slandering a Prince deserues it.
She *Claudio* that you wrong'd, looke you restore.
Ioy to you *Mariana*, loue her *Angelo*:
I haue confes'd her, and I know her vertue.
Thanks good friend, *Escalus*, for thy much goodnesse,
There's more behinde that is more gratulate.
Thanks *Prouost* for thy care, and secrecie,
We shall imploy thee in a worthier place.
Forgiue him *Angelo*, that brought you home
The head of *Ragozine* for *Claudio's*,
Th'offence pardons it selfe. Deere *Isabell*,
I haue a motion much imports your good,
Whereto if you'll a willing eare incline;

What's mine is yours, and what is yours is mine.
So bring us to our palace, where we'll show
What's yet behind that's meet you all should know.[68]

[*Exeunt*]

What's mine is yours, and what is yours is mine.
So bring vs to our Pallace, where wee'll show
What's yet behinde, that meete you all should know.

The Scene Vienna.

The names of all the Actors.

Vincentio: the Duke.
Angelo, the Deputie.
Escalus, an ancient Lord.
Claudio, a yong Gentleman.
Lucio, a fantastique.
2. *Other like Gentlemen.*
Prouost.
Thomas. } 2 *Friers.*
Peter. }
Elbow, a simple Constable.
Froth, a foolish Gentleman.
Clowne.
Abhorson, an Executioner.
Barnardine, a dissolute prisoner.
Isabella, sister to Claudio.
Mariana, betrothed to Angelo.
Iuliet, beloued of Claudio.
Francisca, a Nun.
Mistris Ouer-don, a Bawd.

FINIS.

Textual Notes

As our Series Introduction explains, our modernized edition remains as faithful as possible to its Folio model. Sometimes, however, it is necessary to intercede on its behalf – where the Folio, in other words, makes little or no sense. These notes are designed to explain these decisions as succinctly as possible, by reference to the play's enormous editorial tradition. It has also sometimes been felt necessary to signal those occasions where the Folio reading we retain has been subject to editorial or scholarly contention. It was Dr Johnson's view (1765) that the text of *Measure for Measure*, unique to the Folio, is also uniquely complicated 'by the peculiarities of its author, and the unskilfulness of its editors, by distortions of phrase or negligence of transcription' (see Introduction above, p. xxxviii). Recent scholarship has tended to invest more of its trust in the expressive idiosyncrasies of Shakespeare's compressed style than in any 'negligence of transcription'. This is a policy to which our Folio editions subscribe, and so the majority of the following notes present the argument *against* the Folio text we retain. Each numbered note therefore gives the relevant line from the parallel text (with its act and scene, and page-number): '7. **So long that nineteen zodiacs have gone round,** (1.3, pp. 16–17)'; and where our modern texts overrule the Folio ('F'), our notes highlight the problem by setting the contested word(s) in square brackets: '23. **Grown sere [F fear'd,] and tedious.** (2.4, pp. 62–3)'. Our accounts of these intercessions and alternatives range from simple attributions to previous editions, to lengthier discussions of thornier 'cruxes', while seeking always to defend the absolute necessity of such interference. A chronological list of the texts, editions, and scholarship cited there, from the 1623 First Folio via the two editions, by Brian Gibbons and N.W. Bawcutt, that appeared in 1991, to Frank Kermode's 2000 study of *Shakespeare's Language*, may be found at the end of these notes.

1. **Then no more remains | But that, to your sufficiency, as your worth is able, | And let them work.** (1.1, pp. 2–3)
The Duke acknowledges that Escalus needs no lectures from him in political expertise ('science'), despite the intellect and authority

('strength') with which he now deputes his power to him. Editors have worked hard to introduce grammatical coherence to what follows, suspecting various degrees of textual corruption in this sentence – perhaps correctly, given the awkward length and metre of its second line. Scholarly opinion ranges from the minor treatment of optimistic textual consultants, to the major surgery of textual pessimists.

The diagnoses of Nicholas Rowe (1709) and C.J. Sisson (1956) are elegantly minimal: 'Then no more **remains; | Put** that to your sufficiency . . . ' [= *Then there's nothing more to say; blend my power with your capacity* . . .] (Rowe); 'Then no more remains | But **that. To** your sufficiency . . .' [= *Then there's nothing more to be discussed but this question of power. On, then, to your capable duty* . . .] (Sisson). Samuel Johnson (1765) and George Steevens (1773) favoured a slightly more interventionist procedure, tracing the problem to the Folio's mistaken inclusion of – respectively – 'to' and 'as': 'But that to your sufficienc**ies your worth** is able**d**' (Johnson); 'But **that your** sufficiency as your worth is able' (Steevens) – both meaning something like 'except [to ensure] that your potential is matched in practice by your capabilities'. Thomas Hanmer (1743–5) believed that two half-lines had been omitted from Shakespeare's original, and then promptly composed them: 'Then no more remains | But that to your sufficiency *you joyn* | *A will to serve us* as your worth is able, | And let them work.' N.W. Bawcutt (1991) supported this view (the result of 'compositorial eye-skip') and suggested his own equivalent ('. . . sufficiency *you add* | *A power as ample* as your worth . . .'). (But it must surely have been a *very* tired compositor or scribe who botched the eighth line of a play?)

Our text subscribes to the tradition of editorial optimism, from William Warburton (1747) to Brian Gibbons (1991), that gives the Folio the all-clear – as evidence of the correlation between a character's 'complex and contorted' state of mind and the 'ambiguous and disjointed' nature of their dialogue . The coherence of the Folio principally depends upon 'that' being a pronoun: 'no more remains but *that thing* [the Duke's 'strength'; or possibly the written commission which he now presents], and so let my devolved power work together with your own independent capabilities'. Whatever the truth, the play's abrupt plunge into the deep end of its knotty, intractable manner sets the tone of much that follows.

2. **I thank you. Fare you well.** ***Exit*** (1.1, pp. 6–7)
Here – as frequently throughout the play – F sets stage-directions ('SDs') in advance of their evidently proper place, sometimes with an eye that favoured a page's neatness over the utility of stage-practice. In this example, the Duke apparently exits before he says goodbye. Another example may be found in the next scene (pp. 12–13), where Mistress Overdone the Bawd greets Pompey the Clown before his entrance. Our modern edition silently adopts – without attribution – the reorganization of such effects when they are generally accepted, noting only those occasions that have prompted a substantial difference of opinion (see Textual Note 64 below, for example).

3. **I had as lief be a list of an English kersey as be piled – as thou art pilled [F pil'd] – for a French velvet.** (1.2, pp. 10–11)
The First Gentleman's gibe puns on the 'pile' (or texture) of an expensive velvet and the 'pilled' nature (hairless, as in 'depilation') of Lucio's head, hair-loss being a side-effect of the treatment for the 'French' venereal disease – which is why we follow J.W. Lever (1965) in spelling it out. (A 'list' is the discarded or hemmed edge of a woven fabric.)

4. **and there's Madam Juliet.** ***Exeunt*** (1.2, pp. 14–15)
Editorial tradition since Nicholas Rowe (1709) has overruled the Folio's scene-division here, which seems to have been introduced by Ralph Crane in the transcript he prepared for its compositors. Crane prepared his text with readers in mind, and he has noticed here the shift in both tone and content that follows the Clown's cue; the mood and pitch assuredly modulate from bantering obscenities in prose to a higher-brow blank-verse exposition of the plot.

The inclusion of Juliet and the two Gentlemen in the subsequent entrance, none of whom are given anything to say, has aided speculation that more is textually awry than a superfluous scene-division. Why, for example, does the Bawd enter with news that Claudio has been 'arrested and carried to prison', sentenced to death 'for getting Madam Julietta with child' – but then profess complete bafflement at the Clown's own news ('What? Is there a maid with child by him?') (1.2, pp. 10–13)? And why should Lucio later ask Claudio, 'Whence comes this restraint?' when he has already heard the answer from the Bawd? On the latter point, N.W. Bawcutt (1991) reasonably claims that Lucio 'was not completely persuaded' by her account, and that his quizzing provides Claudio with the opportunity to express his perspective to the play's audience. His argument that Mistress Overdone is 'not . . . particularly quick-witted' (p. 73) provides a useful negotiation of the second anomaly, though he uses the same argument, more convincingly, about the executioner Abhorson in a later textual crux (see Note 53 below). The counterview is presented most extremely by the editors of the Oxford *Works* (1986). They claim that an adapter (perhaps Thomas Middleton) provided 'a new, seedy opening' to 1.2 – in fact the entire conversation between Lucio and the two Gentlemen. Their edition includes as an appendix the 41 lines (rearranged and 'restored' from the Folio's 116) which 'probably represents Shakespeare's original intention' (p. 923). As Bawcutt notes, however, that presumed intention damagingly withholds the information that Claudio has been sentenced to death; and Juliet's mute (visibly pregnant?) presence – which editors and directors have sometimes suppressed – may foreshadow Isabel's comparably ambiguous silence at the play's end.

It seems likely that the relevant Folio sequence (pp. 8–15 of this edition) preserves the forensic evidence of *some* form of revision, whether by Shakespeare or others, at some point(s) between 1604 and 1622.

5. **I had as lief have the foppery of freedom as the mortality of imprisonment.** (1.3, pp. 14–15)
Most editors adopt Nicholas Rowe's 1709 emendation to 'morality' (*moral instruction*) as a more likely contrast for Lucio to make with 'foppery' (*trivial folly*), a reading which is also found in William Davenant's adaptation of the play (1673). The F-reading ('mortality') is vividly glossed by Charlotte Porter and Helen A. Clarke (1909) as 'dead earnest'.

6. **Only for propagation [F propogation] of a dower** (1.3, pp. 16–17)
The Second Folio (1632) supplies the modern spelling of this word, which – as most modern editors comment – sets a keynote to the play's thoroughgoing preoccupation with fertility (both human and financial). Claudio explains that he and Juliet have delayed their marriage, pending the increase in (or simply settlement of) her dowry, which financial arrangement lay in the hands of her initially reluctant kinsmen ('Till time had made them for us'). A series of literal-minded emendations have nevertheless been proposed: 'prorogation' (= *legal*

extension, Malone, 1790); 'procuration' (= *acquisition*, Collier, 1853); 'preservation' (White, 1857–66); 'propugnation' (= *protection*, Staunton, 1858–60); 'propriation' (= *settlement*, John Dover Wilson and Arthur Quiller-Couch, 1922) – all of which make sense, and none of which Shakespeare seems likely to have written. On contemporary matrimonial law, see Ernest Schanzer (1960).

7. **So long that nineteen zodiacs have gone round,** (1.3, pp. 16–17) This apparently innocent line illustrates the flurry of conjecture that the play's relative textual simplicity has generated. For it has been noticed that the Duke himself later complains that the law in Vienna has been flouted only for 'fourteen years' (1.4, pp. 20–21), and not nineteen. The discrepancy has been variously explained as Shakespeare's own inattention; as a mistake in the transcription or typesetting of the play – for in contemporary manuscript forms, both Arabic ('14'/'19') and Roman ('xiv'/'xix') numerals are easily confused; and as an obscure reference to the nineteen-year astronomical phenomenon known as the 'Metonic cycle', as Norman Nathan proposed in 1969: 'for as long a time as it would take the sun and moon to run their full cycle into realignment. This seems similar to saying that the law is enforced once in a blue moon.'

8. **There is a prone and speechless dialect** (1.3, pp. 18–19) The word 'prone' (with its contradictory associations of inertia and alacrity, lent tang by a floating sense of sexuality) has caused much critical discussion, and a series of editors has conjectured its replacement, Samuel Johnson proposing 'power' or 'prompt' (1765), and C.J. Sisson 'grace' (1956). Frank Kermode (2000) offers an inspiriting defence of the Folio reading, 'where distortions make poetry': 'an excellent example of Shakespeare at his richest, for at such times he will not settle for a single, simple sense, though he leaves one around to keep the reader or auditor quiet; and in this respect the passage is characteristic of the play itself' (pp. 150–56).

9. **The needful bits and curbs to headstrong weeds,** (1.4, pp. 20–21) Though the Second Folio (1632) retains 'weeds', editors since Lewis Theobald (1733) have noticed that the imagery of 'bits and curbs' sits rather oddly with 'weeds', as does their description as 'headstrong'. Theobald shrewdly suggested 'steeds', and this long remained the standard reading – though 'wills' and 'deeds' have also been posited as (rather flat) substitutes. J.W. Lever (1965) plausibly suggested 'jades' (= fractious, wilful horses), calling in evidence

Marlowe's description of 'headstrong jades' as 'wanton' (*2 Tamburlaine*, 4.3), and citing *A Mirour for Magistrates of Cyties* by George Whetstone (1584): 'althoughe, a Braynsicke Iade, wyll ronne with a Snaffle, a sharpe Bitte wyll bridle him'. Pompey the Clown later uses the same word ('No, no, let car-man whip his jade', 2.1, pp. 42–3), and so the emendation seems persuasive – though Lever's description of the F reading as a 'pointlessly mixed metaphor' overlooks William Empson's scintillating discussion of this crux (1953). Empson notes that 'wicked weedes' feature in a comparable passage in the source play, Whetstone's *Promos and Cassandra* (1575): Shakespeare, he argues, with 'the image of *weeds* lying about in his mind' (pp. 84–5), suddenly applied it in the place of the 'steeds' he had originally conceived; and Theobald inadvertently reconstructed the momentary train of his mercurial thought.

10. **in time the rod | More mock'd than fear'd – so our decrees,** (1.4, pp. 20–21)
Alexander Pope (1723–5) suspected an omission here, on the grounds both of metre and grammar, and most subsequent editions follow him in supplying the wanted verb: 'in time the rod | *Becomes* more mock'd than fear'd'. The Oxford *Works* (1986) supplies an arguably smoother variant ('More mock'd *becomes* than fear'd'), but Brian Gibbons's generally non-interventionist edition (1991) wins sense from F by the punctuation we have adopted, as a complementary subclause.

11. **Upon the sisterhood [F Sisterstood], the votarists of Saint Clare.** (1.5, pp. 22–3)
We follow most editors in assuming, with F2 (1632), that 'Sisterstood' is a simple misreading of 'sisterhood' – in some contemporary manuscript forms the letters 'h' and 'st' are very similar. The fact that Isabel herself later uses the same word ('in probation of a sisterhood', 5.1, pp. 146–7) perhaps tilts the balance away from J.W. Lever's dissenting view (1965) that the line's grammar allows 'sisters stood' (= *wishing that a stricter regime circumscribed the nunnery*). T.H. Howard-Hill pronounces the result 'cacophonous' (1972, p. 126).

12. **[*Enter* LUCIO]** (1.5, pp. 24–5)
Nicholas Rowe's supply of Lucio's entrance (1709) is surely correct, since his opening lines ('as those cheek-roses') strongly suggest a face-to-face meeting, and the rest of the scene would be oddly static if he remains '*within*'. But the exit Rowe provides for the Nun

beforehand is less certain. As J.W. Lever (1965) persuasively notes, she would be remiss in her duty to leave Isabel alone with any man, and especially a man like Lucio. Lever accordingly specifies that the Nun '*Retires*' after her final line.

Rowe's subsequent emendation of F's 'steed' ('can you so steed me') to 'stead' (meaning 'assist', with useful associations of substitution) is evidently correct. Brian Gibbons (1991) notes that 'F spells this verb "steed" seven times, "stead" twice, and "sted" once.'

13. **Or that the resolute acting of our blood** (2.1, pp. 30–31) Editors have generally agreed that the rhetoric and sense of the passage as a whole demands support for Nicholas Rowe's 1709 emendation of 'our' to 'your', a reading that gains further likelihood from William Davenant's 1673 adaptation. It is also true that the answer to Escalus's hypothetical question (*Is it not possible that you yourself might have yielded to the same desires* ['the resolute acting of your blood'] *as Claudio has done?*) is shortly to be proved all too pertinent. Since our editions constantly lend the Folio the benefit of the doubt, however, we follow Peter Alexander (1951) in retaining the Folio reading (despite the slight jarring of the rhetorical accumulation) to mean something like *the active submission to those bodily urges which we all sometimes feel*. The distinction between 'your' and 'our' (we may add) is in any case less absolute than it might seem: 'There are more things in heaven and earth, Horatio,' says Hamlet in his play's Second Quarto (1604–5), 'Than are dreamt of in your philosophy' (1.5): 'Not some particular philosophy of Horatio's,' comments Harold Jenkins in his 1982 edition, 'but philosophy in general, *your* being used in the indefinite sense then common' (p. 226). The Folio changes 'your' to 'our' (see our Shakespeare Folios edition of *Hamlet*, pp. 52–3).

14. **Some run from brakes of ice, and answer none, | And some condemnèd for a fault alone** (2.1, pp. 32–3)
This couplet – perhaps extemporized by Escalus following the *sententia* (or moral proverb) he offers in the preceding line (see Introduction above, p. xxxix) – has inspired a complicated sequence of editorial debate. The matter rests upon a satisfactory interpretation of the phrase 'brakes of ice', and commentators have generally agreed that one or other of the nouns requires surgery. Nicholas Rowe (1709) led the field by supposing that 'ice' had been misprinted for 'vice', retaining 'brakes' (= hedgerow thickets), and then changing F's 'from' to 'through': *Some emerge unscathed through*

the thorny bushes of vice . . . George Steevens (1778) qualified this reading by interpreting 'brakes' as 'engines of torture', and thus precariously retained F's 'from': *Some flee severe punishment for their vicious living . . .* 'Brakes' may also mean 'bridles' or 'curbs' (*Some flee the restrictions placed upon their vice . .*). But perhaps 'ice' *is* correct, after all – as Steevens had originally thought (1773), and as J.P. Collier later and influentially agreed (1842–4). Given 'ice', therefore, the thought naturally turns to 'breaks' (rather than 'brakes'): 'The fool slides o'er the ice that you should break,' says Ulysses to Achilles in the play Shakespeare had recently finished (*Troilus and Cressida*, 3.3), as C.J. Sisson (1956) pointed out in support of Collier's reading ('breaks of ice'): *Some hack away at the ice (on which they stand), and escape scot-free, while others plunge down into the depths after a single chip* ['fault' = flaw]. Since 'breaks of ice' sounds almost identical to 'brakes of vice', however, such discussion must yield to the momentary effect the line made (and makes) to audiences, upon whom the full range of these incompatible associations (thorn-bushes or sheeted ice) must surely remain available. Our modern edition retains the Folio reading, following Lever (1965), on the arguable grounds that 'brakes [in the sense of *constrictions*] of ice' so vividly anticipates Claudio's own fearful description of the 'thrilling region of thick-ribbèd ice' that may await his soul (3.1, pp. 82–3).

15. **Sir, we had but two in the house, which at that very distant time stood,** (2.1, pp. 34–5)
The F2 editors (1632) corrected Pompey's 'distant' to 'instant', which certainly makes better sense, and J.W. Lever (1965) noticed that the confusion may have arisen if Crane (or Shakespeare) had spelled the latter word with a contraction as 'īstant'. Yet it is a bold spirit who ventures into the morass of Pompey's endlessly frustrating shaggy-dog story, and – as Brian Gibbons (1991) points out – it is possible that 'distant' is a deliberate parody of Elbow's malapropisms ('notorious benefactors', pp. 32–3).

16. ***Provost* [*Aside*] Heaven give thee moving graces!** (2.2, pp. 48–9)
It is an unusual feature of this scene that each of its main characters except Isabel at some point speaks out of earshot of the others ('*Aside*') – everyone has something to hide, it seems. Such directions are only rarely specified in the 1623 Folio, and audiences accept their artificiality more readily than readers. It should be noted, however, that Lucio's first comments, and his later advice that ''Tis well. Away' (56–7), are evidently addressed to Isabel, though his

other lines may just as well be choric interpolations for the sole benefit of the audience.

17. **May call it again. Well, believe this:** (2.2, pp. 50–51)
The editors of the Second Folio (1632) restored a regular metre to this line by supplying 'back' ('May call it *back* again . . .'). Some of their modern counterparts tend to prefer what C.J. Sisson (1956) called the 'marked and dramatic pause' that the Folio provides in its place. (The verb 'longs' in the following line means the same as 'belongs' but is not, apparently, a contraction of that word.)

18. **Either now, or by remissness new-conceiv'd,** (2.2, pp. 52–3)
The sense of the argument is plain: Angelo is distinguishing between two 'future evils', one already growing, the other at the point of sinful ('by remissness') conception – 'And so, in progress, to be hatch'd and born'. F lays great weight (in both metre and sense) on the word 'now' ('Either [*such an evil that is already*] now [*growing*], or . . .'), and editors since Alexander Pope (1723–5) have felt the need to lessen that burden. Pope perceived the need for a rhetorical repetition ('*Or new*, or by remissness *new*-conceiv'd'), at the same time tidying up the metre by using 'Or . . . or' in the standard Jacobean sense of 'Either . . . or'. J.W. Lever (1965) contrasted the 'well balanced' repetition of 'new' to the 'awkward repetition' of 'now' later in the speech ('Are now to have . . .'), and therefore favoured Alexander Dyce's 1857 more conservative reading: 'Either *new*, or by remissness new-conceiv'd . . .' Others have spelled out the sense with various degrees of literal-mindedness: 'Either now *born*, or by remissness new-conceiv'd' (Thomas Keightley, 1864); '*Eggs* now, or . . .' (John Dover Wilson and Arthur Quiller-Couch, 1922), a reading which spells out the subsequent 'progress to be *hatched* and born'; the Oxford editors (1986) ingeniously suggest 'Either *raw*, or by remissness . . .'

The last line of the same speech (F 'But here they liue to end') has also divided editors. Thomas Hanmer (1743–5) noticed that while F makes a sort of sense (= *But are here brought into embryonic life only to die*), the line would more effectively – more compactly – read 'But *ere* they live to end' (= *But die before they even live*). N.W. Bawcutt (1991) cites a close analogy in *All's Well That Ends Well*, where Bertram seeks to 'End ere I begin' (2.5). (It is of course something of an irony that a line about alternative moral origins should have sponsored so many editorial efforts to retrieve Shakespeare's original conception of it.)

19. **Not with fond sicles of the tested gold,** (2.2, pp. 56–7) Alexander Pope (1723–5) chose to refine 'sickles' to the more biblical '*shekles*' (i.e. the biblical currency of *shekels*). The Latin root-word is '*siclus*'; the English form 'sicles', William Aldis Wright notes, is the form in which Shakespeare 'would hear it read in church from the Bishop's Bible' (1891–3). A buried reference to 'testicles' is not impossible (Brian Gibbons, 1991).

20. ***Enter* DUKE [*as Friar Lodowick*] *and* PROVOST** (2.3, pp. 58–9) William Davenant's adaptation (1673) first specified the Duke's disguise ('*as a Friar*'), whose alias ('a meddling friar') is given in the final scene (5.1, pp. 150–51). His initially clumsy assumption of his role is rather nicely observed in his first line, where he greets the Provost – then remembers that the fictional 'Friar Lodowick' has never met him.

21. **Must die tomorrow? O injurious love,** (2.3, pp. 60–61) Thomas Hanmer's emendation of 'love' to 'law' (1743–5) in this line is one in a series of such tentative corrections in the scene, each of which has usually been resisted since. Thus Samuel Johnson (1765) defended F's 'love' by explaining that Juliet's own 'execution was respited on account of her pregnancy, the effects of her love'. N.W. Bawcutt (1991), however, claims that 'emendation to *law* gives a richer meaning to *injurious*'.

    The word 'spare' in the Duke's earlier line ('Showing we would not *spare* heaven, as we love it,') was conjecturally replaced by 'seek' by Alexander Pope (1723–5), and both 'serve' and 'share' by J.P. Collier (1853) – despite F carrying the sense of something like *Demonstrating that we can scarcely refrain from vexing heaven by the extent of our sins – for all that we love God*.

    Alexander Dyce (1857) similarly felt the need to divide the Duke's exit-line (F 'Grace goe with you, *Benedicite*') between Juliet ('Grace go with you!') and the Duke ('*Benedicite*' = 'Bless you').

22. **Anchors on Isabel – heaven in my mouth,** (2.4, pp. 62–3) This line is one of the strongest pieces of evidence in favour of the theory that the script Shakespeare composed was subsequently trimmed of its expletive oaths. The 'Name of God in Stageplayes' was specifically forbidden by James I's 1606 Act (see Introduction, p. xxxiv), and J.W. Lever (1965) provides a relevant quotation from James's own book on kingship, *Bazilikon Doron* (1599) – 'Keepe God

more sparingly in your mouth, but aboundantly in your harte' – which paraphrases Jesus's words in Matthew 15, 8 (in the King James version): 'This people draweth nigh unto me with their mouth . . . but their heart is far from me'. 'Heaven' is certainly the customary substitute for 'God' between the 1604-Quarto and 1623-Folio texts of *Hamlet*; and the next line ('As if I did but chew *his* name') provides strong internal support for the theory. It has recently been suggested that the scribe Ralph Crane may have taken it upon himself to expurgate the plays he transcribed, quite independently of the 1606 Act (which in any case seems not to have applied to printed texts) (Honigmann, 1996, pp. 77–80).

23. **Grown sere [F feard,] and tedious.** (2.4, pp. 62–3)
The Folio scarcely makes sense – for in what sense can a frequently-read maxim inspire both fear and boredom? – so editors must choose between 'sere' (= dry, desiccated), a reading given in Henry Hudson's edition (1851–6); and 'sear'd' (= dried out, withered), the reading given in Nicholas Rowe's 1709 edition – though this may itself have been a misprint – and then adopted by Thomas Hanmer (1743–5). Macbeth famously uses 'sere' in one of his final reflections, where its Folio spelling perhaps illuminates the process of error here: 'my way of life | Is falne into the Seare, the yellow Leafe' (5.3). (For a comparable *s/f* confusion, see Note 30 below.)

24. **As to put mettle in restrainèd means** (2.4, pp. 64–5)
Contemporary spelling made no distinction between 'mettle' (= courage, spirit) and 'metal' (the substance of which coins, among other things, are made), and Shakespeare's imagination plays freely between them here – as it does at 1.1 (pp. 4–5): 'Let there be some more test made of my metal [F mettle]'. Frank Kermode (2000) provides a useful account of some of the implications of this quibble, including Angelo's name, which may be related to a coin known as an 'angel' (p. 147).

25. **Now took your brother's life; or, [F and] to redeem him,** (2.4, pp. 64–5)
F unfortunately botches the crux of Angelo's (so far hypothetical) demand, though it was not until 1709, and Nicholas Rowe's edition, that the proper reading was restored – as it had been in Davenant's 1673 adaptation of the play.

26. **Let me be [F Let be] ignorant, and in nothing good** (2.4, pp. 66–7)
The editors of the Second Folio (1632) first corrected this obvious inattention, whether Ralph Crane's or the First Folio compositors'. Compositorial errors often come in spates, and many editors accordingly group this one with F's rather awkward use of the word 'crafty' in the previous line: Davenant's adaptation (1673) reads 'craftily', which makes the smoother rhythm – though Shakespeare often used adjectives in an adverbial sense: 'Which are as easy broke as they make forms' (2.4, pp. 70–71).

27. **Proclaim an enshield [F en-shield] beauty ten times louder** (2.4, pp. 66–7)
The meaning of Angelo's figure may be paraphrased: 'like those black masks that women wear nowadays, which provoke admiration of their wearers' beauty far more than their faces alone ever could.' (Angelo's observation, perhaps revealingly, anticipates Roland Barthes's analysis of strip-tease in his 1957 *Mythologies*.) Zachariah Jackson (1819) suspected that the reference was to the black habit that Isabella wears as a 'probated nun'. But what can F's 'en-shield' mean? 'Shielded' is an obvious answer, and, as Brian Gibbons notes (1991), heraldic imagery was one of Shakespeare's regular resources (''Tis not the Devil's crest', 2.4, pp. 62–3); but the awkwardness of 'enshield' for 'enshielded' is plain (despite Edward Capell's deft apostrophe in 1767–8: 'enshield' beauty'). A distraction was provided by Dover Wilson and Quiller Couch in 1922, who scented a reference to Ben Jonson's *Masque of Blackness* (F: 'these blacke Masques'), which was performed at court within a fortnight of *Measure for Measure* itself and therefore suggest 'enshell'd' – which occurs, in reference to snails, in *Coriolanus*: 'Thrusts forth his hornes againe into the world | Which were In-shell'd' (4.6). Others have proposed 'enciel'd' – by analogy with Lucio's earlier description of Isabel as 'enskied' (1.5, pp. 24–5) – with the sense 'canopied' (the English word *ceiling* and the French word *ciel* [= sky] being related).

Such editorial word-association prompts the thought that the word 'conceal'd' (though altogether blander) performs all the duties made of it by the sentence. 'And what says | My conceal'd lady to our cancell'd love?' exclaims Romeo of Juliet (3.3), whom he had met at a masked ball.

28. **Of the all-binding law [F all-building-Law];** (2.4, pp. 68–9) There are good reasons for accepting the emendation that Dr Johnson proposed in 1765, following Styan Thirlby's earlier conjecture. Firstly, according to Johnson, 'Mr. Theobald has *binding* in one of his copies' – of the First Folio, presumably, though no such variant has subsequently been traced in surviving copies. Second, the 'manacles' of the previous line sit rather oddly with an 'all-*building*' law, for all that W.H. Durham (1926) otherwise reasonably paraphrases that reading as 'upon which all is founded'. (*Measure for Measure*, after all, is perhaps uniquely preoccupied with the neighbouring architecture of Bankside.) But third – and surely definitively – the scholarship of John Russell Brown (1964) has established that John Webster's *The Duchess of Malfi*, which was also first printed in 1623, was also typeset from a transcript prepared by Ralph Crane (see Introduction, p. xxxi). That Quarto contains an identical crux ('How can the church bind [Q build] faster?'), in which the printed text is similarly 'not meaningful'. Mario Praz's suggestion (1937) of 'All-bridling' (as 'more satisfactory palaeographically') would also be true to a stream of the play's imagery (see Note 9 above).

29. **My body up to shame.** (2.4, pp. 68–9) The Folio sets '*Ang.* That' as the catch-word (see Series Introduction, p. xiii) at the bottom of F5r, but it seems more likely that this is a compositorial error (for 'Then') rather than the ghost of a missing line.

30. **For thine own bowels which do call thee sire, [F thee, fire]** (3.1, pp. 74–5) F's punctuation (the comma before 'fire') represents an attempt to wring a kind of burning sense from the original confusion of 's' for 'f' ('fire | The . . . effusion of thy . . . loins'); but the structure of the preceding sentence dictates otherwise, as the editors of the Fourth Folio belatedly noticed in 1685. J.W. Lever (1965) presents a grim diagnosis of the symptoms presented in the passage.

31. **for all thy blessèd youth | Becomes as agèd, and doth beg the alms | Of palsied eld;** (3.1, pp. 76–7) F may be paraphrased, *since your entire state of youthful happiness resembles old age in its dependence on the charity of senile parents for its*

support. (J.W. Lever notes a submerged pun, by which the 'palsied' (tremulous or paralysed) 'alms'-givers might likewise beg the use of 'arms' from the young.) Nevertheless, commentators have suspected textual corruption in the first phrase. F's use of the word 'blessèd' must be understood as ironic, but the irony was lost on William Warburton (1747), Samuel Johnson (1765), and J.P. Collier (1842–4), who respectively proposed 'blazed' (vaunted, paraded), 'blasted' (assailed), and 'boasted'. The compact density of the phrase 'Becomes as aged' has also attracted a range of scholarly emendation that seeks to simplify the construction, lending 'Becomes' its more familiar sense: thus youth, in time, variously becomes 'assuaged', 'engaged', or 'abased'. Alexander Pope (1723–5) assumed that the arguably superfluous word 'yet' in the following sentence ('. . . To make thy riches pleasant. What's yet in this . . .') was introduced by mistake – possibly from 'compositorial anticipation' of the next line ('Yet in this life'), as N.W. Bawcutt (1991) points out. The Folio, perhaps suspiciously, uses 'yet' three times in as many lines.

32. ***Isabel* [*Within*] What ho, peace here, grace, and good company!** (3.1, pp. 76–7)
As Edward Capell first noticed (1767–8), the context ('Who's there? Come in') insists that Isabel speak this line '*within*', though someone, Crane probably, assumed otherwise. Reason likewise dictates that the Duke and Provost later withdraw, but do not leave, since each man subsequently comes forward, having heard the outcome of Isabel and Claudio's meeting ('Son, I have overheard what hath passed between you and your sister'). The F2 editors (1632) have them exit the stage, perhaps as a result of the simple but radical mistake in the Duke's subsequent instruction, detailed in the following note. N.W. Bawcutt (1991) points out that the eavesdroppers' visible presence on-stage might be a distraction, notes that the Duke wishes to be 'conceal'd', and therefore provides them with an exit and subsequent entrances. In practice, the distinction between a withdrawal and an exit can only be demonstrated – if at all – in production.

33. **Bring me to hear them [F them to hear me] speak where I may be concealed.** (3.1, pp. 76–7)
It is unfortunate that the necessary stage-business has been muddled by the simply transposed error in this Folio line. The problem was identified by the F2 editors (1632), who spelled out the situation

('Bring them to speake, where I may be conceal'd, yet heare them') but compounded the error by having the Duke and Provost then exit. George Steevens's conjectural solution, subsequently adopted by Edmond Malone (1790), is both elegantly and logically correct, and has become the standard reading.

34. **Through all the world's vastidity you had,** (3.1, pp. 78–9) Most editors prefer Nicholas Rowe's 1709 emendation of 'Through' to 'Though', so carrying the sense, *Yes, indeed! Permanent imprisonment – a sentence which, despite your universal freedom in the world, would be confined by the fixed penalty of your guilt*. As Brian Gibbons (1991) admits, however, this is merely an editorial preference. F might therefore mean, *Yes, indeed! Permanent imprisonment – a sentence you would bear through the universal world that once was free to you, namely the fixed penalty of your guilt*.

35. **Nips youth i'th' head, and follies doth enew [F emmew]** (3.1, pp. 80–81)
Shakespeare retained an enduring fascination with, and knowledge of, the art of falconry – *2 Henry VI*, one of his earliest plays, features a bold theatrical scene in which the characters converse while enjoying this sport; and a falcon 'at shake' featured on his coat-of-arms (See Katherine Duncan-Jones, 'Shakespeare among the Heralds', *Times Literary Supplement*, 20 April 2001). As the sequence of this sentence demonstrates, his mind returned to the subject here: 'enew' (as Thomas Keightley first proposed in 1864) is a specialist term used to describe the way in which hawks deflect their prey. F's 'Emmew' probably reproduces Ralph Crane's eccentric spelling of the associated term 'enmew' (= to keep a hawk in a close coop) which he seems to have substituted.

36. **The princely [F prenzie,] Angelo?** (3.1, pp. 80–81)
This crux is surely the most baffling of the whole play, and one stressed by the appearance of the same word just three lines later (F 'In prenzie gardes'). There are two strands of thought. The first – properly perplexed by what on earth 'prenzie' may mean – remembers the Duke's earlier description: 'Lord Angelo is precise' (1.4, pp. 22–3). ('Precise' means pedantic, austere, 'tight-assed', and was often applied to Puritans in the period.) But if Crane understood and transcribed the word there, why has the word been so botched (twice) here? Arguably, because this Folio-page was typeset by a

less gifted compositor – but since no consensus exists as to the distribution of these artisans (see Introduction, p. xlv, n.60), we are thrown back onto the rocks of speculation. How does Claudio describe Angelo here – and in such a way as to provoke an echo in his sister (always assuming, of course, that the underlying manuscript intended such an echo)? What is certain is that F's 'prenzie' sounded meaningless within a decade, since the F2 editors (1632) twice substituted 'Princely', which, though bland, may be the best that can be done. The word 'prince' was not limited to specific royalty, but carried its etymological sense of 'primary authority' – the authority with which Angelo has been invested (hence the subsequent imagery of clothing: 'guards' = hems). Thomas Hanmer (1743–5) suggested 'priestly'; J.P. Collier's assumption (1842–4) that Shakespeare suddenly availed himself of usefully bisyllabic Italian ('The *prence* [= prince] Angelo') inspired a sequence of related support. 'Proxy' and 'phrenzied' represent wilder guesses, and demonstrate the range of the feasibly intended meaning.

37. **A kneaded clod, and the delighted spirit** (3.1, pp. 82–3) The vexed and snagged nature of this desperate speech have prompted a series of editorial interventions. The spirit, released from the mortal body, is 'delighted' (F), apparently, because it is capable of, attended by, or endowed with delight. The impression of the word seems to include *bright* (not dark 'in cold obstruction'), *weightless* (not a 'kneaded clod'), and *bliss* (but now bathed 'in fiery floods'). It may also mean 'beloved', as J.W. Lever (1965) notes, who also points out that Thomas Hanmer's 'dilated' (1743–5), with its contrast to the body's constriction, 'fits the context better'. Samuel Johnson's 'delinquent' (= full of offence) (1765) is resonant but unlikely.

Nicholas Rowe (1725) ('in thrilling regions'), Lewis Theobald (1743) ('incertain thoughts | Imagine howling'), and James Halliwell (1854) ('incertain thought | Imagines howling) have each sought to wrest a coherent syntax from subsequent lines. Most editors introduce a punctuative break at the end of the sentence ('Imagine howling – 'tis [F howling, 'tis] too horrible!). As Brian Gibbons comments (1991), 'the speaker is becoming excited to the point of hysteria and the seeming breakdown of coherence here reinforces the impression'.

It was the F2 editors (1632) who first supplied 'penury' to Claudio's subsequent list ('That age, ache, penury [F periury], and imprisonment'). It is true that Shakespeare had imagined a terrible afterlife for perjurers ('false, fleeting, perjur'd Clarence' dreams of being seized by 'a legion of foul fiends' in *Richard III*, 1.4); but Claudio is here contrasting earthly pains to posthumous agonies. The graphic similarity between the words is plain to see.

38. **that the time may have all shadow and silence in it, and the place answer to convenience.** (3.1, pp. 88–9)
M.R. Ridley (1935) detected an oddity in this line (both *places* and *times* may be convenient, but only *places* shadowy and silent), and assumed a scribal/compositorial transposition. The conjecture found its way into J.W. Lever's 1965 edition, though it is perhaps significant that the Folio reading passed through the often literal-minded eighteenth century unimproved. But surely, say, four o'clock in the morning may reasonably be described as having 'shadow and silence in it'.

39. **and the corrupt Deputy scaled.** (3.1, pp. 88–9)
Most recent editors agree that F's 'scaled' carries a compressed reference to the Scales of Justice (the Duke will weigh Angelo in the balance), though both the sense of the word and the word itself have been contested. Interpreters have imagined Angelo being violently scattered or dispersed; being gradually approached via a step-ladder; and being prepared for the table, as a fish, 'his scales of sanctity being stripped off' (Halliwell, 1853–65). Interventionists have suggested substituting 'foiled' (Richard Grant White, 1857–66) and 'sealed' (Howard Staunton, 1858–60).

40. ***Enter* ELBOW, CLOWN, *and officers*** (3.1, pp. 90–91)
Alexander Pope (1723–5) signalled a change of scene here – '*The Street*' as opposed to '*The Prison*' (where Nicholas Rowe's 1709 edition had set the previous exchange); and Edward Capell (1767–8) accordingly introduced a new scene-number (3.2). But the Duke remains on stage following Isabel's exit, and the scene is continuous – as testament both to the fluid auspices of contemporary theatre-practice, and the counterpointed theme of corruption in high (Angelo) and low (Lucio) places that Shakespeare has built into the architecture of his play.

41. **the merriest was put down and the worser allowed, by order of law, a [F Law; a] furred gown to keep him warm – and furred with fox on [F and] lamb-skins too, to signify that craft, being richer than innocency, stands for the facing.** (3.1, pp. 90–91)
F's – presumably Crane's – punctuation diminishes both the force and sense of the Clown's paradox: the legal system has always punished one sort of prostitution, while surreptitiously rewarding another. 'The Vsurer hangs the Cozener,' as Shakespeare was soon to rephrase the thought: 'Robes, and Furr'd gownes hide all' (*King Lear*, 4.6). Joseph Rann (1786–94) first took up John Monck Mason's suggestion by setting 'fox *on* lambskins', and so lending sartorial precision to the idea: crafty fox-fur provides an opulent trimming ('stands for the facing') to innocent lambskin: usury is a wolf in sheep's clothing.

42. **I drink, I eat, array [F eate away] myself, and live.'** (3.1, pp. 90–91)
Lewis Theobald's was the first edition (1733) to correct the Folio reading here. The apparent potential for confusion in manuscript between *rr* and *w*; the line's recapitulation of the Duke's previous argument ('What 'tis to cram a maw or clothe a back'); together with a persuasive analogy (Mark Eccles, 1980) in Ben Jonson's contemporary *Epigram* ('. . . he liues, eates, drinkes, arrayes | Himselfe') – have all ensured that the intervention is 'unchallenged' (J.W. Lever, 1965).

43. **From our faults, as faults from seeming, free!** (3.1, pp. 92–3)
The Second Folio editors (1632) sought to improve the metre of this couplet by giving 'Free from our faults, as faults from seeming free!' – the first in a sequence of such tamperings ('Free from all faults, as faults from seeming free!', Fourth Folio, 1685; 'From our faults, as from faults seeming, free!', Thomas Hanmer, 1743–5; 'From our faults, or faults from seeming, free!', Samuel Johnson, 1765), none of which affects the intrinsic sense: *would that all men were as free from sin as sin should be from dissembling*. It seems likely that he is thinking in the first instance of Angelo, and in the second instance of Elbow.

44. **for putting the hand in the pocket and extracting clutched?** (3.1, pp. 92–3)
It is Nicholas Rowe's suspicion (1709) that the word 'it' has been accidentally omitted from F ('extracting *it* clutched'), though

J.W. Lever (1965), who is generally more suspicious of that text, here trusts it ('"extracting" may be an elocutionary simplification'), and N.W. Bawcutt (1991) defends F as being potentially Shakespearean. It should be noted, however, that Brian Gibbons (1991), who is generally eloquent on the compressed impressionism of the Folio text, feels the need to adopt Rowe's reading. (The hand is 'clutched' because clenched around the coins retrieved to pay prostitutes.)

45. **and he is no [F is a] motion generative – that's infallible.** (3.1, pp. 96–7)
Opinion is divided – as so often in both the text and theme of *Measure for Measure* – between two entirely contradictory readings. Eighteenth-century editors found it strange that Lucio's account of Angelo's cold-blooded nature ('stockfishes' are dried salt-fish, a Jacobean version of Bombay duck) concludes with his 'motion generative', or sexually fertile disposition. Lewis Theobald (1733) accordingly appended an 'un-' to the Folio text ('he is a motion *un*generative'), and this is broadly the standard reading. The fact that the Folio sets 'generatiue' on a new line may suggest a lapse in compositorial concentration. Thomas Hanmer (1743–5) suggested an alternative route of error by changing 'a' to 'no' – the reading we adopt on the basis that certain handwriting-forms of the period may explain the error – presumably misread by Crane from Shakespeare's manuscript. Of recent editors, J.W. Lever (1965) glosses Theobald's emendation as 'a puppet without power of generation'; N.W. Bawcutt (1991) retains F, but glosses it to mean 'sexless puppet'; Brian Gibbons (1991) also retains F, but his gloss feels more tentative: 'puppet or automaton, despite having the organs of generation'.

46. **Love talks with better knowledge, and knowledge with dearer [F deare] love.** (3.1, pp. 98–9)
Thomas Hanmer's emendation (1743–5) is the standard and unchallenged reading – correcting a casual flourish of Crane's pen.

47. **Can tie the gall up in the slanderous tongue?** (3.1, pp. 100–1)
William Warburton (1747) proposed an interestingly radical intervention at this point. He noticed that the Duke's four lines here closely match the six lines he speaks at 4.1 (pp. 110–11), when Isabel briefly leaves the stage with Mariana to catch up on the plot. The 'full' speech would therefore read approximately as follows:

O place and greatness! Millions of false eyes
Are stuck upon thee; volumes of report
Run with these false, and most contrarious quest
Upon thy doings; thousand escapes of wit
Make thee the father of their idle dream,
And rack thee in their fancies.
No might nor greatness in mortality
Can censure 'scape. Back-wounding calumny
The whitest virtue strikes. What king so strong
Can tie the gall up in the slanderous tongue?

The theory goes that a subsequent editor or adapter played fast and loose with Shakespeare's original script; but having 'restored' this (rather impressive) speech, the question arises as to whether it should be spoken *in extenso* here or at 4.1: either solution leaves a greater gap than the original problem. (For a related theory of adaptation, see Note 49 below.)

48. **Novelty is only in request, and, as it is, as [F and as it is as] dangerous to be aged in any kind of course as it is virtuous to be constant in any undertaking.** (3.1, pp. 102–3)
Innovation is the only thing people want, and (this being so) [*it is*] *as dangerous to persevere in any course of action as it is virtuous to be constant in anything.* The majority of editors prefers to assume, with the Third Folio editors (1663–4), that the first 'as' ('and as it is as dangerous') is a scribal or compositorial error – not implausibly since the sentence is such a difficult one, and F requires 'it is' (square-bracketed above) to be implicitly understood. The standard reading is therefore 'Novelty is only in request, and it is as dangerous to . . .'. H.N. Hudson (1851–6) also changed 'constant' to 'inconstant' (which changes the construction into a more conventional opposition: it is as dangerous to persevere in any course of action as it is [considered] virtuous to be unreliable and irresolute).

49. **He who the sword of heaven will bear** (3.1, pp. 104–5)
Scholars have detected four substantial textual complications attaching to this remarkable speech. Is it by Shakespeare? Was it written at the same time as the rest of the play? Is it complete? Is it in the right place?

H.C. Hart (1905) cast doubt upon its Shakespearean authorship, a theory pursued by Arthur Quiller-Couch and John Dover Wilson (1922). (The choruses to *Pericles*, which was published in a 'bad'

Quarto in 1609, are written in the same metre – but arguably not by Shakespeare.)

Mary Lascelles (1953) agreed with Hart that the speech was an 'interpolation', but not that it was a 'needless' one. Noticing that Puck's and Prospero's epilogues to *A Midsummer Night's Dream* and *The Tempest* use the same octosyllabic couplets, she suggested that the lines were introduced – by Shakespeare – for a subsequent revival of the play that for some reason incorporated 'a formal pause' half-way through the performance. (Prologues and Epilogues certainly were commissioned for particular performances in the period.)

J. W. Lever (1965) discounted both these theories, but persuasively advanced one of his own. Noticing that the speech falls into four distinct sections (of six, six, four, and six lines respectively), and that the third section ('How may likeness . . . ponderous and substantial things?') makes enormous demands of a reader wishing to understand it, Lever proposed that the Folio has omitted two lines – a lost couplet that would restore both a ready sense and a symmetry to the original 24-line speech. As our facsimile page shows (see below, p. 210), the speech ends flush to the end of a Folio page: does the finger of suspicion therefore point to a negligent compositor? Crane's transcript having been 'cast off' (see above, p. xxii, n. 17), might he have suddenly realized that he was two lines adrift, and quietly suppressed the relevant lines? Whatever the cause, N.W. Bawcutt (1991) accepts the disheartening prognosis that the missing lines are beyond recovery; Brian Gibbons (1991) valiantly paraphrases the relevant section: 'How may criminal seeming practise deception on the world, and thereby get control and possession of important matters by a deceptive appearance of lightness and triviality?' The construction 'How may likeness . . . *To* draw . . . ?', however, seems very strange – and even when such emendations as 'To-draw' (a single verb meaning 'pull apart') or 'So draw' are introduced, the sense remains elusive (though still somehow impressive).

As detailed in the following note, the Shakespearean authenticity of the Boy's song has long been questioned. The editors of the Oxford *Works* (1986) assume that the act-break, the song, and the subsequent conversation between Mariana and the Duke are all subsequent interpolations; and argue that the Duke's soliloquy here has 'evidently been transposed' with his shorter speech ('O place and greatness!') at 4.1 (pp. 110–11). Such an arrangement would certainly afford a more realistic amount of time for Isabel to explain to Mariana the Duke's plan: but since we are being asked to believe that Angelo has sex with Mariana under the illusion that it is Isabel, issues of realism are perhaps best ignored.

50. **Take, O take those lips away,** (4.1, pp. 106–7)
Shakespeare's authorship of this song has been the subject of much scepticism, and the theory – first asserted by James Boswell the younger (1821) – that it was inserted into Shakespeare's script without his authority still divides editors. The central piece of evidence is the fact that the same song appears (with an extra stanza) in the 1639 Quarto of *Rollo, Duke of Normandy*, a collaborative play by John Fletcher, Ben Jonson, George Chapman, and Philip Massinger which was first performed around 1616 (the year of Shakespeare's death). John Benson included both stanzas in his *Poems written by Will. Shakespeare, Gent* (1640), and William Warburton (1747) included the second verse in his edition ('part of a little sonnet of *Shakespear*'s own writing, consisting of two Stanzas, and so extremely sweet, that the reader won't be displeased to have the other'):

> Hide, O hide those hills of snow,
>   That thy frozen bosom bears,
> On whose tops the pinks that grow,
>   Are yet of those my April wears;
> But first set my poor heart free,
> Bound in those icy chains by thee.

(Mariana's command to 'Break off thy song' may indicate that whoever wrote this dialogue – whether Shakespeare or his adapter – knew that the song had more than one verse.) The Oxford editors (1986) emended the song's last line by reference to the 1639 text of *Rollo*: 'Seals of love, though [F but] seal'd in vain, seal'd in vain') – though they treat the first twenty-odd lines of the scene as a later addition, printing the sequence 'as we believe Shakespeare to have written them' in an appendix (p. 924).

51. **Good friar, I know you do, and have found it.** (4.1, pp. 110–11)
J.W. Lever (1965) reasoned that a 'monosyllabic word like "so" or "oft" seems to have dropped out of F', and plumps for the former: '. . . and *so* have found it.'

52. **Run with these false, and most contrarious quest** (4.1, pp. 110–11)
The editors of the Second Folio (1632) assumed that 'quest' was a noun and should be plural ('these . . . quests'); Thomas Hanmer (1743–5) solved the problem by changing 'these' to 'their'. Alfred E. Thiselton (1901) chose to explain rather than alter: 'quest' is a second verb (said of hunting dogs when they chase after, or bark at, game): *rumours run like hounds in pursuit of what is falsely discerned.* On possible revision, see Textual Note 47, and Introduction, pp. xxxvi–xxxvii, above.

53. **If it be too little for your thief . . . every true man's apparel fits your thief.** (4.2, pp. 114–15)
Most editors agree with Edward Capell (1767–8) that the Folio's assignment of these lines to the Clown is inexplicably erroneous: he has just asked for 'Proof' of Abhorson's statement that the art of execution is a 'mystery' (or skilled trade), after all. N.W. Bawcutt (1991) points out that the same Folio page (G2v) contains another error in attribution (see Note 56) – though his edition retains F's sequence on the grounds that 'it could be that Abhorson rather ponderously launches into his syllogism, only to have it snatched from his mouth by the quick-witted Pompey' (p. 236). It is certainly true that Abhorson is elsewhere humourlessly taciturn, and the mercurial quibble – which obscurely likens the crimes of thieves to the craft (or 'mystery') of tailors, then to that of the hangman, whose perks of the job included their victim's clothes – better suits the 'snip-snap style' (Charles and Mary Clarke, 1864) of the Clown's agile wit (see 2.1, pp. 42–3). Perhaps still more of the play has been lost: William Warburton simply marked a lacuna after the Clown's words, 'if I should be hanged I cannot imagine' (1747).

54. **you shall find me yare [F y'are].** (4.2, pp. 114–15)
The oddity of the Clown's word ('yare' = *brisk, nimble*) seems to have caused confusion in the compositor's mind rather than in Crane's, for it appears three times in the first ten lines of *The Tempest*, which is thought to be the first of the transcripts he prepared for the Folio. Lewis Theobald (1733) first restored the proper sense. (It is necessary to postpone Abhorson and Pompey's subsequent exit until after the Provost's instructions.)

55. **That wounds th'unsisting postern with these strokes.** (4.2, pp. 116–17)
Once again, while the broad sense of the Folio's wording is vivid, editors have struggled to explain quite how. The door ('postern') is being hammered on so urgently that it reveals the haste of the visitor; and the door itself is somehow unyielding: but what precisely does 'unsisting' mean? If F is correct, it is probably an abbreviated form of 'unassisting' (= *unavailing, helpless*), which H.C. Hart (1905) accordingly spelled 'un'sisting'. Emendations include 'insisting' (= *standing firm, persistent*, F4, 1685); 'unresting' (Thomas Hanmer, 1743–5); 'unshifting' (= *unyielding*, Edward Capell, 1767–8); 'resisting' (J.P. Collier, 1853); and 'unlisting' (= *unbending*, Richard Grant White, 1857–66).

56. **This is his lordship's [F Lords] man. | *Duke* [F *Pro.*] And here comes Claudio's pardon.** (4.2, pp. 118–19)
Editors agree with Nicholas Rowe (1709) in expanding F's 'Lords' – perhaps the result of Crane's mistaken interpretation of Shakespeare's manuscript abbreviation ('Lo.' or 'Lord.'). More damagingly, the Folio also has the Duke recognize the Messenger as Angelo's man (despite this blowing his alias), and the Provost suddenly reverse his pessimism ('No such example [of a reprieve] have we'). The often persuasive Joseph Rann (1786–94) restored what seems the proper sequence. (The source of the problem is probably simply that the Messenger's entrance interrupts a verse line, which Crane or compositor mistakenly sought to tidy up.)

57. **Then have we here young Dizzy [F *Dizie*],** (4.3, pp. 126–7)
Although the names in this speech are purely fictional, their Folio spelling sometimes obscures for modern readers the comic point. The choice of joke here is between 'Dizzy' (= *giddy, foolish*), following Alexander Pope (1723–5), and 'Dicey' (following George Steevens's conjecture adopted by Isaac Reed in 1803), which would carry an association with dice-playing, and mean something like 'gambler'. It likewise seems necessary to spell the name of the Folio's 'braue Mr *Shootie*' as 'Shoetie' in order to finesse the reference to the fashionably extravagant shoe-laces to which Hamlet also refers (see p. 242 of our Shakespeare Folios edition).

William Warburton (1747) suggested that Master Forthlight the tilter's name should properly be 'Forthright' (apparently an allusion to the horizontal position of the jouster's lance); and Ernst Leisi

(1964) followed suit in rechristening the murderer of lusty Pudding 'young Drophair' (apparently an allusion to the hair-loss brought about by syphilis; see Note 3 above). 'Droopheir' has also been proposed, by analogy with 'Starvelackey' (profligates both, who respectively neglect their heirs and starve their servants). Such emendations perhaps restrict the free play of Shakespeare's imagination: the comic names may have more in common with Dickensian novels than Restoration comedies.

Scholarly opinion is divided as to who or what was 'stabbed' by 'wild Halfcan'. Some assume that he 'stabbed pots' (or sold short measures – though this practice was more usually known as 'nicking'); others imagine a more violent crime – that he 'stabbed [a man called] Pots', which, as Brian Gibbons notes (1991), may be a generic name for a 'pot-boy' (= *lowly barman*), by analogy with the Bawd's reference to Pompey the Clown as '*Thomas* Tapster' (1.2, pp. 14–15). (All these men are 'for the Lord's sake' because that was the cry of the inmates begging passers-by for food from London's prisons.)

58. **After him, fellows, bring him to the block.** (4.3, pp. 128–9) Commentators since Samuel Johnson (1765) have suspected that this line more properly belongs to the Provost, who has just entered to discharge his duty, than to the Duke, whose own duties – disguised as the visiting father-confessor – scarcely extend to such orders. If the Provost speaks the line, it might carry a melancholy tone of 'I told you so' to the Duke, as J.W. Lever (1965) puts it; if the Duke speaks the line, it may perhaps represent a subtle slip in his disguise (see Note 20 above). The Duke immediately issues further orders ('Dispatch it presently', pp. 130–31), and the possibility remains that the Provost quietly sees through the disguise.

59. **To yonder [F yond] generation,** (4.3, pp. 130–31) There is an editorial consensus that F's immetrical 'yond' derives from scribal or compositorial negligence. Shakespeare may well have written 'yond^{r}', and there seems little dramatic point in introducing a metrical hesitation here. Nicholas Rowe (1709) first emended the line. 'Yonder generation' refers to the inhabitants of the world outside the prison, on whom daylight shines. Thomas Hanmer (1743–5) suspected further corruption, reading 'Th'under-generation' (= *the inhabitants of this nether-world*).

60. **And why meet him at the gates and reliver [F re- | liuer] our authorities there?** (4.4, pp. 136–7)
The OED records, as rare, the verb 'reliver' (= *give up again, restore*), and cites this passage, though the earliest previous citation is dated 1473. The word certainly baffled the Second Folio editors (1632), who corrected it to 'deliver'. Most modern editors give 'redeliver', following Edward Capell (1767–8), in part because F sets the word over a line-break, followed by a botched spacing ('ou rauthorities'), which perhaps suggests a spell of compositorial fatigue. Might Shakespeare have originally written 'relieve' (*Hamlet*, 1.1: 'Who hath reliev'd [F, Q2 relieu'd] you?')?

61. **For my authority bears of a credent bulk,** (4.4, pp. 138–9)
The Fourth Folio editors (1685) give 'my authority bears *off* a credent bulk' – a reading supported by the 1986 Oxford editors; Lewis Theobald (1733) simply deleted 'of' ('bears a credent bulk'); Peter Alexander (1951) tidied up the sense well enough ('my authority bears a so credent bulk'); and J.W. Lever (1965) gives 'my authority bears so credent bulk'. The sense is plain (*For my power carries with it the force of credibility*). But the compressed sense that the Folio carries well sets up the ensuing expostulation in which Angelo's turmoil unravels.

62. **Go call at Flavius' [F *Flauia*'s] house,** (4.4, pp. 138–9)
The description of this house-owner is revealed as male in the very next line ('And tell *him* . . .'), and he is subsequently named as '*Flauius*'. Nicholas Rowe's 1709 emendation is obviously necessary. What precisely these Ancient Romans – Flavius, Valencius, Crassus, Varrius – are doing in seventeenth-century Vienna (or London) has been supposed a Shakespearean eccentricity; it should not be forgotten, however, that in legal and political documents of the period English names were customarily latinized: the foreshadowing of the Duke's re-assumption of ('Jacobean') power?

63. **Give me [F we] your hand,** (5.1, pp. 142–3)
This simple slip was first corrected in the Third Folio (1663–4). J.W. Lever (1965) chose a different course by reading 'Give we our hand', which would anticipate the Duke's use of the royal 'we' four lines later.

64. **Till she herself confess it. [*Exit* ISABEL *under guard*]** (5.1, pp. 152–3)
F specifies that Isabel re-enters with the Duke a hundred lines later (pp. 158–9) but does not provide her with an earlier exit. Editors must therefore locate a suitable moment in proceedings for her to leave. The Duke describes Isabel as 'this woman here' on pp. 150–51, and as 'her that's gone' shortly before his own exit (pp. 158–9). Edward Capell (1767–8) therefore directed her exit where we set it. The counterview – proposed by John Dover Wilson and Arthur Quiller-Couch (1922) – places her withdrawal from the action immediately after her last comment in this sequence of the action ('One that I would were here, Friar Lodowick', pp. 150–51).
The Oxford editors (1986) further specify that Friar Peter exits following the Duke's 'Good friar, let's hear it', and then re-enters with Mariana.

65. **First let her show her [F your] face, and after speak.** (5.1, pp. 152–3)
This simple slip was corrected by the editors of the Second Folio (1632). J.W. Lever (1965) suggested that the manuscript (or transcript) read 'h^{r}', which was subsequently misread.

66. **Go, do it instantly. [*Exit one or more*]** (5.1, pp. 158–9)
Someone must obey the Duke's command, and exit, and the choice is between one of the mute '*lords*' (or unspecified attendants) who enter at the beginning of the scene, and the Provost himself, as Edward Capell (1767–8) suggested, after including him in that first general entrance (pp. 140–41).

67. **Although by confutation they are ours,** (5.1, pp. 168–9)
The Second Folio editors (1632) emended to 'confiscation', which makes the readier sense, since it is Angelo's 'possessions' which, now that the case of his innocence has been *confuted*, will be *confiscated*. Subsequent editors tend to dismiss Edmond Malone's 1790 defence of F ('by confutation' = 'by his being confuted or proved guilty of the fact which he had denied'), but the compressed sense is arguably typical of the play's mannerist style throughout.

68. **What's yet behind that's [F that] meet you all should know.** (5.1, pp. 176–77)
Editors are agreed on the grammatical necessity of F2's 1632 correction.

Authorities Cited

F	*Mr. William Shakespeares Comedies, Histories, & Tragedies* [The First Folio] (1623)
F2	*Mr. William Shakespeares Comedies, Histories, and Tragedies* [The Second Folio] (1632)
F3	*Mr. William Shakespeares Comedies, Histories, and Tragedies* [The Third Folio] (1663–4)
Davenant	William Davenant, *The Law Against Lovers* [*c.* 1662], in *Works*, Part II (1673)
F4	*Mr. William Shakespeares Comedies, Histories, and Tragedies* [The Fourth Folio] (1685)
Rowe	*The Works of Mr. William Shakespear*, ed. Nicholas Rowe, 6 vols (London, 1709)
Pope	*The Works of Shakespear. Collated and corrected by the former editions*, ed. Alexander Pope, 6 vols (London, 1723–5)
Theobald	*The Works of Shakespeare. Collated with the oldest copies and corrected*, ed. Lewis Theobald, 7 vols (London, 1733)
Hanmer	*The Works of Shakespear*, ed. Thomas Hanmer, 6 vols (Oxford, 1743–5)
Warburton	*The Works of Shakespear. The Genuine Text*, ed. William Warburton, 8 vols (London, 1747)
Johnson	*The Plays of William Shakespeare*, ed. Samuel Johnson, 8 vols (London, 1765)
Capell	*Mr William Shakespeare his Comedies, Histories, and Tragedies*, ed. Edward Capell, 10 vols (London, 1767–8)
Steevens (1773)	*The Plays of William Shakespeare . . . with . . . Notes by Samuel Johnson and George Steevens*, 10 vols (London, 1773)

Steevens (1778) *The Plays of William Shakespeare . . . with . . . Notes by Samuel Johnson and George Steevens*, 2nd ed., 10 vols (London, 1778)

Rann *The Dramatic Works of Shakespeare*, ed. Joseph Rann, 6 vols (Oxford, 1786–94)

Malone *The Plays and Poems of William Shakespeare*, ed. Edmond Malone, 10 vols (London, 1790)

Reed *The Plays of William Shakspeare . . . Revised and augmented*, ed. Isaac Reed, 21 vols (London, 1803)

Jackson Zachariah Jackson, *Shakespeare's Genius Justified: Being restorations and illuminations of seven hundred passages in Shakespeare's Plays* (London, 1819)

Boswell *The Plays and Poems of William Shakspeare*, ed. James Boswell the younger, 21 vols (London, 1821)

Collier (1842–4) *The Works of William Shakespeare: The text formed from an entirely new collation of the old editions*, 8 vols, ed. J.P. Collier (London, 1842–4)

Hudson *The Works of Shakespeare. The text carefully restored according to the first editions*, ed. Henry N. Hudson, 11 vols (Boston, 1851–6)

Collier (1853) *The Plays of Shakespeare: The text regulated by the old copies*, ed. J.P. Collier (London, 1853)

Halliwell *The Works of William Shakespeare; the text formed from a new collation*, ed. James O. Halliwell, 16 vols (London, 1853–65)

Dyce *The Works of William Shakespeare. The text revised*, ed. Alexander Dyce, 6 vols (London, 1857)

White *The Works of William Shakespeare. The plays edited from the folio of MDCXXIII*, ed. Richard Grant White (Boston, 1857–66)

Staunton *The Plays of Shakespeare*, ed. Howard Staunton, 3 vols (London, 1858–60)

Keightley — *The Plays of William Shakespeare. Carefully edited*, ed. Thomas Keightley, 6 vols (London, 1864)

Clarke and Clarke — *Cassell's Illustrated Shakespeare. The Plays of Shakespeare*, ed. Charles and Mary Cowden Clarke, 3 vols (London, 1864–8)

Wright — *The Works of William Shakespeare*, ed. William Aldis Wright, 9 vols (London, 1891–3)

Thiselton — Alfred E. Thiselton, *Some Textual Notes on 'Measure for Measure'* (R. Folkard & Son, 1901)

Hart — *Measure for Measure*, ed. H.C. Hart (Arden, 1905)

Porter and Clarke — *Measure for Measure*, ed. Charlotte Porter and Helen A. Clarke (New York, 1909)

Wilson and Quiller-Couch — *Measure for Measure*, ed. John Dover Wilson and Arthur Quiller-Couch (Cambridge, 1922)

Durham — *Measure for Measure*, ed. W.H. Durham (Yale, 1926)

Ridley — *Measure for Measure*, ed. M.R. Ridley (New Temple, 1935)

Praz — Mario Praz, '"All-Bridling Law"', *Times Literary Supplement*, 13 February 1937 (p. 111)

Alexander — *The Complete Works*, ed. Peter Alexander (Collins, 1951)

Lascelles — Mary Lascelles, *Shakespeare's 'Measure for Measure'* (Athlone Press, 1953)

Empson — *Seven Types of Ambiguity: A Study of its Effects in English Verse*, 3rd ed. (Chatto & Windus, 1953)

Sisson — C.J. Sisson, *New Readings in Shakespeare*, 2 vols (Cambridge, 1956)

Schanzer — Ernest Schanzer, 'The Marriage Contracts in *Measure for Measure*', *Shakespeare Survey* 13 (1960), 81–9

Leisi — *Measure for Measure: An Old-Spelling and Old-Meaning Edition*, ed. Ernst Leisi (Heidelberg, 1964)

Brown	John Webster, *The Duchess of Malfi*, ed. John Russell Brown (Revels Plays, Manchester, 1964)
Lever	*Measure for Measure*, ed. J.W. Lever (Arden, 1965)
Nathan	Norman Nathan, 'Nineteen Zodiacs: *Measure for Measure* I.ii.172', *Shakespeare Quarterly* 20 (1969), 83–4
Howard-Hill	T.H. Howard-Hill, *Ralph Crane and some Shakespeare First Folio Comedies* (Virginia, 1972)
Eccles	*A New Variorum Edition of Shakespeare: 'Measure for Measure'*, ed. Mark Eccles (New York, 1980)
Oxford	*The Complete Works*, gen. ed. Stanley Wells and Gary Taylor (Oxford, 1986)
Bawcutt	*Measure for Measure*, ed. N.W. Bawcutt (Oxford, 1991)
Gibbons	*Measure for Measure*, ed. Brian Gibbons (Cambridge, 1991)
Honigmann	*The Texts of 'Othello' and Shakespearian Revision* (Routledge, 1996)
Kermode	Frank Kermode, *Shakespeare's Language* (Penguin, 2000)

Luc. Sir, I know him, and I loue him.

Duke. Loue talkes with better knowledge, & knowledge with deare loue.

Luc. Come Sir, I know what I know.

Duke. I can hardly beleeue that, since you know not what you speake. But if euer the Duke returne (as our praiers are he may) let mee desire you to make your answer before him: if it bee honest you haue spoke, you haue courage to maintaine it; I am bound to call vppon you, and I pray you your name?

Luc. Sir my name is *Lucio*, wel known to the Duke.

Duke. He shall know you better Sir, if I may liue to report you.

Luc. I feare you not.

Duke. O you hope the Duke will returne no more: or you imagine me to vnhurtfull an opposite: but indeed I can doe you little harme: You'll for-sweare this againe?

Luc. Ile be hang'd first: Thou art deceiu'd in mee Friar. But no more of this: Canst thou tell if *Claudio* die to morrow, or no?

Duke. Why should he die Sir?

Luc. Why? For filling a bottle with a Tunne-dish: I would the Duke we talke of were return'd againe: this vngenitur'd Agent will vn-people the Prouince with Continencie. Sparrowes must not build in his house-eeues, because they are lecherous: The Duke yet would haue darke deeds darkelie answered, hee would neuer bring them to light: would hee were return'd. Marrie this *Claudio* is condemned for vntrussing. Farwell good Friar, I prethee pray for me: The Duke (I say to thee againe) would eate Mutton on Fridaies. He's now past it, yet (and I say to thee) hee would mouth with a beggar, though she smelt browne-bread and Garlicke: say that I said so: Farewell. *Exit.*

Duke. No might, nor greatnesse in mortality
Can censure scape: Back-wounding calumnie
The whitest vertue strikes. What King so strong,
Can tie the gall vp in the slanderous tong?
But who comes heere?

Enter Escalus, Prouost, and Bawd.

Esc. Go, away with her to prison.

Bawd. Good my Lord be good to mee, your Honor is accounted a mercifull man: good my Lord.

Esc. Double, and trebble admonition, and still forfeite in the same kinde? This would make mercy sweare and play the Tirant.

Pro. A Bawd of eleuen yeares continuance, may it please your Honor.

Bawd. My Lord, this is one *Lucio's* information against me, Mistris *Kate Keepe-downe* was with childe by him in the Dukes time, he promis'd her marriage: his Childe is a yeere and a quarter olde come *Philip* and *Iacob*: I haue kept it my selfe; and see how hee goes about to abuse me.

Esc. That fellow is a fellow of much License: Let him be call'd before vs. Away with her to prison: Goe too, no more words. Prouost, my Brother *Angelo* will not be alter'd, *Claudio* must die to morrow: Let him be furnish'd with Diuines, and haue all charitable preparation. If my brother wrought by my pitie, it should not be so with him.

Pro. So please you, this Friar hath beene with him, and aduis'd him for th'entertainment of death.

Esc. Good euen, good Father.

Duke. Blisse, and goodnesse on you.

Esc. Of whence are you?

Duke. Not of this Countrie, though my chance is now
To vse it for my time: I am a brother
Of gracious Order, late come from the Sea,
In speciall businesse from his Holinesse.

Esc. What newes abroad i'th World?

Duke. None, but that there is so great a Feauor on goodnesse, that the dissolution of it must cure it. Noueltie is onely in request, and as it is as dangerous to be aged in any kinde of course, as it is vertuous to be constant in any vndertaking. There is scarse truth enough aliue to make Societies secure, but Securitie enough to make Fellowships accurst: Much vpon this riddle runs the wisedome of the world: This newes is old enough, yet it is euerie daies newes. I pray you Sir, of what disposition was the Duke?

Esc. One, that aboue all other strifes,
Contended especially to know himselfe.

Duke. What pleasure was he giuen to?

Esc. Rather reioycing to see another merry, then merrie at anie thing which profest to make him reioice. A Gentleman of all temperance. But leaue wee him to his euents, with a praier they may proue prosperous, & let me desire to know, how you finde *Claudio* prepar'd? I am made to vnderstand, that you haue lent him visitation.

Duke. He professes to haue receiued no sinister measure from his Iudge, but most willingly humbles himselfe to the determination of Iustice: yet had he framed to himselfe (by the instruction of his frailty) manie deceyuing promises of life, which I (by my good leisure) haue discredited to him, and now is he resolu'd to die.

Esc. You haue paid the heauens your Function, and the prisoner the verie debt of your Calling. I haue labour'd for the poore Gentleman, to the extremest shore of my modestie, but my brother-Iustice haue I found so seuere, that he hath forc'd me to tell him, hee is indeede Iustice.

Duke. If his owne life,
Answere the straitnesse of his proceeding,
It shall become him well: wherein if he chance to faile
he hath sentenc'd himselfe.

Esc. I am going to visit the prisoner, Fare you well.

Duke. Peace be with you.
He who the sword of Heauen will beare,
Should be as holy, as seueare:
Patterne in himselfe to know,
Grace to stand, and Vertue go:
More, nor lesse to others paying,
Then by selfe-offences weighing.
Shame to him, whose cruell striking,
Kils for faults of his owne liking:
Twice trebble shame on *Angelo*,
To vveede my vice, and let his grow.
Oh, what may Man within him hide,
Though Angel on the outward side?
How may likenesse made in crimes,
Making practise on the Times,
To draw with ydle Spiders strings
Most ponderous and substantiall things?
Craft against vice, I must applie.
With *Angelo* to night shall lye
His old betroathed (but despised:
So disguise shall by th'disguised
Pay with falshood, false exacting,
And performe an olde contracting. *Exit*

Actus

*Mr. William Shakespeares Comedies, Histories, & Tragedies (*1623), G1v;
pp. 98–107 of the present edition.